At the end of the seventies, Christov Rühn was nominated the best Under-Thirteen soccer player for the Ile de France region and subsequently passed the entrance trials for a place at the National Institute of Football. Because of a knee injury, he had to stop playing at the age of sixteen. He turned to music, his other passion, and moved to London, where he stayed for five years, to learn his trade.

As an avant-garde DJ and producer in Paris, he has worked with the likes of Mory Kante, the African singer best known for his worldwide hit 'Yéké Yéké'; IAM, the number one hip-hop group from Marseilles; Judge Jules; Roy the Roach; Charlie Hall from the Drum Club and others. He was the first DJ to introduce Garage music to Paris around 1992. He influenced the local fresh funkhouse scene, Daft Punk and Stardust, with the regular clubs he hosted in the French capital (Radical Chic, Zoom, Jelly Baby's, Funky People and Fantazzia), inviting and spinning alongside Armand van Helden, CeCe Rogers, Robert Owens, Blade (Jestofunk), Laurent Garnier, Keoki and many others.

Rühn wrote a specially commissioned piece, 'Lost in Music', and also interviewed Marcel Desailly, for *XCiTés: The Flamingo Book of New French Writing*, edited by Georgia de Chamberet. He lives in London, and supports Olympique Marseille and Arsenal.

Le Foot

The Legends of French Football

Edited by Christov Rühn

Introduction by Irvine Welsh

An *Abacus* Book

First published in Great Britain in 2000 by Abacus

Compilation, editing and preface copyright
© Christov Rühn, 2000
Introduction copyright © Irvine Welsh, 2000
Afterword copyright © Daniel Bernard, 2000

For further detailed copyright information about individual
contributions see pages 297–300

A CIP catalogue record for this book is available from
the British Library.

ISBN 0 349 11270 3

Typeset by Solidus (Bristol) Ltd
Printed and bound in Great Britain by
Clays Ltd, St Ives plc

Abacus
A Division of
Little, Brown and Company (UK)
Brettenham House
Lancaster Place
London WC2E 7EN

Contents

IV Les Coaches

V Les Scandales

VI Les Supporters

To Martin Luther Rühn

Preface

The idea of *Le Foot* came to me a few months after Les Bleus' outstanding 1998 World Cup victory, which I followed with great passion from my newly found English residence. The reaction generated on both sides of the Channel by the winning of this trophy was exceptional. French football, generally perceived to be a poor relation of the European game, no longer provoked mockery among British sports journalists and fans but a genuine interest bordering on admiration. This was a new development, since until then, French football was known only through the dramatic performances, week in, week out, of French performers in the English Premier League.

Eric Cantona had been the one to pave the way. The rebel from Marseilles disembarked in the north of England to become a legend in his own lifetime, alongside those other number 7s George Best and David Beckham. Before this move Cantona had threatened to quit the game for good because he had felt less than happy playing on his home turf. No doubt Cantomania will be remembered as the beginning of a special bonding between French football and its British counterpart. 'King Eric' conquered British hearts and British football, a fact borne out by his recently being voted Manchester United's player of the twentieth century. In 1996, Arsène Wenger, dubbed 'the Professor' by the Gooners, was appointed manager of Arsenal FC. English football culture had traditionally embraced the stereotypes of lad culture. Thanks to Wenger's professional, even scientific, approach to training, the north London team began to play a modern game of continental flair and skill. The club became infinitely more attractive to the fans than the 'boring, boring Arsenal' of the George Graham era. The Gunners won the Double, masterfully powered by one of the finest pair of midfielders to perform for a Premiership team in a long time: Emmanuel Petit and Patrick Vieira.

Even as a fanatical schoolboy player and a dedicated supporter of Olympique Marseille, any French victory had been nothing more than a mere fantasy to me. French sides would only rarely qualify for the second round of any major competition. Nobody outside France had ever heard of those footballing heroes who sported names like Georges Bereta or Charly Loubet. So, in 1998, as a French exile living in the native land of football, I proudly watched the tremendous exploits of my compatriots while witnessing my homeland get into the international groove. Emotional overflow. Intense joy. At last! The timing was right to tell an incredible story. Inspired and spurred on by the boundless energy of my agent, Georgia de Chamberet at BookBlast, I threw myself into what seemed to be the craziest of adventures. To unite British and French novelists, journalists, players, fans and movers and shakers and inspire them to participate in the realisation of this book. To bring alive through their experiences and vision, in specially commissioned pieces and exclusive interviews, the legends of French football, transcending national boundaries and identities. The contributors to *Le Foot* are truly world class. Now, when I look back, I can't help thinking that this all happened as a sheer miracle. Their passion for and vast knowledge of the game, their varied writing and voices coming from many different horizons, shaped *Le Foot: The Legends of French Football*.

During the last quarter of the twentieth century, a tremendous revolution took place in French football. In the early 1970s, fans were desperate to see their teams win trophies and accolades at international level. But France had become a second-rate footballing nation. Then, to everyone's surprise, in 1975, Les Verts from St Etienne reached the European Cup final and the whole nation took to the game, just when football's core supporters had almost completely lost faith in a sport which promised so much but frequently delivered so little. Patience was yet to be learned and confidence to be developed. *Le Foot* tells the story of how France went from being second rate to a major footballing superpower. The founding of the Auxerre Youth Academy, the European Nations Championship victory in 1984, the first win over Brazil in Guadalajara during the 1986 World Cup, the reign of Michel Platini in the *calcio* of the 1980s and Marseille's European Cup win in 1993 all contributed to the renaissance of the French game. Sometimes France's worst defeats led to amazing victories, the most obvious example being the contentious World Cup semi-final at Seville in 1982, in which France's controversial loss to Germany was to reveal the best-ever national side, featuring Platini, Giresse, Tigana and Fernandez. Although scandals of corruption and embezzlement erupting out of Tapie's Olympique Marseille and Rocher's St Etienne threatened to put the clock back, they could not stop France's inexorable rise to glory.

The example and influence of several remarkable individuals contributed towards building a strong national identity for the French game and received respect from the international football community. *Le Foot* tells their stories, and more – from Michel Platini to Zinedine Zidane, Eric Cantona to Marcel Desailly, Frank Leboeuf, Franck Sauzée, the Anelka brothers, Aimé Jacquet, Arsène Wenger, Gérard Houllier, Laurent Perpère . . . It shows how 'Magic' Chris Waddle rocked Marseilles; how Roger Milla led the way for so many and how José Touré became a fallen hero who had too much too soon. It looks at the demise of hooliganism; it also celebrates the fans, from the followers of RC Lens – 'the best public in France' – to the millions who invaded the Champs Elysées to cheer the new world champions.

Le Foot is dedicated to the infinite pleasure and phenomenal passion which surrounds the 'most universal game known to man', to the lovers of the beautiful game, to its converts and to a multiracial France at the heart of Europe, a France that wins. From Marseilles to Liverpool, Edinburgh to Paris, London to Manchester, Madrid to Monaco, a powerful mosaic of voices unites.

Sometimes, dreams do come true. Football is not only about big business, as Michel Platini tells us, it is about togetherness. It unites people of all ages, all colours, all sexes from all over the world. It belongs to all of us. This is what I have come to understand through everybody I have had the honour to meet and work with during the past year while compiling *Le Foot*. And I send a special thanks to all those who supported and encouraged me in the realisation of this book, which was initially just an incredible dream. A vision. In all humility, I shall make my own, for always, the words of the late Albert Camus: 'All I know for certain, about the mortality and the obligations of men, is that I owe it to football.'

Acknowledgements

All my love to: Roxane, André & Madeleine, my brothers and sisters and family and my son, MLCR.

Respect and thanx to: Lol, Pepe, Amy, Giles and Philippa: you are such incredible friends.

Big up to: G@BB (Madame Bookblast!): what would I have done without your incredible support? Alan Samson and everyone at LB: thanx for believing in me. Michel Platini, Olympique Marseille, Arsenal FC, Les Bleus for the fantastic emotions they have given me through the years.

Special thanx to: Marcel Desailly, Caroline Duret, Jean-Michel Larqué, Alain Leiblang, Philippe Tournon, Laurent Perpère, Didier Anelka, Françoise Rust-Fourteau, Laure de Gramont, Christel Paris, Mounsi, Q, Irvine Welsh, Daniel Bernard, His Excellency the French ambassador, Quitterie Pinçon, Gordana, Kal Touré, Stéphanie and Edouard, Torty and Nigel, Tam Dean Burne, Tania Glyde and everyone on both sides of the Channel who helped me through *Le Foot*.

Keep it real.

By way of an Introduction: Confessions of an Embittered Scottish Schemie (Vol. 6015)

IRVINE WELSH

When I first started to get published, make a bit of cash and generally receive a bit of recognition in the writing game, I set myself three rules. These rules were a type of insurance policy, a very crude device to keep me operating in the social milieu in which I prefer to write, or, if you like, to stop me from becoming a poncey literary type. They were: 1) Never set foot in the Groucho, 2) Never write for *Granta*, 3) Never do anything for a publication which celebrates 'football'.

Much to the chagrin and bemusement of visiting overseas publishers, I've managed to keep to number one. Number two was no problem; that was never going to be a marriage made in heaven. Why number three? Well, in the current climate, it seems to me that writing which celebrates 'football' is now invariably just free PR for one of the richest, most élitist and exploitative industries around. The trouble is, even though I detest this industry it's becoming increasingly indivisible from, I've always been well into football.

So, after thinking a bit about that magical time I had over in France in 1998, bang goes number three, my resolve crumbling like old dental fillings in the wake of a cocaine binge. I was able to rationalise this sell-out by reasoning, well, this is about French football, and it's not like over here in the UK, where TV money has rendered the game's outcomes predictable. In French domestic football more than one team can still win the League, and the final table doesn't necessarily correspond almost perfectly to a ranking order of the club's wage bills. Also, unlike in the UK, the French have a national football side which can rise above mediocrity and play with great skill and flair.

While the media circus of France '98 did nauseate, and although I seldom follow the fortunes of the Scottish national team, I felt I just had to be there. Paris in the summer. Do you need an excuse? Anyhow, about a week before the game, I was offered tickets for Scotland–Brazil, the first match of the tournament, to mark the opening of the new Stade de France. Obviously, I was tempted, but I declined, electing to watch with 5,000 other ticketless fans on a huge screen in the Place de l'Hôtel de Ville.

Prior to the game I was sitting outside a café in the Rue St Opportune, pretending to my other ticketless companions that I wasn't now lamenting my daft stance. But the words 'spite', 'face' and 'nose' played in loop in my head as kick-off time approached. I watched, with growing envy, the crowds filing into the Châtelet–Les Halles métro station opposite. That swift RER line would take them out to the new, state-of-the-art stadium and the opening match of France '98.

However, continuing to observe the crowds, I began to feel better, convinced, in fact, that I'd made the right decision after all. The Scotland supporters who piled on to the station opposite our bar, although I'm sure there must have been a few punters in the mix, seemed corporate bods to a man. Their accents suggested more familiarity with a different-shaped ball. It took more than a profusion of ridiculous See-You-Jimmy hats to give me an inkling that we were all Scots fitba fans together.

So it slowly and implacably resonated that the only thing to do with football, as I knew it, would be happening on the park. 'Football' to me has always been a broad package, with the actual match and the players just a small part of it. Most of all it's been about the fans: your own, and those sad,

deluded fuck-ups who support the opposition. That afternoon in the Rue St Opportune, the real fans seemed to me to
be the ones who were staying back, getting bevied and sorting
out the carry-outs for the street parties at the various screens
dotted around Paris. They were the ones who'd been priced
out of the footballing market, disenfranchised into the role of
viewers, watching in the streets over here, or back at home, in
their houses or local pubs. The saddest thing was the attitude
of the ordinary punters who were milling towards the big
screens. Most just laughed in the face of the odd naïve idiot
who framed the question, 'Have you got a ticket?' Not so
long ago the reply would have been, 'Why, have you got any
going spare?' Now it was just accepted that physical attendance
at the match was an option only for the connected, the professional celebrators everywhere, who just had to be at the
next big tourist/media event. So I hit the square via the offie,
glad that I had avoided the queues and the trains.

It was strange to watch the game on a big screen outdoors,
but from the start I could tell my personal France '98 World
Cup campaign was going to have a surreal edge to it. As we
waited in the bar at Waterloo Station to board the Eurostar, a
squad of bears with East of Scotland accents came marching
in, displaying the sense of purpose traditionally associated with
Scots football supporters and drink. One guy stole straight up to
the bar and asked the English student-type bartender for six
pints of lager and six whiskies. The student gaped at him for
a second, bemused. The guy repeated his order. The student
nodded and came back with six pints of lager and six small
packets of biscuits, the kind that usually accompanies railway
coffee. The Scottish boy's face dropped several inches as
resounding laughter from his mates reverberated around the
bar. Funnily enough, the Auld Alliance sprang into operation,
as it was a French barman who was able to correct his
colleague's mistake, pacifying the outraged bear and sending
over the water of life.

But, as the pundits would say, let's get back to that opening
match and the screen at the Place de l'Hôtel de Ville. One

great thing about Scotland, post Ally McLeod and Argentina '78, is that we have no imperialistic delusions of grandeur. We may be able to get half-decent results away from home against minnow outfits on the fringes of Europe (think about the creditable 1–1 draw against the Faroe Islands and the 1–0 win over England), but basically, we know our place. Apart from the ditty which set the unsavoury precedent in mass fan folklore by linking soccer opponents and paedophilia, our main number on the Parisian streets was the self-deprecating 'We're shite, but we'll beat Brazil'. Incidentally, I maintain that it was the paedophile song, and the gusto with which it was sung along those sunny boulevards, which caused poor Ronaldo to have his breakdown, thus effectively handing the World Cup to France on a plate.

You have to feel sorry for the Brazilians; they just keep running into us Scots in the World Cup. Over the years we've come to believe a lot of our self-generated propaganda that we are Brazil's soccer and cultural soul-mates. If so, we were definitely short-changed. Why did we get that hideous, dirgey bagpipe music when they got samba? And what about Ronaldo versus Billy Dodds? Rivaldo or Gary McSwegan? Aye, for all our Scottish festive bonhomie, you can't help thinking that the Brazilians must occasionally ask themselves, just who are those strange, drunken transvestites who insist upon dancing in front of us at international football tournaments? Fortunately, the footballing connection does have some basis in fact. The British Championship-winning Hibernian team of the fifties, who became the first British club to tour Brazil, played a quick, interchanging passing game. (I say British, as they defeated the then English champions, Manchester United's 'Busby Babes', 7–2 in the unofficial decider.) The Hibs tour, though ignored by the Scottish (Glasgow) press, was so influential with their counterparts in Brazil that Hibs became heralded as the prototype of the great Brazilian side of the seventies. The watershed game for the South American press on that occasion was the 'Famous Five's' 3–3 draw with Vasco de Gama in the blistering heat of the Maracana Stadium.

But we have to stop you there, Irvine, because we're ready to go back to the Place de l'Hôtel de Ville, Paris, Scotland versus Brazil. If you could just talk us through this. Certainly, Des. In the apocalyptic, frenzied build-up to the contest, nerves were kicking in. In order to combat this, I had drunk the best part of a bottle of Jack Daniels by the time ex-Hibernian player John Collins gave Scotland the lead against Brazil. After the game I staggered back to my hotel room and fell into a deep slumber. It could have been hours or minutes later when my phone rang. It was my buddy from London, Alex, and he said that he had somebody with him who wanted to speak to me. So he put on Kate Moss, who told me that she was in town and having a do with some of the girls from her modelling agency in a restaurant a couple of stops away on the métro. Kate demanded my presence. 'Get your arse up 'ere, Welsh!' Well, being an obliging sort, I got it together and stumbled blearily out of the hotel. Then I decided that I couldn't face either the métro or a taxi without a fortifying drink.

The bar I chose was possibly the ugliest, grimiest dive in Paris. It looked like it had been transported straight from Leith Walk. It even had a Scottish barman. Almost as soon as I got my bearings, I heard a familiar Glasgow voice: 'WELSHY YA CUNT!' I hadn't seen Andy Sim and his crew for an age, and it seemed as good a time as any to catch up. 'Fuck the models, Welsh, ya Embra bastirt, thair only eftir ye fir yir boady. We wahnt ye fir yir money. Git thum in!' So instead of being sur-rounded by supermodels in an upmarket restaurant, dining on the finest French cuisine, I was screaming football songs at maximum volume with a load of my drunken country-men. Of course, it felt just right. It felt like I'd gone the full circle.

I grew up in an Edinburgh housing scheme near the Firth of Forth. I remember the arguments we used to have, as wee kids, about the county of Fife, which stretched before us over the waters of the Forth estuary. That was England across there, some kids ventured. But I wasn't having that. It was France for definite over there, simply because, as everybody knew,

there was no water between Scotland and England, only hills.
It might have been Ireland, as some did suggest, but I knew
better because I'd been over there, and it was much further
away. My geography's got a little better since then, that is
until Jack Daniels decides to lend a hand.

Growing up as a fitba-crazy kid in those days, you never
really perceived France as a power in the game, although Rheims
did beat Hibs in the first European Cup semi-final, only to
lose narrowly to the mighty Real Madrid. My first direct experience of French football was being taken to Parkhead in Glasgow
to watch St Etienne defend a two-goal lead against Jock
Stein's Celtic. It's inconceivable that Celtic could overturn a
two-goal deficit against even a French works team these days,
but remember, this was the Stein era. Post-Stein, Celtic, like
Aberdeen post-Ferguson, may be just another mediocre club
in a poor League, but the Big Man had a way of working
magic. (If you don't believe me, consider the 2–0 Hibs victory
he conjured up against the then-champs of Europe, Real
Madrid.) As soon as you heard Jock's gravelly tones on the
radio stating: 'SINT ENTY'S A GUID TEAM', you sensed that
the French outfit were doomed. So it proved, as wee Jimmy
Johnstone ran amok on a magical night.

My second direct encounter with French football was at
Easter Road in 1976, when Hibs beat Sochaux in the UEFA
Cup, the tightness of the margin being the only surprise. So
that was France: beautiful girls, fantastic wine, excellent food,
did the right thing with their monarchy, but, please, leave the
fitba to the beer-guzzling, socially repressed nations. The real
watershed for French football came two years later when Hibs
failed to pull back a two-goal deficit and were beaten 2–1 on
aggregate by Strasbourg. The weird thing was that this was
actually considered a shock result at the time. (Well, it shocked
me, anyway.) Aye, the French game has never looked back since
then. St Etienne (or Sint Enty, as we call them in Scotland),
came to Hampden Park and narrowly lost the European Cup
final to Bayern Munich. What visiting French supporters must
have made of that massive toilet (I mean Hampden, not

Glasgow, yes I do! yes I do!) is something worth considering.

Then, of course, came Marseilles' European triumphs and finally France '98, where the French game was somehow condescendingly acknowledged to have 'come of age' by English commentators. This was not just an admission of French brilliance, though it would now be exceptionally churlish to dispute this, given the status of French players in the English Premiership from Cantona onwards. It also served as a tacit recognition of England's relative decline as a footballing power.

The French have always had catholic sporting tastes. Games like rugby and cycling, which real people in Britain don't seriously take part in, have traditionally enjoyed just as high a status as the Beautiful Game in France. For France to win the World Cup was a marvellous achievement, made all the more impressive by their lining up in the final with a centre forward who couldn't score bad Es in a dodgy nightclub. I hate to go on about this, but once again, you have the Scots to thank for neutralising the Ronaldo threat.

An interesting point, Irvine, but we're going to have to move on. Specifically, back to this anthology. Well, what can I say Des/Gary/Alan/Jim? It's as diverse as French sporting tastes and is of Platini or Zidane quality, brilliant interviews with both of those masters featuring in its pages. Yes, it's that excellent; it has the capacity to affirm, surprise and irritate. It's also not frightened to stray from well-worn Media Central routes, as in Tam Dean Burn's piece on Franck Sauzée. Additionally, it looks at old issues in a completely fresh way. I thought I'd read and heard roughly fifty times more about the Nicolas Anelka transfer saga than I wanted to in my lifetime, but Q's offbeat piece has achieved the near-impossible by managing to breathe new life into possibly the most played-out affair in the modern game.

There's something for everyone and the standard of writing is very high, which is my way of saying don't let this introduction put you off. And personally, I'm now very glad that I broke one of my own rules. After all, that's what they're there for.

I

Les Clubs

1

The Legend of Les Verts – St Etienne

CHRISTOV RÜHN

'He is what I want to be, as brilliant and powerful as he is,' Jimmy Kunte would chant to himself every Sunday, like a prayer, as he walked on to the main pitch of his football club, the pride and joy of the local community. 'He' was Salif Keita, the wonderful young African star of the French football champions and formidable striker for the renowned Association Sportive de St Etienne. Jimmy's idol.

In the heart of the sixties, Jimmy lived with his two sisters, young brother and parents in an old house on the edge of a peaceful little provincial village. They were newcomers to this backwater, which had the air of having strayed unintentionally to the outer limits of that utterly Parisian region the Ile de France. Here all was lush greenery. Jimmy played for Racing Club de Verniers, whose grounds lay on the outskirts of the village. Like a great raft, the pitch was set in the brown and ochre patchwork of those fields on which Normandy cows chewed the cud with such resigned boredom. A vast green field, it seemed to float on land farmed pitilessly, without joy or respite, by huge Massey-Ferguson tractors. Barely 300 metres lay between the young Jimmy's front door and what for him was a fabulous playground. Two white metal goalposts. The penalty box. The touchlines. The centre circle. Enormous, awe-inspiring goalmouths like gaping giants' caverns. Perfection in an imperfect world.

With the down-to-earth common sense natural in the country, the locals referred to the football pitch as 'the stadium'. In such small villages there is usually only one of anything. The only school was therefore referred to as 'the school', 'the church' was an ancient thirteenth-century abbey, which crumbled a little more by the day, and 'the hairdresser' a terrifying old headshrinker who freely plied his trade between the police station and the butcher's, and terrorised successive generations of kids.

Jimmy's first experiences were played out within the boundaries of 'the stadium'. It was here that he discovered the infinite pleasures of football; the first excitement which follows victory; the bitter tears which accompany unfair defeats; the joy of the goalscorer after a strike. All infused his mind with indelible memories – to such an extent that, today, when a football skims the net, a great tremor passes through him. He sees himself as a child again, facing those huge goals at the end of the road. Jimmy adored this place.

Football matches were seldom broadcast on TV. Over interminable weeks, the little ones and the grown-ups would keep an impatient lookout for them, in the hope that these encounters from the other side of the world would offer up to their wondrous gaze a fantastic show. The magic created by great footballers incited an unrivalled excitement among the spectators.

Jimmy was fascinated by the action, the shirts, the public, the suspense. Everything.

'The through ball flies down the touchline from Tostão to Jairzinho. He dribbles past one, two, then three defenders. A storm is brewing.'

Suddenly, like a sign from the gods, a wind rises over Mexico and Brazil picks up speed.

'Sublime. La Séléçao seem to be everywhere at once; truly blessed by the heavens. It looks as though twenty Brazilians

are on the pitch . . . a cross from Jairzinho . . . Pelé stretches and springs . . . way above the other players . . . Oooh! High in the air he controls the ball on his chest with a mind-blowing gesture and passes it backwards to Rivelino, who appears from nowhere . . . the favelas' favourite glides into the box and with a stupendous shot, at 200km per hour, places the ball with his left foot into the top right-hand corner of the goal . . . Gooooaaaal!'

Hearing the commentators going bonkers, Jimmy would suddenly metamorphose into one of those jubilant victims, willing prisoners of that unbearable suspense which reigns during the last minutes of a match. He lived these moments with a religious fervour infinitely more intense than that prevalent at Sunday Mass, to which his mother dragged him insistently.

'The crowd stands as one and hails the new Lords of the stadium.'

Images fused across the small screen with supersonic speed, came to life, merged and confounded reality in his child's brain. The second the referee blew the final whistle, Jimmy fled surreptitiously through the french windows behind his house, jumped on his bike and joined his friends, who were already forming teams in the municipal park. Ready for action. They would replay the match, goal for goal, free kick for free kick, and adopt the names of the star players.

Jimmy would be Salif the Great.

If the score at the end of their game was different from the one on TV it didn't matter at all. Jimmy wanted one thing and one thing only: to score the winning goal which gave his team the World Cup.

School was a mediocre pastime in comparison to the achievements of his studded heroes. Jimmy thought about nothing but football. All week he would conjure up different moves and one-twos enabling him to dribble successfully the following

Sunday against his opponents, who he'd eliminate one by one, to end up confronting, alone, the goalkeeper. And score an historic goal.

Jimmy Kunte was one of those destined to cultivate that superlative love of the leather ball from a tender age. Fascinated by the perfect spherical shape of this object endowed with supernatural qualities, he lovingly cherished it. In turn, it could be received, controlled and kicked far away in a single movement without even falling to the ground. These actions immediately placed him in a mystical relationship with the rest of the world. Football had cast a spell on him. The ball obsessed him and also played the dual role of confidant and best friend. This wondrous sphere filled with air concealed at its very centre most of his child's secrets and the essentials of his dreams of glory.

A flawless passion gripped Jimmy. He would spend hours contemplating his football; envied it as it flew high into the sky; admired it as it fell back to earth, slow yet swift; followed its trajectory accompanied by that faultless gravitational pull. It would return to him only to bounce off his attentive forehead and he'd send it even higher than before, the prelude to a dance he wished were never-ending. He stroked this ball and coveted it in order to juggle it for as long as possible. Football made of Jimmy Kunte 'a different man', if one can say such a thing of an eleven-year-old boy.

His name began to be heard along the edge of the green grass. Some saw in him the makings of a future great player. He was filled with pride. This was a pleasant contrast to those stupid supervisors at school who stopped at nothing in their mission to punish him for insignificant trifles linked to his favourite sport. Football was a game universally appreciated, yet seemingly little valued by the authorities who ran his *lycée*, who considered it common and anything but educational. Jimmy was most decidedly not suited to school.

'Monsieur Kunte, come and see me in my study and bring your football. You know full well that it is against school regulations to bring it into the precincts of this establishment!' the tetchy headmaster would bellow, tin-pot dictator disguised as educator.

Sunday at last. 'Les Cars François' arrived. These coaches regularly ferried the under-thirteens from RC Verniers to take part in the region's junior championships at other local clubs. The point of departure and return was the village square, opposite the Café des Sports, also known as Chez Tonton, which served as a meeting place for club managers and self-styled football experts. Mayhem. Laced with booze, these pseuds considered their knowledge to be virtually divine, but it was the wine talking. Jimmy didn't like the smell of alcohol and this revulsion would stay with him always. He couldn't stand those braying fools, either. The genuine supporters, though, clearly recognised his striking talents, thereby protecting him from the ear-bashing which assailed the team when they lost. He had become untouchable. Sacred.

'He's good the little one, talented,' said the old boys.

'Very, very talented,' came the echo.

It was crucial that Jimmy should continue to score goal upon goal in order to maintain his status as local star. But that wasn't a problem since he lived for such exalted moments – heart pounding against his ribs; all fear banished; the individual at one with himself. Executing the *coup de grâce*. Taking life, giving life. Jimmy Kunte: a born predator, a real goalscorer.

If he hadn't known about Salif Keita, Jimmy wouldn't have known where Mali was. He had little interest in the geography taught at school, an omission reflected in his school reports. Africa was miles away and its football was as yet unknown in Europe.

To emulate his hero, Jimmy chose the number 10 shirt. He liked to lead. They may have shared the same number, but Salif's was infinitely more beautiful. It seemed to radiate a million flames, embroidered in big figures on that famous green shirt with its blue, white and red border: the celebrated colours of the French champions.

'Me too,' declared Jimmy. 'I'll play for St Etienne.'

Like Salif Keita, he loved great open spaces, those solitary runs towards the goal and that one-on-one contest with the goalkeeper. Week after week, at Verniers as at St Etienne, it rained goals. Jimmy had pace, was agile and powerful. A merciless executioner of the opposition. Each match made of him an ever greater sensation. Scouts began to prowl along the touchline. The way he moved and the magic tricks he displayed on the pitch strengthened his resemblance to St Etienne's black star.

Jimmy wanted to be the best. To achieve this he would happily spend hours alone with his football, alternating shots between his right and left foot, acquiring a perfect mastery over his body and its movements. These solitary periods in the fresh air, far away from everything, taught Jimmy that the price of freedom is hard work; the source of that psychological strength so particular to champions.

His friends, jealous of his growing fame, nicknamed him 'Négus'. He was unsure how he should deal with this. Perhaps his mates chose it to take the mickey out of him, or perhaps because he was the only mixed-race kid in that godforsaken backwater. Either way, he could have done without it. Yet most of his idols were black: Martin Luther King, Cassius Clay . . .

At a time when African players were thin on the ground, considered disorganised and undisciplined and were as yet unknown to the general public, Salif Keita established his reputation with his magnificent touch. St Etienne had discovered a rare pearl. He was a prodigious athlete, a football wizard who possessed the sinuousness of a black panther, the speed of a leopard and the majesty of a lion. In the penalty box he was king. His phenomenal shooting power terrified the best goalkeepers of the First Division* and his unnerving dribbles sowed panic at the heart of the tightest of defences. Never had a player demonstrated such natural class.

---

*In the French Championship the First Division is the equivalent of the Premier League in Britain.

To the great dismay of Jimmy's mother, who disapproved of the holes he made in his wall with drawing pins, his bedroom was covered in posters of football stars. Les Verts of St Etienne took pride of place over his bed, as though to watch over his dreams and keep them whole and pure. The players in the photograph held themselves straight as posts, looking attentive and well behaved, like children in an end-of-year school photograph wearing the smug smile of school favourites. A black-and-white chequered football was wedged tightly between the legs of the kneeling attackers, while in the background the defenders stood tall. Salif Keita radiated from the middle of the picture.

The centre forward from Mali had been signed up by l'ASSE in the mid-sixties. He had never left his homeland and was a stranger to the customs of the Old Continent, but to play in France had always been one of his most cherished dreams. The day he landed at Orly for the first time, on board a DC10 from Bamako, no one was there to meet him. Freezing cold and disorientated, he went in search of a taxi. He extended a piece of paper to the first driver he found. On it was scribbled an address 600 kilometres away. To begin with the driver thought he was dealing with a madman, but he soon realised that the destination in question was the French champions' club and fulfilled his commission with good grace. After all, he was probably transporting a future star. At the end of an interminable drive they finally arrived in St Etienne. The managers had to dig deep in their pockets, but the bill was paid. Welcome, Salif!

No one had any cause for regret, such were the numerous talents subsequently displayed by the black pearl every time he made an appearance on the pitch at the Geoffroy-Guichard Stadium. He captivated the entire arena.

'Goal by number 10 – Saliiiif . . . Keita!'

During his time at St Etienne, where he stayed for a few of seasons, he scored over 100 goals and passed into the legend of Les Verts. Not everything was that easy, but he ended up taking the place of Rachid Mekloufi, the exceptional Algerian player, in the hearts of the Stéphanois, the inhabitants of St Etienne and its hinterland.

To the Stéphanois, the main attraction of St Etienne was the Geoffroy-Guichard Stadium, baptised the 'green cauldron' by the team's loyal supporters, most of whom worked in the Manufrance hardware factory, whose founder gave his name to the stadium. This town of middling importance was reminiscent of those of the River Mersey. Every weekend, the Geoffroy-Guichard Stadium welcomed around 25,000 enthusiastic fans for whom football was often the only family outing. Thanks to St Etienne's standard-bearing team, which pulverised all opposition, football flourished: the pride and joy of the Stéphanois, who basked in its glory for many years. Les Verts brought to the capital of the Forez region titles of great distinction and, for a while, made it the most famous town in France.

This legendary team soared over the French Championship in the First Division. It seemed as though nothing or no one could stop it. Les Verts won the title for four consecutive years from 1966 to 1970, picking up two French Cups on the way. Jimmy had learned by heart the names of its players from the pages of the daily sports paper *L'Equipe*. In goal was Georges Carnus, first-choice goalkeeper of the Tricolores, and at the back the Yugoslavian Vladimir Durkovic and Robert Herbin, the 'Ginger Sphinx', who was to coach Les Verts in the 1970s. They surrounded Bernard Bosquier, the sturdy captain of the French national team, Aimé Jacquet, who matured in a midfield defensive position with, at his side, the young Jean-Michel Larqué, who became legendary captain of St Etienne in Glasgow in 1976 and, twenty years on, the most famous sports commentator of the small screen. In attack were Patrick Parizon and Hervé Revelli, the greatest Stéphanois striker of all time, and let's not forget the stunning and talented Georges Bereta on the left wing. Albert Batteux was the coach of this renowned side.

At the epicentre of this dream team was Salif Keita, who scored a total of 42 Championship goals during the 1970–71 season. Never before had such a haul been seen in the First Division – yet he finished only second in the goalscoring table, just behind the Yugoslavian Josip Skoblar, Olympique Marseille's international player, who also enjoyed an exceptional season. He scored 44 goals and claimed the European Golden Boot for that year, a fabulous record which remains unequalled to this day.

The most heated encounters were those between Les Verts of St Etienne and Les Blancs of Olympique Marseille. The frenzied atmosphere of these matches was palpable.

To everyone's surprise, in the early seventies Bosquier, Carnus, Keita and Bereta joined the arch-rival Phocaean club. Les Verts subsequently experienced a fall in form but soon regained their national supremacy with the help of new players from the local youth academy. They went from strength to strength just as French supporters were agonising at their favourite teams becoming regular losers on the international scene. In 1975 St Etienne reached the semi-final of the European Champions Cup against Bayern Munich, then considered the world's best football club.

A year later Les Verts got to the final at Glasgow's Hampden Park. After an epic battle they lost narrowly, by 1–0, to the German giants, having hit the woodwork a couple of times. The following day, St Etienne paraded down the Champs Elysées in an open-topped limo, to the enthusiastic applause of the entire nation, thanking its heroes for having come within a hair's breadth of glory. As a result of this final, lost in such an heroic manner, St Etienne would find a place in the hearts of the French for ever. Yet it signalled the beginning of the end, for in 1977 the French champions' European campaign was prematurely halted by that second-leg 'match from hell' at Anfield Road, and Les Verts would never again be on top. The winner of that year's competition, Kevin Keegan's impressive Liverpool Reds, eliminated the Stéphanois in the quarter-final despite a great effort by Michel Platini, who had joined the Forezien club that year, wearing the famous number 10 shirt which made him a megastar.

*　　*　　*

In 1970, when the legend of Les Verts was already flourishing, Jimmy Kunte's parents were telephoned by a major club's
talent scout who wanted their son to take part in a trial for its
youth academy. He had to pass a medical, and a technical
competence test. No details were given other than that the
club's colours were green.

It seemed that young Jimmy Kunte's dreams were about to
come true. He was outside when his mother called out to tell
him the news. He heard nothing. He was smiling to himself,
playing alone with his football, dreaming of being Salif Keita.
He was happy because a few minutes earlier he had scored
the goal in the final which brought Mali the World Cup.

2

Olympique Marseille – The First French European Cup Victory

ALAIN PECHERAL

Olympique Marseille: a club in a class of its own

'We weren't going to wait 107 years . . .' In Provence, people are fond of using this expression to make it clear that things had dragged on long enough; it did not escape many of them that they had to wait until the 106th European final, in 1993, to witness the first victory of a French club.

One hundred and six finals and thirty-seven years: an interminable wait to which, when you think about it, Olympique Marseille was the perfect team to put an end.

For OM, a side you could describe as many things – except a club like any other – has always played a special role in French football. A bit like those brilliant but boisterous students who, depending on the whims governing their behaviour, may come top of the class one year but have to repeat the next year all over again.

An impressive list of achievements and idiosyncrasies attests to this very singular status: founded in 1899, twenty-five years later OM became the first provincial club to win the French Cup, a feat until then the prerogative of Parisian teams. OM was also one of the first clubs to take part in the competition. It has gone on to win the Cup ten times, and has held the record for the number of Cup wins since 1938, the year that saw its fifth triumph.

For many years it was the proud boast of the Marseilles side that it had never been relegated to the Second Division. Especially since, when it eventually did slip down in 1959, it was the only club to have held out for so long. Indeed, OM was one of the pioneers of professional football in France, introduced in 1932. In the twenties, the club was already practising a policy of spectacular and high-priced transfers – and on a far grander scale than any other side.

The international players Edouard Crut, Jean Boyer (who, as a twenty-year-old scored the goal on 5 May 1921 that gave France its first-ever win over England) and Jules Devaquez were lured away from Paris to play a decisive part in the club's first successes: three victories (1924, 1926 and 1927) in the French Cup, the only major national competition of the era. Their first unleashed an indescribable wave of enthusiasm in the country's most venerable city (founded by Greeks from Phocaea in 600BC, the city of Marseilles has just celebrated its 2,600th birthday): over 100,000 people turned up at the station to wait for the return of their conquering heroes and accompanied them in triumph to the club's headquarters, then located two steps away from the Old Port at the foot of the city's most famous avenue, La Canebière.

It has to be said that the supporters' devotion has always been one of the club's strongest characteristics. No other side in France has ever aroused such passion, let alone such loyal and enduring passion. Teams such as Reims, Lille, St Etienne and Bordeaux, to name but a few, have had their turn at dominating French football, but their supremacy has never lasted longer than ten or fifteen years, whereas OM has sailed through the century winning at least one national title each decade. Always making its presence felt, sometimes down on its luck but more often scaling the heights, the Marseilles club never fails to provoke a reaction. Love it or hate it, just about everyone has something to say about it.

OM's run-ins with the national authorities – along with its

budgetary follies and irresistible attraction to players from outside France – are the last of the great traits that make it stand out from the crowd. Well before the arrival of the colourful Bernard Tapie, OM had known plenty of outspoken presidents; its existence has almost always been enlivened by controversies and sanctions, dramas and schisms. Maybe it has something to do with the Mistral, that violent wind from the north which now and then arrives to purify the blue skies of Provence but which also, according to local tradition, lies behind the hot-tempered character of the region's people.

Added to this explosive mix is a deep-seated antagonism towards the capital city, an emotion that runs much deeper than football. France is an excessively centralised country and there is no denying that far too often the inhabitants of Paris tend to look down their sophisticated Parisian noses at the rest of the nation. It is an attitude which goes down badly in the provinces, specifically in Provence, where people react to this issue with all the sensitivity of somebody being flayed alive. For example, fans of the club have always called it OM, whereas those who dislike it merely use the term 'Marseille' with a lack of warmth that borders on the scornful. It's like saying 'Munich' when talking about Bayern, 'Amsterdam' instead of Ajax or 'London' to describe Arsenal.

Between the southerners who feel neglected and the northerners who accuse them of being paranoid, a chasm of misunderstanding has opened up which is nowhere near to being bridged. The Marseille victory of 1993 in the Champions Cup – a first for a French club in a European Cup – is a perfect illustration of this: the entire country went wild with joy – except for the capital.

Unlucky finalist in the same competition in 1991, having been unjustly eliminated from the semi-finals by Benfica the previous year (with a 'hand of God' goal by the Brazilian Vata), this was an OM that successfully combined great entertainment with impeccable results – and it did not get to the top by accident.

This is demonstrated by the resounding initial victory in

spring 1991 (1–1, 1–0) over the footballing gods of AC Milan. All thanks to the unstoppable Jean-Pierre Papin and his best mate, the mischievous and brilliantly unpredictable Chris Waddle.

Two years later, in Munich, the two clubs faced each other once again in the final and another Marseille success (1–0, from a Boli header) sent the city to new heights of joy, even for a place used to Roman-style triumphs. The day after this historic win the players brought their trophy home to the Stade Vélodrome, full to bursting.

Two days later, in an atmosphere of rapturous delight, they defeated their deadliest rivals, Paris St Germain, by 3–1 to take their fifth consecutive title as champions of France. The next day the players had to make their way through a great flood of people to reach the Old Port and the city hall, where, to describe the scene with just a hint of Provençal exaggeration, the entire city awaited their conquering heroes. Sadly, this was an honour of which the club was subsequently stripped following a corruption scandal centring on a match against Valenciennes.

Though less celebrated at the time than the prestigious Milan players, that OM team nevertheless took up their rightful place in football history alongside that most famous of Marseille footballing sons Zidane, who has in fact never actually played for OM.

Barthez, the architect of countless exceptional saves throughout a long and faultless career (against, for example, Glentoran, Dinamo Bucharest, Glasgow Rangers, CSKA Moscow, FC Bruges), became at twenty-one years old the youngest victorious goalkeeper in the European Cup with Marseille, before going on to save goals for France, the world champions, five years later. Angloma, Di Meco, Boli, Deschamps, Durand and Sauzée all played for the national team, and Desailly was to join them a few weeks later after his transfer to Milan. The Croat Alen Boksic – at twenty-three years old the top striker in the French Championship (the only French competition in which he was eligible to compete), went on to a bright future in Italy and with his own national side. The German Rudi Völler, the wily old fox of the playing field, who already had a long list of achievements to his name, travelled the opposite direction, coming to France to take part in, and win, his first-ever Champions Cup. And let's not forget the Ghanaian Abidé Pelé, winner of the African Golden Ball in 1991, 1992 and 1993.

As for Didier Deschamps, the first French captain to hold aloft a European trophy before receiving the World Cup, his destiny was to prove to be nothing short of spectacular . . .

In July 1998, at the moment that ushered in the global triumph of Les Bleus, Deschamps, the most capped of French players, did not fail to pay homage to the white OM strip, declaring: 'It's from OM that we learned how to win!'

3

Auxerre: The Ultimate Youth Academy

JEAN-PHILIPPE RETHACKER

In France, and particularly in the Burgundy region, the Association de la Jeunesse Auxerroise (Association of Auxerre Youth) is generally known simply as AJA. What this abbreviation stands for is therefore sometimes forgotten. The word 'youth' in the club's name is the symbol of an entire philosophy. AJA's beginnings, its lifeblood, its success have been engendered, enriched and embellished by young footballers.

Let us go back to the very earliest days, when the motivating forces behind the foundation of the club were both political and religious. In 1905, the French government decided to separate the roles of Church and State. The official announcement, made in Auxerre by the president of the Council of State, Emile Combes, immediately provoked the anger and indignation of a local cleric, one Abbé Deschamps, who wanted to protect the young Auxerrois from the dangers of secularism. He decided to found a sporting club with the aim of saving all these imperilled young souls.

Thus was born the AJA, whose mentoring spirit has always respected and nurtured the ideas and work of its founding father, Abbé Deschamps. A former notary's clerk, he was also an astute businessman who had the foresight to purchase the first patches of ground where the flourishing stadium that bears his name stands today. Some years later, another priest was to continue the work he started. Abbé Bonnefoy, a holy man who devoted his life to good causes, was also a lover of football and of the AJA. In 1961 these twin passions moved him to offer board and lodgings in his presbytery to young footballers from the club who found themselves far from home.

Such were the foundations of the training centre at Auxerre, which became fully operational twelve years later, after many false starts and difficulties. In 1980 the club suddenly found itself sitting on a small fortune – 1,200,000 francs – thanks to a run in the 1979 French Cup that took them all the way to a final against Nantes and promotion to the First Division.

The question facing club president Jean-Claude Hamel and coach Guy Roux was what they should do with the money. Should it be spent on strengthening the team by signing a new, quality player? Or maybe it would be better to use it to purchase the 3.5-hectare farm adjoining the ground so that they could build the training centre they'd dreamed of for so many years and which they sorely needed. The two men hesitated for a long time before reaching their decision. They even decided to put it to the vote. Agreement was reached by a margin of 2–1: the training centre it would be.

The year 1983 saw the inauguration of what the locals refer to as the Pagoda because of its highly distinctive architecture and wonderfully exotic roofline. Guy Roux appointed Daniel Rolland to the new centre as his assistant. Rolland, a former club player, still works at the centre today, having seen through training an entire galaxy of future Auxerre stars in an atmosphere inevitably somewhat akin to that of a boarding school. Pranks and schoolboy escapades were very much the order of the day at the centre, from illicit nocturnal jaunts via the roof to trips out on motor scooters, which were expressly forbidden for fear of accident – especially as far as one Basile Boli was concerned.

It was into this environment that a young man named Eric Cantona gained his first true introduction to the world of football. Eric had been spotted by Jean-Pierre Dubord, one of Guy Roux's scouts, at a junior selection camp. After discussing the matter with his parents and grandmother at one of the best restaurants in town, they signed the lad up. In those days he was a rangy youth, 1.78 metres tall yet weighing only 55 kilos. He dribbled with the agility of a child and the insolence of an old hand, and at sixteen years of age he was already wilful and strong-minded.

At eighteen Eric became a professional footballer, for once and for all. For seven seasons he brought the good times to AJA, punctuated by a single season spent with Martigues in the Midi, where he went to woo and wed Isabelle, the sister of his Auxerre team-mate Bernard Ferrer. Eric gave a lot to AJA, up to and including the cash from a big-money transfer to Olympique Marseille, a sum which helped further to swell the coffers of the Burgundy club. OM had taken much (and paid handsomely for it) from the club on the banks of the River Yonne. Basile Boli and Jean-Marc Ferreri also made the journey from Auxerre to Marseilles, developing their brilliant national and international careers and in the process seriously improving the health of AJA's bank balance through the size of their transfer fees.

It is this aptitude for rearing youngsters that is the secret of Auxerre's success, for its aim is not to retain them to form the basis of a top international club side, rather to move them on to provide the club with revenue for ultra-modern facilities. This policy has borne fruit beyond anybody's wildest dreams. Stands at the ground have been enlarged year by year and can now welcome a crowd of 21,000, all of them seated as demanded by European regulations. It's an astonishing capacity if you consider that the population of Auxerre itself is only 39,000. But here we touch on the unique aspect of AJA's supporters who, on match days, converge on the town from all the *départements* of the region from a radius of 200 kilometres. It's a faithful crowd, hospitable, friendly, decent, perfectly at one with the traditions and philosophy of the club.

As well as being wisely used to renovate the old ground, the money generated from transfers has also returfed several other pitches and training areas to an immaculate standard (one of Guy Roux's passions: as well as being a qualified geologist, he also happens to be a specialist in agronomy). The changing areas, too, have been carefully updated, with treatment rooms and a balneotherapy facility. Finally, Auxerre became the proud owner of a giant indoor sports hall complete with a half-size pitch to help with winter training sessions when it's wet and cold in Burgundy.

This policy of carefully husbanding their resources, a concept dear to the hearts of country people, is a product of Guy Roux's character. Roux, the undisputed 'Monsieur AJA', is a character who really stands out in the world of French football, first of all because, quite exceptionally, he's been coaching Auxerre for almost forty years. He became the club's technical director in 1961 at the age of twenty-three after the premature curtailment of a respectable amateur playing career. And the boss he will always be, overcoming obstacles, overseeing more successes than failures, imposing and sustaining the training policies he believes are the only way forward for AJA. He is the man you see today thanks to his roots, and especially to his rural upbringing, a childhood spent with his smallholder grandfather who taught him about life, money, property and love of nature, woodland, and the fields. He is a true countryman, yet operates comfortably right at the heart of French professional football, a sport that is increasingly being invaded by big money and big businessmen. His appearance says all there is to say about him – the stolid trencherman, uncomfortable in suit and tie, his hooded, mischievous eyes shining with intelligence and guile. He has the air of a straightforward man out of place in the cut-throat world of football. But be in no doubt: he has understood all there is to understand, and has been able to make the best of the situation, and of the differences that make him stand out. It's the same with the cameras and microphones that seek him out because he is straightforward, visionary in his judgements, striking, amusing, camera- and media-friendly, very much a man of the times, even though he always arrives straight from the Appoigny countryside of his birth, from the small village where he grew up and where he now owns a lovely little lake and a handful of fertile pieces of land. AJA, too, is his inheritance, a property he's been canny enough to allow to prosper and grow over the years.

From time to time Guy Roux has had to deviate a little from his clearly defined path and from the Pagoda in order to maintain credibility in the minds of the public and so as not to die disappointed, without trophies or titles. To this end he has taken two or three gambles, summoning to his school a handful of seasoned pros who needed to recharge their batteries in Burgundy. As a result the Abbé Deschamps ground has seen the appearance and resurgence of Alain Roche, Frank Verlaat, Enzo Scifo and Laurent Blanc, all class players with international reputations, but players who were struggling to make their names elsewhere and who enjoyed a second youth and renewed acclaim with Auxerre. It is thanks to such names that AJA was able to cock a snook at the bigger French clubs by taking the French Cup twice – in 1994 and in the double year of 1996, when they won the Championship as well – and by qualifying eleven times in fourteen years for the European Cup-Winners' Cup.

Nonetheless, it is at the Pagoda that the Guy Roux School will remain long into the future. This is the place which trained Cantona, Boli, Ferreri and other French and overseas internationals from Martini to Diomède, via Vahirua, Prunier, Charbonnier, West and Goma, and where the pros of tomorrow will continue to flourish.

Auxerre is rightly proud of its record in junior competition, at which level it beats the other French professional clubs every year. Its scouts scour France ceaselessly, especially the lle de France region where the African and West Indian immigrant communities have proved such an abundant source of talent for French football, as evidenced by the triumphant World Cup-winning side of 1998 featuring Thuram, Desailly, Vieira, Diomède and Zidane.

To get the most out of such extremely talented players, you simply need to find them and work intensively with them – and they are now an increasingly common sight on AJA's fields. The club's professional reserves have been winners of the Third Division title (open to professional reserves in France) in 1984, 1986, 1988, 1990, 1992, 1994 and 1996. And Auxerre's under-seventeens recently won the 1999 Gambardella (junior) Cup, as they did in 1982, 1985, 1986 and 1993. Sadly, though, while only ten years ago the brightest of the club's hopefuls were happy to advance slowly up the ladder to the first team, their successors in the year 2000 are tempting the palates of large overseas clubs at an increasingly young age. A case in point is Mexès, the captain and sweeper of the 1999 junior team, who AC Milan has already tried to lure from AJA.

This is the pattern of modern football, the avid devourer of talent, however young and unformed. Yet it will not affect the policies and outlook of a club that is so deeply rooted in its region, a club that intends to go on garnering its strength and its glory from local sources, mirroring the way the rich lands of the Yonne itself offer up the Chablis and Irancy of which the region is so proud.

4

A TV Show Called Paris – Canal Plus Buys Paris St Germain:
Interview with Laurent Perpère, Chairman of PSG

CHRISTOV RÜHN

PSG is one of the richest French clubs. Where does it stand in European terms?
The most recent figures I have place it thirteenth. I think that French clubs will become a lot richer, because in the past French TV rights were considerably undervalued compared to what clubs in Spain, Italy or England receive for them. Within the next two to three years we'll see a process of revaluation. This should be enough to put us back up among the leading clubs in Europe.

Canal Plus is the leading TV sports channel in France. Was it really essential to buy a football club?
Back in 1990–91, PSG was on the point of bankruptcy. The management at the time, along with representatives from the Paris City Council, came to see Canal Plus and stressed how risky the current situation was for everybody concerned. They asked whether Canal Plus would be willing to take over the reins. It would have been a disaster for the channel's sub-scribers if the French First Division Championship, which at

the time was shown exclusively on Canal Plus, went ahead without a Paris-based team. The 10 million population of the Ile de France region would have been deprived of a local club to support. So in order to keep the Championship – the cornerstone of Canal Plus's programming – alive, the channel decided to apply its expertise in events management to support PSG. It was a successful decision, as the figures show that PSG is France's most successful club of the nineties, alongside Olympique Marseille. During the Canal Plus era, PSG have won the French Cup three times, in 1993, 1995 and 1996, as well as the League Cup in 1995 and 1998. PSG were also French champions in 1994, won the Cup-Winners' Cup in 1996, and were beaten finalists the following year, 1997.

A major portion of PSG's budget is covered by income from TV rights. What's the situation here, given that as Canal Plus you pay out for the rights, and as PSG you receive money from their sale?
The income from TV rights is, of course, divided equitably between all the clubs in the First Division. We receive a lot less for PSG than we pay out as Canal Plus. In July 1999, the value of the contract signed between the National Football League and Canal Plus was increased significantly. PSG gets exactly the same amount of money from the National Football League as every other club. The only slight difference in payment is related to a club's league position at the end of the season.

Other European countries use different systems. In England, the Premier League allocates 50 per cent of TV income equally to member clubs, with 25 per cent awarded according to final league positions and the remaining 25 per cent in relation to a club's share of the TV audience. In Italy, each club controls its own TV rights and income from them depends on the deals they agree with TV channels. The income the League can split between the clubs is generated by only a tiny number of games. In Spain income from TV rights is not divided equally, either.

In my capacity as executive president of PSG, I'd naturally

prefer it if we owned our TV rights. However, if I were in charge of a club like Nancy or Le Havre, this would obviously not be in my interests. The major clubs find themselves in an awkward position, for although we compete in a national competition, what's really vital for us is to finish high enough to qualify for Europe. This can be a major handicap. PSG finished the 1998–9 season in ninth place, and although we haven't lost audience, the fact that we weren't engaged in a European competition lost us a major source of revenue. The difficulty for a club like PSG lies in the fact that we have to measure ourselves simultaneously against Le Havre, a modest-sized League club, albeit the longest established, and against international clubs like Arsenal and Real Madrid. Sadly for us, the financial set-up in France favours the National League at the expense of European competitions. The English system is the best all round, and I think that this fact is beginning to sink in over here.

As for TPS, a competing satellite service that has followed our lead in transmitting pay-per-view games, I'm not in the slightest bit concerned. On any one League day there are going to be three decent games, two of which will be covered exclusively by Canal Plus and the other by TPS. [*Like Sky TV in the UK*.] Some matches shown on Canal Plus are transmitted outside the normal League kick-off times. Only Canal Plus does this. TPS doesn't have this advantage: they broadcast a match at the same time as the other games kick off, and are penalised as a result. Subscribers and supporters know what's best for them – it's Canal Plus they look to.

What's more important for club profitability, deep pockets or sound management?
Both. There are considerable improvements to be made in the way clubs are managed, and every club is moving in this direction as the League takes a very close interest in what goes on. This isn't to say that club management is free from hare-brained schemes, but things like the OM–Valenciennes match-fixing or the scandal of the bungs at St Etienne seem to

have pretty much disappeared from the scene. What does still need to be improved is the legal status of the clubs. Most are run as non-profit-making associations under a law dating back to 1901. They often suffer from weak management and are not run as proper businesses which now need to go out and find new revenue streams beyond the usual subsidies and TV rights. What is absolutely vital is to take the core formed by the team and develop your brand around it, with merchandising and season-ticket systems that both increase your net take per season ticket-holder and attract sponsors. This is the example set by English clubs like Arsenal and Manchester United, who are leaders in this field.

Does PSG need stars in the same way that Canal Plus does?
If we have things working properly, it's not the stars that make PSG, but rather PSG that makes the stars. We're selling a dream, and stars are a vital part of a team that gives the public something to dream about: great characters in a great side. However, I prefer a set-up with slightly fewer stars, if it works well and plays attractive football, to a team packed with big names who have no real understanding of each other. A team works well when everything around it clicks. Back when Canal Plus took over the club, the budget was bigger than at any other French club at the time and PSG became the club all the great players such as Ginola, Weah, Djorkaeff and others wanted to play for. Despite the fact that we achieved great things with these star players, especially on the European stage, at the end of the day we won the French Championship only once during this period.

Since those days, other French clubs have increased their budgets to match ours, and the big names don't necessarily look to us any more as they can earn the same money at other clubs. The Bosman ruling* has had the effect of driving a lot

---

*The Bosman ruling, delivered by the European Court at Luxembourg on 15 December 1995, decreed that players at the end of their contracts would be free to circulate within the European Union.

of players away from France for financial reasons. We can't afford to compete with the wage policies in force in some other European countries. The French tax system is pretty severe, and we're doing everything we can to lobby the government to make some changes. But it's not a simple matter in a country with an 11 per cent unemployment rate. It's very hard to defend the idea that somebody earning 1 million francs a month shouldn't be taxed. You've got to keep a sense of decency. However, I hope that we'll find a solution in the not-too-distant future and that the current situation will improve.

Do sales of replica strips and merchandising represent a significant part of your operating budget, as is the case at clubs like Manchester United and Barcelona?
We were the first French club to venture into this area, but nowadays we're not alone. OM and RC Lens have caught up with us. OM's results show annual merchandising sales of 50 million francs, as opposed to 40 million for PSG and 20 million for RC Lens. We're a long way from the sales generated by Manchester United, which amount to close to 300 million francs, and it'll be difficult for us ever to achieve that level. British football benefits from considerable exposure in the former British colonies. Manchester United even have a shop in Hong Kong. PSG only have one shop, on the Champs Elysées, and most of the sales there are to tourists looking for a souvenir of Paris – in this case the city's team strip.

Why doesn't PSG own its ground? Are there any plans in the pipeline?
Very few clubs actually own their ground. We use the Parc des Princes, which we lease from the Paris City Council, and which is currently undergoing extensive renovation. The cost of the work is shared between the council and us. We've got a deal for the Parc with fifteen years left to run. It's just like having your own ground. We'd gain nothing by purchasing it.

Although Paris is the capital city of France, it has only one major team, unlike cities such as Madrid and London. Why do you think this is?
Football in France is currently enjoying a surge in popularity and there's definitely a market for a second Parisian team. The problem is that it would require a very large investment to found a new club and the returns are limited. I can't imagine any entrepreneur who is going to be prepared to sink almost 1 billion francs into creating a second team in Paris. For PSG, it would be fantastic to have another team, as it would make things more exciting; you'd get derbies just like in London or Milan. The Stade de France, too, is desperate to attract a resident team, but so far without success.

What is the exact nature of the relationship between Canal Plus and PSG? What is the set-up at PSG?
I was appointed executive president of PSG, but I am also financial director of Canal Plus. [*This interview was held in September 1999. Laurent Perpère is now senior executive vice president of Canal Plus development and international affairs.*] My job at the TV company takes up an enormous amount of time, which is why we're talking here, at the Canal Plus building; otherwise I'd be out at Boulogne, where the club is based. I'm lucky to be able to rely on Jean-Luc Lamarche, the club manager, who came to us from Lens, as well as on our coach Philippe Bergeroo, who was assistant coach to the French World Cup-winning side. The three of us spend a lot of time discussing sporting matters. Everything else is run in the normal way by a top-class team, just like in most major companies.

What's the status of the PSG youth training centre?
We're currently in the process of renovating it and giving it a new sense of mission. A truly major professional team can't solely exist on, or justify itself by, results on the pitch. Beyond the entertainment aspect, professional football must also take the lead in the educational and social fields. In the minds of

the public, footballers are role models, and they must represent a force for the good. Youth training centres are part of
this; they offer an outlet to youngsters who love football and
who often have nothing else to strive for in their lives. What
we want is for young footballers who live in the Paris region
to dream of being recruited by PSG. We're developing ever
deeper links with the entire Ile de France region. You must
remember that youth training begins with spotting the raw
talent, and around Paris there's a terrific reservoir of that.
We're doing everything we can to make sure that these
youngsters end up at PSG. In the past, when players were
cheaper to acquire, youth development programmes were not
so important, but today they are a vital part of the club's
financial stability. Bringing on young talent doesn't come
cheap, but it's still a lot cheaper to bring one or two talented
players into the first team from our own ranks than to buy
players once they've left somebody else's training programme.

*If that's the case, why on earth did you release a player like
Nicolas Anelka, who was trained at PSG and is now worth a
fortune?*
Well, there were a number of factors in play. First of all, PSG
made a big mistake in not recognising the player's tremendous potential and in not immediately giving him his chance.
However, Anelka was just seventeen and a half years old at
the time and was demanding to be the first-choice striker for
the A team. The management at the time agreed with the
coach that it was a little early to agree to this. Secondly, he
wasn't yet contracted to our club, and there was no way
legally that we could stop him leaving. Finally, PSG wasn't
prepared to accede to the financial demands of Nicolas and
his family. It's not really possible to hang on to a player
against his will, and anyway, as everybody saw, the same
thing happened again, in a pretty surreal way, when he went
to Arsenal.
    In football, the people who advise players are terribly
important and I feel that although Nicolas is perfectly straight,

despite himself he finds he's the victim of circumstances that are somehow larger than his desire to play football, which is probably very sincere.

Transfer fees in excess of 200 million francs are far removed from any economic reality. When you think that the average price of a first-team player, if you want to put together a side that's competitive nationally and in Europe, is around 70 million francs, and that you need around twenty of them, then a club needs an annual budget of close to 800 million francs. Now that's a great deal of money. Even Manchester United don't have that kind of cash. If everybody goes around artificially inflating transfer prices, the only thing that happens is that the players' agents make a bigger profit. It's an irrational system based on speculation, and at any time it could collapse like a house of cards. Clubs that have paid out top dollar to build a powerful team and then can't sell enough players to finance their outgoings will pay the price.

Opel are sponsors of Bayern and AC Milan as well as of PSG. Do you have a special relationship with these clubs when it comes to buying players? Does Canal Plus sponsor any football clubs?

We take part every year in the Opel Masters. PSG enjoys excellent relations with AC Milan and we often exchange players with them. As German football is very different, we don't have the same type of relationship with Bayern Munich when it comes to exchanging players. Canal Plus are sponsors of the French national side.

The Swiss club Servette de Genève is owned by Canal Plus. Are there any others?

Servette de Genève is effectively owned by Canal Plus, and although we don't own the majority of the shares, we do own close to 50 per cent of them. The club president is a Canal Plus man and we're represented on the board by Michel Denisot and myself, among others. Le Servette and PSG exchange players and we often send youngsters to

Switzerland to gain experience. It's harder for us at PSG to take Swiss players as Switzerland is not a member of the EU. The quotas for non-EU players are very restrictive, so it's not as advantageous for PSG as it would be if Canal Plus owned, for example, a Belgian or an Irish club. PSG has never faced Servette de Genève in a European competition so we haven't yet had to deal with any problems arising from owning more than one club, and we hope not to have to.

It's the first time that Philippe Bergeroo, PSG's current trainer, has had a job at this level. Isn't PSG taking a big risk?
He isn't the first. Ricardo, a former PSG and Brazilian international player, and Alain Giresse, a team-mate of Michel Platini's in the French European Championship-winning team of 1984 and current manager at Toulouse FC, both started out as coaches with PSG, though with varying degrees of success.

[*Ricardo led PSG to the final of the 1997 Cup-Winners' Cup, where they lost narrowly, 1–0, to Barcelona. Under his guidance PSG won the League Cup and the French Cup. Alain Giresse lasted three months before being sacked during the tenure of former PSG president Charles Biétry.*]

Yours hasn't been the classic route into football. How did you end up as executive president of PSG?
I've been involved with PSG for almost three years and was a board member in my capacity as a director of Canal Plus. When it came to choosing a successor to Charles Biétry, Pierre Lescure, the head of Canal Plus, considered that I had the leadership and management qualities needed to run the club. It was also thought that I was sufficiently versed in the ways of PSG not to repeat some of the errors made in the past. Finally, I'm a Canal Plus man, and it had to be somebody from Canal Plus.

[*Charles Biétry is the former head of sport at Canal Plus and was appointed to the PSG hot seat at the start of the 1998–9 season, after a long campaign of scheming within Canal Plus.*

He lasted only six months before being forced to resign because of the club's poor results and a lack of support both within the club and from the owners. That season saw PSG slump to ninth in the Championship, their worst result since the Canal Plus takeover in 1990–91. Biétry also resigned from Canal Plus and headed for TF1, a competing channel, owners of the TPS satellite service and bitter rivals of Canal Plus.]

I am a financial manager, and PSG is a commercial operation. At the time, Michel Denisot [*the first president of PSG-Canal Plus and a sports journalist*] also had to make the transition and become a financial manager. Despite the fact that he was a man of many qualities, Charles Biétry didn't have enough time to change his mindset to approach football as a business when he'd come from a different background, journalism in his case. He wasn't able to correct the mistakes he made, and as things move very quickly in the world of football he soon found himself in an unstoppable downward spiral. Another problem was that a lot of people were waiting for him to trip up. As a journalist he was always quick to call people to account, and his friends in the press, jealous of his promotion, didn't hesitate to take their revenge and ripped him to shreds. He ended up resigning because he knew he'd hit the buffers and that there was no way back.

When will we see PSG as champions of Europe?
It will probably be a few years before PSG, or any other French team, become European champions. French clubs need more time to build teams capable of challenging the supremacy of the big clubs in Europe. I'm thinking especially of the Italian Serie A teams, which I personally consider to be the best club sides in the world. In France we don't currently have the qualities needed to reach this standard. There's still a little something missing.

These days French football can't afford players as expensive as Anelka or Desailly, for example, and for as long as that remains the case we can't reasonably expect to consider ourselves the equals of our European colleagues. It will take time for

PSG to build a great team, and even if we were suddenly given unlimited funding, which is not likely, you'd have to allow a minimum of three years before you'd have all the pieces in place.

But the day will come when the five biggest clubs in France will have sufficient resources to be able to hang on to the players we trained as youths. I'm not in the slightest bit worried about the future.

II

Les Bleus

5

Unjust Rewards: Harald Schumacher's Foul on Patrick Battiston, World Cup 1982

DAVID BADDIEL

It might be quite hard to explain to someone with no know-ledge of the game why exactly it is that Germany are the villains of world football. You could begin by pointing to the fact that they are, more or less, the villains of world history. You could bring up their irritatingly fine record at international level – three World Cups and three European Championships making them effortlessly the most successful team in Europe – a record linked in the football fan's mind not, as in the case of Brazil, with wild, radical skill but with ruthless efficiency. You could try to describe Rudi Völler's facial hair. Or you could just show them a video of the 1982 World Cup semi-final.

In Freudian analysis there is a famous syndrome known as transference, where, in the absence of a loved object, the emotions it would normally inspire are projected on to another, present one. During the 1970s, English football fans underwent a *lot* of transference. That was the only way of watching that decade's two World Cups: to transfer the emotions inspired by the so, so absent object – the English national side – on to a present one, Brazil, normally, or, at a pinch, Holland. In 1982, I had hardly got used to the extravagant idea of actually being able to support England in a World Cup when they got knocked out in the second round, a result of two 0–0 draws and an infamous missed header by Kevin Keegan. Almost immediately, the years of living without them came into play; transference kicked in, and before I knew it – Brazil having already been knocked out following some classically Brazilian defensive errors against Italy – I was supporting France. This was not a hard choice in 1982. The French team at the time were Brazil, anyway, Brazil in blue – or rather, they were the perfect combination of seventies Brazil and seventies Holland, of dancers like Tigana and visionaries like Platini; of rock 'n' roll pin-up boys like Rocheteau and *enfants terribles* like Didier Six and eccentric elfin character-players like Alain Giresse. One of the best sides of all time; certainly France's best side, much better than the journeyman side that won the World Cup in 1998, characterised by Aimé Jacquet's utterly unGallic only-one-flair-player-per-eleven quota. And then, in the semi-final, this side was drawn against Germany: or *West* Germany as they were then, the adjective conveying just that extra bit of cultural and economic superiority required to maximise their hate-object status.

I was eighteen. Many of my initial attempts to create for myself a social life had revolved around football, and on 8 July 1982, that social life converged upon my parents' house in Dollis Hill, north London: five tortured-by-testosterone English adolescents, all supporting France. There was no question of anyone supporting Germany; apart from the engraved-in-stone football fact that the transference never goes there, we were all Jews – on the one hand the Dreyfus affair, on the other. . .

Let's cut to the chase: it's less painful. Germany won. France played some beautiful football, but then a combination of complacency and Karl-Heinz Rummenigge destroyed their two-goal lead in extra time, and once it went to penalties, there was only ever going to be one winner: winning penalty shoot-outs is what the Germans do, it's in their genes along with moustaches and soft rock. But the critical moment of this game was not a goal, nor a penalty. In the fifty-eighth minute, with the score at 1–1, Platini lifted a ball from the right wing towards the German penalty area. The French substitute Patrick Battiston, who at that point had been on the field for approximately seven minutes, ran on to it in space. It is a little-remembered fact that his shot from this position went wide. He should, actually, have scored, and no doubt, if he could, would have reproached himself. But Patrick Battiston couldn't reproach himself, because he was unconscious.

Something that really doesn't help the negative German paradigm this game represents is the look of their then goalkeeper, Harald Schumacher. A brown-blond mullet-and-moustache combo isn't great in any circumstances; think of it atop one of the squarest faces in history, itself atop a body built like a brick *Scheissehaus*. And now think of the whole lot coming towards you at 500 miles an hour. That was what Battiston saw, or would have seen if his eyes had not been on the ball. Perhaps it's better that he was spared it.

The French players surrounded not the ref, as they would do now, but the prone figure of Battiston. In Dollis Hill, we waited with bated breath to see what was going to happen to Schumacher, who was standing by the edge of his 6-yard box as if nothing had happened. What punishment would be meted out by the Dutch ref, Charles Corver? A sending-off? A life ban? Six months in prison? After Battiston had left the field on a stretcher – concussed, not just for the rest of the game, but for the rest of the night, with four broken ribs and five lost teeth, injuries that were to cost him his place in the Monaco side for the opening half of the following season – Charles Corver waited a couple of seconds and then awarded . . . a goal kick.

A goal kick. Not even a foul. My friend Richard Gerard was so disgusted he got up and walked out of the room. I don't think I can remember him more outraged. And he didn't even like football. That's the problem, of course, when refs bottle it. They have to go completely the other way. If Mr Corver was to admit that Schumacher's tackle had been a foul, he could hardly have dismissed it as a slightly clumsy challenge. A sending-off would only have started to balance the scales of justice: and a sending-off in a World Cup semi-final is a big deal, especially taking into account the basic leniency refs tend to show goalkeepers. That's the only explanation I can offer. The other possibility is that Mr Corver was a fucking idiot. You take your pick.

Who knows what difference it would've made if the referee had made something approaching the right decision? If Schumacher had been sent off . . . if Platini had taken the resulting free kick . . . and other might-have-beens the stuff of football daydreams.

Looking back, this is probably the single most scarring international football memory I have outside of the terrible tapestry that is England's latterday World Cup history. Because actually, France started to play better after the Schumacher foul. The first half had been fairly even, and it was only after Lopez replaced Battiston that the blue flair really started to outfox the white regimentation. It was as if God had looked at the ref's decision, and thought, that's it – I knew this free will was a bad idea. I'm giving the French the run of the ball. That was what was so painful about the final outcome. Miscarriages of justice, they normally take years to be put right, but this one, it seemed to be being put right here and now, in front of our eyes: and then of course that turned out to be wrong. Because not only did Bossis miss the sixth penalty. Harald Schumacher saved it. He was not, as he should be, the villain of the night, but the hero. As the Germans ran from the centre circle to embrace him, I turned the TV off, and we all sat around in silence, learning a lesson I guess: the lesson that there is no levelling, no Aristotelian evenhandedness to be had in football, or anywhere else, in fact. It's all accidents and bad decisions. Hope is an error, surpassed only by the idea that there is a moral order to the universe. I'm not sure all this was entirely clear to us at the time, but without doubt we were a bit depressed.

However: when I recreated this incident for BBC 2's *Fantasy Football* in 1998, I met Patrick Battiston. And to be honest, he didn't seem that bothered about it any more. His teeth were OK now, his ribs were fine, and the nightmares about a moustachioed figure bearing down on him were gone. He even told me he'd gone to Harald Schumacher's wedding, where apparently Harald had mistaken the imprecation 'You may now kiss the bride' and shoulder-barged her to the floor.

Admittedly, it's sixteen years later, and a mature person would – should – have got over it. But somehow I'd have preferred it if he wasn't so mature; if he was still resentful, still bitter, still raging somewhere in the wild heath of his heart at Germany, at Charles Corver, and at injustice, the injustice that hung over Seville that night like the scent of rotting oranges.

6

The Fab Four – France Wins the 1984 European Championship

PATRICK BARCLAY

In 1984, according to a forecast in George Orwell's novel published thirty-five years earlier, ignorance would be strength. And this certainly appeared to be the basis of England's attitude to the 1984 European Championship. As the tournament destined to become the most enthralling of its kind got underway in the Parc des Princes, Paris, British television companies seemed oblivious of it, and the senior correspondents of the national newspapers were otherwise engaged in South America, covering a tour by the England team which had failed to qualify for the event in France.

As deputy to the *Guardian*'s David Lacey, I benefited from this island mentality, being among a handful of second-string reporters who crossed the Channel to be there from the start. Lacey and company were to arrive later, in time for France's glorious semi-final with Portugal, but they missed several other treats. Our little advance party had abundant opportunity for fun because in those days, before television had broadened the English public's view of the game and indirectly funded the proliferation of imported players, there was deemed to be scant interest in the foreigners playing it. Our editors wanted only brief reports and so, armed with the Michelin Guide, we built into our itineraries some wonderful restaurants in out-of-the-way places.

On one occasion in rural Alsace, while diligently fuelling ourselves in preparation for the meeting of Denmark and Belgium in Strasbourg, we were brought a wooden board that, although stout, was almost audibly groaning under the weight of local *charcuterie*. Boggle-eyed, we polished off the lot before realising from the waiters' resigned expressions that it had been intended to suffice for the entire restaurant. We lived and learned. And at the same time our love of football was satisfied by a month that, although dominated by the ascent of Michel Platini to unquestionable greatness, contained much more. There was always plenty to discuss while lingering over the *cassoulet* and *coq au vin*: the heroics of Denmark's dashing Preben Elkjaer, the last-minute knock-out blow delivered by Spain's giant central defender Antonio Maceda to the West German holders, the emergence of Portugal as dark horses. And France. Always France, always with Platini to the fore.

In truth it was unforgivable, even in those blinkered days, for England to take so long to notice that something special was happening across the water. The English, or to be more accurate, the British, had been warned that France were on the march, for after England had succumbed to two Platini goals, from a free kick and a flying header, in Paris at the end of February, a run of four consecutive wins by Michel Hidalgo's team in pre-tournament friendly matches was to culminate in the slaughter of Scotland. On a bowling green of a Marseilles pitch that was ideally suited to France in general, and Alain Giresse in particular, the Scots were subjected to sublime torture. It was one of the most one-sided internationals I have witnessed and, from the Scottish point of view, one of the luckiest escapes: the record books show that, like England, they lost 2–0, but only merciful providence knows why France were restricted to goals by Giresse and Bernard Genghini.

We understood then that France had been endowed with

one of the finest midfield quartets ever to grace the game. There had been much evidence to this effect at the World Cup in Spain two years earlier, where France lost only on penalties to West Germany in a thrilling semi-final marred by German keeper Harald Schumacher's appalling, unpunished body-check on Patrick Battiston. And this both matured individually and was communally strengthened by the familiarity of its exceptional technicians Platini, Giresse and Jean Tigana. At the hub was Giresse: compact and balanced, a master of clever and penetrative distribution. To the right was the more mobile Tigana, lithe and quick, supplying width; to the left, Luís Fernandez, who had become the first-choice enforcer, leaving the versatile Genghini to fill in behind when the team's needs dictated. And leading from the front was Platini, who had the freedom to do what he did, which could only be described as everything.

Never in the history of major football tournaments has one man exerted such influence as Platini's in 1984. Not even Pelé in the 1970 World Cup; he was complemented by Jairzinho's goals and Gerson's architecture. Not even Diego Maradona in the 1986 World Cup, though claims on the Argentine's behalf would have to be taken seriously given that, even when close-marked by Lothar Matthäus in the final due to the Germans' fear of his dribbling, he still had a hand in all three goals. But Platini's contribution was demonstrably, statistically, overwhelming. In five matches he scored nine times. In all but one of those matches, his goals were manifestly fundamental to the outcome – and the arguable exception was a 5–0 victory over Belgium in which he per-formed the first of two hat-tricks.

It is, of course, true that outstanding teams usually require more than one leader. Without the craft of Giresse, the verve of Tigana and the industry of Fernandez, Platini could not have been expected to devise his extraordinary dovetailing of two functions: playmaker and striker. Nor should anyone neglect the significance of Maxime Bossis, an assertive, enter-prising and hugely intelligent force at the back. But even a dedicated striker would not be required to average nearly two goals a match in the finals of the European Championship. What Platini delivered went beyond the wildest dreams of a country that had designed the modern game, prompting the formation of international competitions, but was not to win any of them until 1984. In a sense, to paraphrase the English slogan at a later European Championship, Platini brought football home. When the World Cup was won fourteen years later, also on home soil, the credit was shared amid much socio-babble about Europe's rainbow nation. Zinedine Zidane had played very well indeed, but without standing head and shoulders above the rest, as if to demonstrate that the game had changed and the simplicity of old-fashioned heroism had been lost.

Platini, like France, began in less than devastating style. Late in a slow burner of an opening match, he struck to overcome Denmark, who had lost Allan Simonsen with a broken leg. The show moved to Nantes, where Giresse and Fernandez supplemented Platini's three goals in the rout of the Belgians, then on to St Etienne and more troublesome opponents in the form of Yugoslavia, who led at half-time only to be beaten 3–2 as the question of what Platini could do for an encore was answered by a second successive hat-trick. This put France in the semi-finals, and the drama continued to build, for a feeling that the hosts had been favoured by the draw which paired them with Portugal in Marseilles – Denmark, splendidly resurgent, and Spain were to meet in Lyons the following night – proved overoptimistic.

The initial hero of this event was destined to be over-shadowed. Jean-François Domergue, a relatively unsung left back, procured the opening goal from a free kick and was later to rescue France by cracking in their second in extra time, thus setting the stage for Platini to provide an immortal climax. By now even the English were taking notice of the tournament. Their manager, Bobby Robson, had returned from South America and was in the Stade Vélodrome along with my colleague Lacey and the rest of England's press sages, whose underlings had the privilege of keeping a watching brief as a classic match of twists and turns unfolded. For an hour it was fairly routine, but then Portugal brought on the veteran Nene and his enthusiasm spread through their ranks. Within ten minutes Jordão had equalised, dictating extra time, in which the Portuguese were first to find the net, again through Jordão, whose mishit shot crept almost apologetically past the French goalkeeper, Joel Bats. The response to this crisis was reminiscent of Portugal's in normal time: France drew heart from a substitute, Bruno Bellone, and achieved equality through Domergue. The match now took on a life of its own. We were just a minute away from a penalty decider – though whether any Frenchman had the composure to recall that this device had brought their World Cup downfall two years earlier was doubtful – when Tigana popped up on the right flank to send the ball into the danger area. Who was there to receive it? None other than Platini. He tamed it, took his time – an age – and suddenly the roof of the net was billowing. The roar that hit the Mediterranean sky confirmed that France were in the final.

In Burgundy the next day, we pondered whether they would be reacquainted in Paris with the doughty Danes, and there was soon an indication that this would prove the case as Soren Lerby scored after a few minutes. Denmark were a substantial side, extremely hard-working yet endowed with the subtlety of Morten Olsen, perhaps the cleverest *libero* since Franz Beckenbauer defined the role. But they missed chances, and midway through the second half Maceda, whose goal had been responsible for Spain's presence in the semi-finals, scored again. After extra time, the issue went to penalties and poor Elkjaer, one of the tournament's most attractive personalities, drove wildly over the crossbar. So it was France against Spain. Maceda's feelings, however, were mixed, for the blond centre back had been shown the second yellow card of the tournament by the English referee, George Courtney, and would therefore miss the final. The same fate had befallen his team-mate Rafael Gordillo, a wide midfielder who played with his socks rolled down and had the asset of stretching opponents, much as Tigana could do for France. These were not components Spain could afford to lose at such a stage of the championship.

Understandably, perhaps, they arrived at the Parc des Princes with caution uppermost in their minds. More disappointingly, the French were constrained from expressing themselves by the inevitable anxiety of the occasion. To put this in context let it be borne in mind that hosts had not won the European Championship since Italy in 1968 – and no hosts have won it since France. At any rate France were not fired by the proximity of the trophy, nor even by an out-of-touch Platini, in a perturbing first half during which the subdued crowd offered little help. But the many qualities possessed by Platini, it transpired, included the talismanic. When he tried a free kick, the Spanish goalkeeper, Luís Arconada, got down smartly to stop it – only to fumble and let the ball trickle through his arms into the net. At last the accuracy, movement and imagination that had turned France into Europe's best team were liberated. The Spaniards, too, raised their game, but near the end Bellone, served by Tigana, raced through a tired defence to seal the outcome. The crowd were full of passion now and, amid the celebrations that followed the final whistle, Hidalgo's grey suit was soaked with champagne.

His part in the campaign had been noble. Eight years of encouraging creation, of reflecting the French belief in style, had been thoroughly vindicated in a year whose buoyancy was to continue as they began the job of qualifying for the next World Cup with victories over Luxembourg, Bulgaria and East Germany. In all, France played twelve matches in 1984 and won the lot.

May it further be noted, lest we assume that Hidalgo's France were all about the attacking virtues epitomised by Platini, that they conceded goals in only two of those matches: against Yugoslavia and, four days later, Portugal. It should be appreciated that the likes of Bats and Bossis underpinned their triumph, just as Fabien Barthez and Lilian Thuram were to do in 1998. But who can dilute the impact of Platini? France seem for ever to be searching for strikers of appropriate status. In 1998, Aimé Jacquet had to rely on the raw David Trezeguet and Thierry Henry and mundane Stéphane Guivarc'h. In 1984, Hidalgo juggled with four or five front men. And yet the first goal he got from a striker was France's fourteenth, Bellone's – just a minute from the conclusion of the tournament. This is probably the best measure of Platini's gift to the nation. And probably the best testimony to his lieutenants is to say that, since 1984, no discussion of whether a midfield has reached the highest class can have been complete unless it featured the linking of his name with those of Tigana, Giresse and Fernandez.

7

First Samba in Guadalajara – France Beats Brazil in the World Cup, 1986

JEAN-PHILIPPE LECLAIRE

The Tricolores had a less fraught passage into Mexico 1986 than in either qualifying phase of the previous two World Cups. The decisive match, France v. Yugoslavia on 16 November 1985 (2–0, two Platini goals), didn't generate the same level of emotion as 1977's France–Bulgaria game or France against the Netherlands in 1981. There were no tears for new national coach Henri Michel, not even the beginnings of a tickle behind the eyes. The thirty-nine-year-old from Nantes arrived at the head of a national side still basking in the glory of the Olympic title he had won with the French 'hopefuls' side at the LA games. Primed by his predecessor, Michel Hidalgo, it was time for Henri Michel to move up to a higher level: to learn how to lead a squad of strong-minded players, chief among them Michel Platini. Since they had first met, back in 1976, Henri Michel and Michel Platini had got to know each other, but without ever becoming great friends. Platini was unhappy that the Canaries' captain had shown little enthusiasm for his arrival at FC Nantes in the spring of 1979. Seven years down the line, the man from Lorraine still held a grudge, but he also knew that both his and the new coach's personal interests were best served by maintaining good relations.

* * *

It was in this climate of tension that France won their first match of the 1986 World Cup finals, against Canada. Playing a team thought to be among the weakest in the tournament, Henri Michel's men managed only a single goal, ten minutes from full-time, courtesy of their 'joker', Jean-Pierre Papin. Trained at INF Vichy, but subsequently ignored by the major French club sides, the player famous for his 'Papinades' (his now legendary bicycle kicks) had just finished a tremendous season in Belgium. Already signed by club president Bernard Tapie to play his next season with Olympique Marseille, 'JPP' was playing in only his second match for Les Bleus. Despite his eightieth-minute goal, he had a disappointing game, missing an incredible number of chances. The curly-haired centre forward with the jug ears would, little by little, rejoin those players left for ever on the bench. At the sharp end of the French attack he would be first substituted, then replaced altogether, by the Toulouse player Yannick Stopyra.

France qualified for the second round without too many problems, thanks to a 1–1 draw against the USSR and an easy 3–0 win over Hungary. They ended up taking second place in Group C behind the USSR, architects of a memorable 6–0 thrashing of Hungary. The only cloud on the horizon for Henri Michel's players was their next opponents: they were to face world champions Italy in a last-sixteen match that already had the whiff of gunpowder about it. It was a Latin derby of particular importance to Michel Platini.

Arriving in Mexico weighed down by his reputation as 'the best player in the world', the three-times winner of the Golden Ball had never found it so hard to live with his fame. Hidden behind a pair of sunglasses, harassed by journalists and thousands of autograph-hunters, Michel Platini rarely ventured out without bodyguards. All his hopes for evading the crowds, thousands of kilometres from any microphone, were contained in a brown travel bag that he always kept tightly shut. 'It contained his holiday things. It was all he

dreamed of: holidaying in Thailand with his wife,' recalls
Henri Michel. As he waited to discover the temples of Thailand
in the company of Christèle, Platini lived the life of a recluse,
punctuated by press conferences where he strung together a
series of untruths in almost mechanical fashion. 'No, I'm not
upset by not having scored yet.' 'No, the tendonitis in my left
foot isn't a handicap.' And the biggest whopper of them all:
'Truly, sincerely, the fact that we've drawn Italy doesn't make
my motivation any greater.' When operating at such a level of
denial, how could he be believed for one second? Obviously
the match against Italy would be above all his match, a match
for the *Francese*, who had no intention of returning to Turin a
loser.

With Marco Tardelli on the bench and Antonio Cabrini
firmly stuck down his left-hand corridor, Italian coach Enzo
Bearzot decided to nominate Giuseppe Baresi, Franco's
brother, as Platini's marker. With barely fifteen minutes of this
tempestuous match played, the Inter Milan defender found
himself wrong-footed, alone on the outside. The ball was lost
but Baresi junior's famous charge gave him the space to take
a pitch-perfect through ball from Dominique Rocheteau. Con-
trolling the ball with two touches at the edge of the area, he
shot it over the goalkeeper, who had already come off his line
to intercept. First goal of the match to Platini, his fortieth for
France and his first of the competition.

The unofficial assistant coach kept up the pressure on his
team-mates during the half-time break. 'Come on boys! Their
game plan isn't working, and we've got ours spot on. Let's
make the most of it.' Immediately opposite, behind the door
marked 'Italia', Enzo Bearzot was less sure of himself. The
long-faced maestro made a radical change to his strategy,
bringing on Di Gennaro to replace the luckless Baresi. It
made no difference. Michel Platini appeared to be playing
with the legs of a twenty-year-old and as if his heel was
untroubled by tendonitis. Two shots on target, a superb
millimetre-perfect through ball for Alain Giresse, another
player obviously back on form after a long layoff. In the

fifty-ninth minute the other French players had their say, proving that they could succeed without the help of their two stars. Tigana slalomed his way into the Italian defence and passed to Rocheteau, who laid the ball back to Stopyra. His savage grass-high shot clinched a 2–0 victory for France. After the final whistle Marco Tardelli came over and put his arms around Platini's neck, but the great man was far away, detached, floating on his own small cloud. The tendonitis, the anti-inflammatories, the terrible weight of his own repu-tation, had all disappeared. The redeemed champion was in another world, as were the entire French team. Les Bleus had never beaten a defending champion at this stage of the competition. That day, even the notoriously buttoned-up Henri Michel had trouble containing his emotions. 'It was a powerful feeling afterwards in the changing room, as well as later on, when we got back to the hotel. The Mariachis were waiting for us in the lobby and the other guests were applaud-ing us. From that moment we knew that we could go all the way.' Especially as the coach felt that he could again play a Platini who was fully focused, majestic on the field of play and once more at ease away from it. 'I can still see him singing in the bus. He was wearing a blue baseball cap he'd pinched off the Italians. He was never without it for the rest of the tournament. I think he must have even worn it in bed.'

Les Bleus left the Mexican capital and headed for Guadalajara, the city that would stage their quarter-final tie. This magical name, with its 'j' that rumbles in the roof of the mouth, is well known to every lover of football. It conjures up images of another World Cup, that of 1970, the greatest tournament in history. The Jalisco Stadium was home to Pelé's Brazilian team for every one of their games prior to the final. Since then, every inch of the pitch appeared to be haunted by the ghosts of a Jairzinho break, a Carlos Alberto through ball, and, above all, the exploits of Pelé, the king. This stadium, this mausoleum erected in honour of the beautiful game was already known to Platini from an AS

Nancy-Lorraine tour of Mexico seven years previously. Then, respectfully, almost meditatively, the kid who had signed his classroom essays 'Péléatini' had wanted to pay homage to his hero at the famous goalmouth, scene of one of the most celebrated moments in the history of football: the legendary acrobatics of the English goalkeeper Gordon Banks, whose otherworldly, instinctive save deflected a masterful attempt from Pelé as he attempted to bury a close-range header into the back of the English net during the famous Brazil–England game of 1970. 'Was it there, or there?' asked Platini nine years later when he came to the place where the miracle had occurred. 'It was there,' replied the journalist Gérard Ernault, gesturing pretty much at random, not wanting in any way to disappoint the youngster who was dreaming one of football's greatest dreams.

Now summoned in his turn to play a World Cup quarter-final match on the same hallowed turf, Michel Platini was to come face to face with the spiritual heirs of his idols Pelé, Carlos Alberto, Tostão and Jairzinho. The new Brazilians of 1986 were called Zico, Socrates, Muller and Branco, names which, although slightly less legendary, still inspired a mixture of passion and respect. As in 1970, Guadalajara was covered in *auriverde*. The Brazilian party had distributed 6,000 yellow-and-green shirts to local schools as well as quite a few free match tickets. On 21 June, his thirty-first birthday, Michel Platini found the Jalisco Stadium of his childhood memories: *auriverde* right up to the top tier, the sounds of sambas ringing out, an overpowering heat and sense of the event's importance. Two hours later the entire scene had changed: the beautiful *cariocas* were crying their alluring eyes out. Luís Fernandez had just scored the penalty that would see Les Bleus through to the semi-finals. For the Brazilians, the magic of Mexico was spoiled for ever. Jalisco Stadium now belonged to the French. Seville 1982, Marseilles 1984, Guadalajara 1986. Les Bleus had just completed the magical triptych of the Platini era.

* * *

The first ninety minutes of normal time had seemed almost unreal. Rarely has a World Cup quarter-final seen such fluid play. The 'Brazilians from Europe' and the Brazilians from Brazil scarcely committed a foul, there were no yellow cards; it was a symphony of wonderful passes, of perfect through balls, which was to culminate in the first goal, for Brazil. In the sixteenth minute, a one-two between Muller and Junior saw a ball played on to an unmarked Careca. The Séléçao striker opened the scoring with a fierce shot that flew in under the crossbar.

In this game, which appeared to be made for him, played as it was between two teams of artists, Platini was to find himself struggling once again. Those ninety minutes of grace accorded him during the match against Italy were no more than a divine reprieve. The ever-increasing doses of anti-inflammatories he was taking, exacerbated by stomach trouble contracted forty-eight hours earlier, served only to weaken him further. Shadow of his former imperious self though he was, he managed to draw on such strength as he had left to appear at the far post four minutes before half-time. From a Dominique Rocheteau centre, Yannick Stopyra's header rebounded straight off goalkeeper Carlos. The lurking Platini was left with the simplest of tap-ins to bring France back on level terms.

Although at the time he didn't know it, he had just scored his forty-first and last goal wearing the blue shirt of France.

Ever determined, even with only one good foot, Captain Courage painfully played his way through the second half. A cutting remark was made after the match by Alemao, his marker: 'The Platini I was marking didn't pose me any problems. I was even able to give him a little more space without it really affecting our defence.' But France held out against a Brazilian team whose play exhibited passages of fantastic fluency, and who never gave in. 'If you look at the pattern of the game, then you'd say that Brazil should have qualified,' Henri Michel admits twelve years later. Their forwards, Muller and Careca, both hit the post, and Zico, 'the white Pelé', missed a penalty – or, to be accurate, it was Joël Bats, worthy to stand in the footsteps of Gordon Banks, who masterfully turned it wide.

Transformed by this series of miraculous escapes, Les Bleus could even have decided the game shortly before the end of extra time. Released by Michel Platini, Bruno Bellone found himself one-on-one against the Brazilian goalkeeper, Carlos, who launched himself at Bellone like a man possessed. Looking less like a boxer than a judo enthusiast, the big, bald-headed goalie showed no interest in the ball but went instead straight for the French player. Penalty. No doubt about it. But Mr Igna, the Romanian referee, kept his whistle in his pocket. He'd decided to wait for the end of the 120 minutes' playing time before giving Carlos and Bellone the opportunity to confront each other again in a knife-edge penalty shoot-out.

This generation of French players were scarred for life by the memory of what happened in Seville, and they were all remembering their calvary at the Sanchez-Pizjuan Stadium. Didier Six was no longer there, Maxime Bossis looked away, and Henri Michel found himself with the same dilemma Michel Hidalgo had experienced four years before. 'Giresse and Rocheteau should have been our penalty-takers, but I couldn't use them as they'd been substituted.' Happily, Luís Fernandez immediately stepped forward: 'I'll take the last one.' Platini was happy to hand over the privilege; he'd shoot second from last, and all the while Mañuel Amos played it as laid back as ever. 'OK, I'll do whatever you want.' There were still two penalty-takers to be found, and Henri Michel became a little angry. 'I nominated Bellone and Stopyra, and it came as a bombshell to them.' The two players weren't keen, but the coach insisted. 'Don't you think that as you're both forwards it stands to reason that you know how to take a penalty!'

Socrates, for Brazil, is the first to take a penalty, in front of a stand packed with yellow and green. He is class personified. Tall, slim, with a Christ-like beard, he is a qualified doctor, politically active in favour of the marginalised, and to cap it all, a formidably talented footballer. With hardly any run-up, Dr Socrates shoots, and Joël Bats saves – with his wrist. On the bench, Henri Michel felt only a slight sense of relief. 'I'd noticed Stopyra and Bellone walking away with their legs shaking.' Thankfully, Stop calmed down. One powerful kick was enough to chase his fears away, and the ball hurtled in under the bar. Phew! And phew again when, straight after Mañuel Amoros's penalty (flat-footed, to the right), Bruno Bellone, alias Lucky Luke, fired off a shot that travelled faster than his own terror. The ball slammed into the post, hit goalkeeper Carlos on the head, and finally made it over the line.

As Platini steps up for his shot, the two teams are once again level with three successful penalties each. Taking up position in front of the goal, the man who has taken so many decisive penalties – at Seville, at Turin, at Tokyo, and, of course, at Heysel – goes through his usual preparations. He picks up the ball, wipes it, kisses it, then places it on the penalty spot. Michel Platini, the man with nerves of steel, steps back, takes a three-pace run-up, and lets fly with a powerful right-footed shot. The ball raises a small puff of white dust, then sails well over the crossbar. Too high. Way too high – at least a metre over the bar. A staggering moment for the man who has just missed his first penalty in sixty-eight games for France. Later on, he would talk of a ball that 'just as I hit it, moved a quarter turn and settled in a hole'. But that miss was far more than just a dose of bad luck or a hint of a mistake. That tiny hole hollowed into the turf of the magical yet battle-scarred pitch wasn't large enough to contain the dead weight of all the accumulated slog and anxieties of fourteen long years as a professional. The unremitting pressure, the ever-greater responsibilities, the recurrent injuries, as well as the dread ghosts of that night at Heysel; the accumulation of all this could only result in the dulling of his passion, forged in steel though it was. Marking his thirty-first birthday at the Jalisco Stadium, he felt very, very old. 'I was destroyed, in a pitiful state.'

Staring into the abyss, Platini saw the final moments of the match unfurl as if in slow motion as the green-and-yellow flags fluttered in the stands. He held both his hands to his head and walked back towards the centre of the pitch, his eyes cast down. He was enduring an experience he'd never before known: the experience of the poor player who loses a game, the benighted soul who condemns his team and who is in turn consoled by others. Jean Tigana was the first to approach him. But the two men scarcely had time to meet each other's gaze when a deathly hush suddenly enveloped the stadium. Julio César had missed. It now fell to Luís Fernandez, the last French penalty-taker, to comfort Platini. 'Don't worry, this one's going in!'

What strength of character Fernandez showed! Not only was he unfazed by what was at stake, but the terrible tension seemed, if anything, to calm him. The French number 9 un-hurriedly walked the length of the pitch, mesmerising 66,000 people in the crowd and millions of television viewers with his characteristic gait: back arched, socks round his ankles, shorts pulled up to his navel, and a slight nervous tic playing around his shoulders. All that week Fernandez had been practising shooting penalties to the right. And so, as he walks the 30 metres separating him from the little white chalk circle, he is chanting the mantra, 'Go right, go right.' But at the very last moment, without really understanding why, he changes his mind. This son of Tarifa commits the gravest of faults; it is often fatal when taking a penalty to change your mind just before striking the ball. But the ball runs true, to the far left-hand side, sending Carlos the wrong way. Silence reigns, only a sigh ruffles the air: the Brazilian supporters remain transfixed. They, too, have understood: France are through to the semi-finals. From beneath the stands, now plunged into a deathly hush, Fernandez screams out his joy, sprinting flat-out along the touchline. Michel Platini is waiting quietly on his knees, waiting simply to say thank you. The pupil has redeemed the master, the bottle-carrier has saved his hero from a fall.

They rush back to the changing room, wanting to be together. Jean Tigana drums his hands on the massage table singing, 'Brazil! Brazil!', in parody of a popular Brazilian song. Platini, too allows himself to be carried away. Suddenly free from pain, he improvises a few samba steps. His team-mates are delighted to see him dancing and carefree, dressed only in a hideous pair of pastel-coloured boxer shorts and the ever-present Italian baseball cap.

That evening back at the hotel, Les Bleus continue to savour these precious moments of unalloyed happiness. Night-time on the shores of Lake Chapala has never seemed so sweet. For once, even the mosquitoes hold their peace. Inside the dining room of the Hotel Real, Michel Platini, Maxime Bossis and Jean Tigana are cutting their joint birthday cake, a superb slab of chocolate and coffee-flavoured confectionery that, sadly, nobody will ever taste. For the masterpiece of the pâtissier's art has landed plumb in the centre of Luís Fernandez's head. The lad from the outskirts of Lyons replies immediately in kind. Shouts, laughter, happiness.

Four days later, France will play, and lose, by 2–0, their World Cup semi-final against the Federal Republic of Germany.

8

Brothers in Arms: Les Bleus Win the World Cup, 1998

JOSÉ CARLIN

A ceux qui rêvent
A ceux que les rêves d'enfants font avancer
A ceux, comme ces enfants Bleus qui les ont réalisés
Continuons à rêver . . .

He is smiling. There he is, standing up amid a huge crowd. You can bet that he too would have liked to have worn his studs tonight. The entire country is as one, and Michel Platini, from high up in the VIP stand at the Stade de France, savours this victory from across the years. Time has passed but the hurt remains. Nagging, alive. 1982 and 1986, the two semi-finals in which French football brushed the heavens, and surely the very godhead of the round ball itself. On this 12 July, Les Bleus' victory is his victory as well. From up on high he signals to the players to take it all in, to make the most of the moment. With his long experience, he knows that some moments are more important than others. And tonight he is both a player and co-president of the CFO*. He wears the blue shirt next to his heart, under his suit jacket. But there's

---

*Comité Français de la XVIe Coupe du Monde (French organisation committee for the sixteenth World Cup).

59

room for others in his heart as well, especially for Fernand
Sastre, his 'favourite co-president'. 'Merci Fernand' flashes
the giant screen at the Stade de France, written and signed
by Platini himself over a picture of the face of the man who
started it all. It's now an hour since Mr Belqola whistled
for full time, and sent Les Bleus straight to heaven. For all
eternity.

It began in Marseilles . . .

Youssou N'Dour and Axelle Red have delayed their rehearsal.
The Mistral is blowing – blowing away any hopes for a perfect full-scale run-through. It's 3 December 1997, and the
organising committee of the sixteenth World Cup are preparing for their first major event. Tomorrow two stars will
perform the official France '98 anthem from the north stand
of the Stade Vélodrome, weather permitting. There is a plan
B but the organisers are determined to pull off the feat of
making this the first-ever World Cup draw to be staged in a
stadium.

On 4 December, 1 billion viewers tune in to see this unique
event live in globalvision. Marseilles has lifted the curtain
on the France '98 story of Les Bleus, and in a little over six
months, the menu for Jacquet's national side will feature
South Africa and the Mistral as entrées. And these particular
Bleus will prove perfect disciples of Aeolus, god of the wind.

Marseilles, a city at home with every passion and every
excess, is the dream venue for the first match of the competition. As Aimé Jacquet keeps drumming into his players,
'This is the heartland of football.' Zinedine Zidane is at home:
he'll be playing in front of his mates from Castellane, the
neighbourhood where he was born into football.

It's just before kick-off, and everybody is attempting to
relax in his own fashion. Fabien Barthez laughs and laughs,
his way of combating stress, making his Basque team-mate
Bixente Lizarazu, always to be found on his left, crack up as
the anthems are being played. A little further down the line
Emmanuel Petit, hand on heart, sings 'La Marseillaise'. But

the heart of the Arsenal player, high on emotion, seems to be on the right of his chest, where his left hand rests. This caused much mirth in the French camp, although at first the Arsenal player denied that he'd done it deliberately. None of his colleagues was fooled: the team spirit of Les Bleus is already a force to be reckoned with.

Christophe Dugarry pulls a face at the press box up in the stand after quickly opening the scoring for France. This liveliness sets the tone for the spirit that is to galvanise Jacquet's men. The French coach has been heavily criticised for his selections and he has made Dugarry and all the other members of the squad well aware of their responsibilities. Dugarry, who plays for Olympique Marseille, known by his detractors as 'Dugâchis'* tonight has his revenge. Pierre Issa, the South African who plays for Marseille, eases France's passage by deflecting a Djorkaeff shot into his own net. Finally it's the turn of young Gunner Thierry Henry, at the time playing for Monaco, to burn his way into the hearts of the delighted crowd by putting the finishing touches to a fine job. Les Bleus couldn't have dreamed of a better start.

They return to their hotel happy and in high spirits. Vincent Candela has already imported the song that will become the official signature tune of Les Bleus. Gloria Gaynor's iconic disco anthem 'I Will Survive' is sung full-blast over and over again by the twenty-two man squad. They started singing in the changing room and carried on in the coach taking them back to their camp at Moulin de Vernègues, where there was another surprise in store, more Gallic in flavour and, more importantly, more emotionally charged. The players' wives and girlfriends were waiting to serenade their partners with a reworked version of the Joe Dassin number 'Aux Champs Elysées', a musical first.

---

*An ironic reference to his alleged inability to put chances away: *gâchis* means mess or waste.

Zidane sees red

They'd been together since 18 May*, and despite the late
arrival of a few of their number, such as the three players
involved in the Champions' League Final – Christian Karembeu
(Real Madrid), Zinedine Zidane and Didier Deschamps
(Juventus) – it was vital that come the finals, the French
squad was a rock-solid unit. This was what Aimé Jacquet
wanted and demanded of his squad – as well as that they
comported themselves as friends, fighters and professionals.
So the players made the most of such moments with their
partners. There weren't many of them, but they came at finely
judged intervals. It was another successful aspect of Jacquet's
management.

The following day, back on the training pitches at
Clairefontaine, Roger Lemerre and Philippe Bergeroo helped
Jacquet to keep up the pace as France prepared to meet Saudi
Arabia. This was a squad which was allowed no room for
error. All was pressure, relentless pressure.

Apart from 18 June's perfect result (4–0) against the Saudis
at the Stade de France, what really lingered in the mind was
the wholly unnecessary red-carding of Zinedine Zidane.
It's the seventieth minute and the French playmaker is
dangerously tackled by Fouad Amin. Zidane takes his
revenge and runs his studs across his opponent's side. Mr
Brizio Carter, the Mexican referee, sends Zidane off. For
France, the episode is a national drama. As he leaves the
field, Zidane's eyes never meet his coach's. In the dressing room,
the French number 10 seethes within, but he gives no outward
physical sign of his frustration. No plastic water bottles
hurled against the wall, nothing. He knows he is in the wrong.

---

*When the French team first assembled at the Clairefontaine National Technical
Centre, where the national side traditionally gathers, the squad was twenty-eight
strong. On the evening of 22 May, Sabri Lamouchi, Nicolas Anelka, Pierre Laigle,
Martin Djetou, Lionel Letizi and Ibrahim Ba packed their bags after the final
squad was announced.

He can't be unaware of the fact that the injury to his friend Dugarry in the game against South Africa has affected him; that the cause of his bad-tempered gesture, far from malevolence, was not having Dugarry playing alongside him.

The two-match suspension handed down to Zidane the next day forces Jacquet to switch from his first-choice strategy until the quarter-final stage – if France make it that far.

Youri: in the name of the family

The squad travels by high-speed train to Lyons for the Denmark game. At the Château de Pizay, the talk at first centres on which team they are likely to meet in the last sixteen, if they beat Denmark (Nigeria? Paraguay? Spain?), then moves on to the local boy, Youri Djorkaeff, who has just one dream: to score a goal in the World Cup at the Gerland Stadium in front of his family. Anyone laying a bet on Djorkaeff will come out a winner. The Dane Helveg brings down David Trezeguet. Youri Djorkaeff asks if he can take the penalty. Permission granted, and Youri the *gône** realises his dream as he wrong-foots Peter Schmeichel.

After the match, surrounded by his family and cousins from Armenia, he gets the chance to see his eldest son Sacha, on whom he hasn't clapped eyes for a month and a half. The Djorkaeff clan floats on a great cloud of happiness and pride which carries them far from the banks of the River Rhône towards the banks of the River Hrazda. Les Bleus finish their first-round games at around 5.50 pm, beating the Danish Vikings 2–1, to emerge comfortable winners of their group. The vaulted ceiling of the Château de Pizay plays host to another of the squad's family get-togethers.

With their last-sixteen opponent now known – it would be Paraguay – Aimé Jacquet hammered home some hard facts to a squad which up to that point had shown no signs of

---

*A child born in the Lyons region.

faintheartedness: 'From now on, either we win, or we pack our bags.' In the improvised council room at Clairefontaine where Jacquet gathered his players together, he wasn't looking at a team on the ropes, but at a group of men with only one goal in mind: winning. As if taking part in an ascetic retreat, during this period of communal living each squad member instilled in his partners what they needed to make them stronger. Everyone knew who the playmakers were (Deschamps, Desailly, Blanc), and it was up to them to act as go-betweens, translating theory into reality. It was to be from their ranks that France would find salvation. Les Bleus had to undergo trial by Golden Goal. This was the first World Cup to adopt the new rule, which stipulated that the first side to score during extra time would immediately qualify. France were to do well out of it.

Paraguay was a high-octane game and for once the French defence (Barthez, Thuram, Blanc, Desailly and Lizarazu) were irreproachable. It was Laurent Blanc who sent Les Bleus heavenward. During the action that led to the only goal of the match, Marcel Desailly shouted to Laurent Blanc, in the name of the holiest of holy alliances, not to go upfield and leave his central defence position unguarded. The lad from Alès ignored this advice. From a Robert Pires cross, David Trezeguet craftily headed the ball into Blanc's path. His right foot destroyed the hopes of the entire Paraguayan nation, a nation which had ground to an absolute halt for the duration of the match. But the real hero of this game was named José Luís Chilavert.

The Paraguayan keeper repelled the repeated assaults of Les Bleus for a full 114 minutes. He needed only to hang on for another six short minutes to see his team through to a penalty shoot-out. And when it came to penalties, nobody, not even Les Bleus, would have bet on qualifying – the Paraguayan keeper had been awesome in his power and flexibility. But a shoot-out was not needed and France duly qualified for the quarter-finals, where they were to find themselves up against the old friend they loved to hate: Italy.

'Italia parla Francese'

Thierry Henry, sidelined with an ankle injury, watched the Paraguay game from an empty television studio at the ground in the company of a group of CFO volunteers. It was an enormous pleasure for all these young, and not so young, volunteers – the people key to the successful organisation of this World Cup – to rub shoulders with this great player who was also just a young guy like them. But their enjoyment was tempered by anxiety. Was the injury serious? Would 'Titi' be able to return to the squad? Les Bleus' doctor, Jean-Marcel Ferret, quickly made a statement announcing that Henry would be available for the date with Italy five days later.

Once it was clear that France would not now have to play away from their St Denis home ground, Aimé Jacquet allowed his players a little time to relax. Thierry Henry made a sortie to see his childhood friends in the Bosquets aux Ulis estate in the Paris suburbs. Thuram popped into the local hypermarket to pick up some jazz CDs. Everything was going well in the best of all worlds, especially now that Zidane was no longer suspended.

The Italian diaspora was very well represented within the French squad (Boghossian, Candela, Desailly, Deschamps, Djorkaeff, Thuram, Zidane). This latest match between the two nations would obviously also be the stage for a game within a game, pitting club colleagues against each other. This added spice was a source of much pleasure to Aimé Jacquet.

The whole country was behind the national coach and his men. On the stroke of 4.30 pm that afternoon of 3 July, many companies stopped answering their telephones. Even government departments and town halls closed their doors so that those within could watch undisturbed. France–Italy is an affair of state.

Present in the grandstand of the Stade de France were president of the republic Jacques Chirac and prime minister Lionel Jospin, accompanied by numerous members of the government. The teams could not be separated, and the match went to a penalty shoot-out. Moments earlier, the Italian Robert Baggio, who had come on as a replacement for Del Piero, missed a chance to knock France out of the competition when his volley just missed the right-hand upright of Fabien Barthez's goal.

The shoot-out was Dante-esque. Bixente Lizarazu's attempt was saved by Pagliuca, but immediately afterwards it was Barthez's turn to save Albertini's shot, cancelling out the Italian advantage and Lizarazu, the player from the Basque country, could staunch his tears. Les Bleus qualified for the semi-finals with the last kick of the first penalty session. Vincent Candela, the Italian-based player for FC Roma and Les Bleus' DJ-in-chief, announced to his colleagues on the bench that Italy's Di Biagio would miss his penalty. His instinct was right: the ball slammed into the crossbar. Barthez jumped with joy and the bench erupted. A huge roar filled the giant oval of the Stade de France. Victory over Italy meant that the team of 1998 joined the great teams of French football, Kopa's in 1958, and Platini's of 1982 and 1986, all of them semi-finalists in the greatest challenge in the world game. Back in the changing room Fabien Barthez enjoyed a cigarette. It was, thankfully, not the last cigarette of a condemned man.

Thuram's mystical shots

France is floating on cloud nine and the twenty-two heroes have the entire nation at their feet. Although Jacquet's men have still only equalled the feats of the great French teams, they are basking in a feeling of invincibility. It's time for Les Bleus to have their say, and as every microphone is always open to them, they make their feelings known. Deschamps, the team captain, doesn't mince his words: the stadium is too full of people wearing collars and ties. He and his team-mates want to see the public dressed in the brilliant colours this sort of event calls for. Robert Pires goes as far as to declare, 'It would be good to see President Chirac wearing the team colours.' The politicians and the businesspeople who fill a large section of the Stade de France get the message: for the match against Croatia, it has to be blue.

8 July would be Lilian Thuram's day. Thuram, whose friends had always gently teased him about his awkwardness in front of goal; his 'flat feet'. That day he was to strike the ball with mystical brilliance. The Croatian team boasted the competition's leading goalscorer, Davor Suker, a superbly talented player who didn't need to be given much room to open the scoring, and France were behind on the scoreboard for the first time in the tournament. Thuram, a little behind on the action, failed to ensnare the Croatian Gunner in the offside trap, but his will to win, and that of his team-mates, was unbreakable.

Thuram is driven. One minute after the Croatian goal, he wins the ball from Boban and scores. Enlightened, inspired, Lilian Thuram is the messiah. As an offering to Christiane, his mother, and Miles Davis, his musical god, he scores again – the match-winning goal, twenty minutes from the final whistle. Under the spell of one of those West Indian sorcerers who so frightened him in childhood, he seems to be perplexed by his sweeping shot off the inside of the left foot until his team-mates bring him down to earth by throwing themselves on him in celebration. With the index finger of his left hand to his lips, his right arm crossed over his left, he briefly strikes a 'James Bond' pose, enough to tell us that Lilian Thuram has risen above this world.

The joy at France's first-ever qualification for the World Cup final is quite unlike anything else the country has seen. While Jacques Chirac parades around Les Bleus' changing room, pausing to kiss the top of Barthez's head, as Laurent Blanc has been doing since the start of the competition, the streets of the capital are invaded by hordes of red, white and blue scarves and shirts. People embrace to the sound of an orchestra of horns. Aimé Jacquet has already fulfilled one of his challenges: to bring happiness to all and, especially, to bring the French together. This native of Sail-sous-Couzan, a machine-tool operator by training, is already a national hero.

The last to board the coach returning the team to
Clairefontaine is Lilian Thuram. The adoped son of Parma
has been delayed first by a quick session with the test tube for
a routine drugs test, then by the world's media. As he boards
the coach he is applauded and teased by his team-mates. His
invariable response is 'Anything can happen.' The only shadow
has been the unexpected sending-off of Laurent Blanc after
an innocuous contact with the Everton player Slaven Bilic.
Deprived of his sweeper, Aimé Jacquet will be forced to play
Frank Leboeuf – and an excellent choice it will prove to be.

Telling Le Pen where to get off

D-Day is set for 12 July 1998. Even though Les Bleus know
that they have already achieved something special, they realise
that beating current world champions Brazil will be no easy
task. Ever since their victory over Italy, and especially since
they overcame Croatia, the whole of France, man and woman
alike, from worker to politician, is solidly behind Jacquet's
men. The female supporters astonish everyone with the passion
and devotion they demonstrate for the French team, as well
as injecting fresh blood into the traditional cast of supporters.
There is nothing more wonderful than to hear 'La Marseillaise' sung by thousands of women in a stadium.

People have gone crazy about this dream final. The players'
wish to see the stadium filled with colour rather than suits has
been fulfilled. The McDonald's fast-food chain, one of the
sponsors, has offered $1 million to the scorer of a hat-trick in
the match. And nobody could have foreseen the tremendous
surge in popularity enjoyed by the president and the prime
minister. What has become known as the 'World Cup effect'
proves that nothing is more serious than sport. Television
audiences took off during the semi-final stage, and slightly
over 2 billion viewers are expected to watch the final itself.
The whole country has gone completely mad over football.

But all this is secondary to the game itself. Jacquet's men
prepared for the final in the same way as for the other matches.
Although up until then there had been no hint of games-

manship between Jacquet and his Brazilian counterpart, Mario Zagallo, one hour before the match was due to kick off, Laurent Blanc reported to his trainer that the Brazilian teamsheet listed Ronaldo as a mere substitute. It was true that the Brazilian star had scarcely trained since their semi-final against the Netherlands, but it seemed incredible that Brazil would go as far as depriving themselves of the presence in the starting line-up of one of the best players in the world.

Jacquet didn't really believe what he'd been told, but nonetheless planned some changes. Four floors below, Ronaldo's girlfriend, Susana Werner, was weeping in the organisers' office, desperately awaiting news of her partner, who had been taken to hospital several hours earlier after suffering convulsions. Ronaldo eventually reappeared at 8 pm, just an hour before kick-off. The Brazilian teamsheet returned to its original form: Aimé Jacquet had been wise to wait.

As Mr Belqola blew his whistle to signal the start of the game, the models who had just appeared in the Yves Saint Laurent fashion show were still changing in their dressing room. In even more of a hurry than the rest was the future Mme Karembeu, Adriana Zverenikova.

Very soon after the match began, Aimé Jacquet's Bleus found the weakness in Zagallo's system: poor marking from place kicks. Didier Deschamps and his team heeded their coach's advice; all that was left for them to do was to fire the machine called Zidane into orbit.

The kid from Castellane was the undisputed hero of the final. He scored twice, with two searing headers from corners, giving Les Bleus a comfortable lead as the teams left the pitch at half-time. The other unforgettable image is of Fabien Barthez soaring above an out-of-sorts Ronaldo, who was nevertheless only two fingers short of stopping French celebrations dead in their tracks. Emmanuel Petit rounded off the scoring in this sixteenth World Cup final. The national team had achieved one of the greatest victories in the annals of French sport.

France went mad. In Marseilles, Lens, Toulouse, and Bordeaux the landmark town squares were invaded. The historic moment was celebrated across the land, in town and countryside alike. Rouget de Lisle had not been thinking of the World Cup when he described the feeling in the French national anthem, but this too was truly a time when *'le jour de gloire est arrivé'*. In Les Bleus' changing room the joy was unrestrained. Chirac and Jospin couldn't keep away, and the champagne flowed non-stop. The Champs Elysées was overrun by a jubilant crowd chanting 'Zidane President,' and the same message was taken up on the electronic display at the Arc de Triomphe.

Even compared to the jubilation that followed Les Bleus' victory over Croatia, this was celebration on a colossal scale. And what a kick in the face for all those facists, in their various guises, to see black, white and Arab marching hand in hand, shoulder to shoulder. From the Kanak to the Armenian, the Spaniard and the Ghanaian, this French team represented the victory of an entire multicultural generation, a generation others had been too ready to characterise as ruined or lost. The world's most beautiful streets hadn't seen such crowds since the Liberation. And indeed French football had put an end to the lean years of disappointment and was free again.

The team coach took almost three hours to reach Claire-fontaine, where a dinner was laid on for the players and their partners. The night was still young and France was embarking on a well-deserved binge. And Platini was smiling.

III

Les Stars

9

The Greatest: Michel Platini
Interview with Michel Platini

CHRISTOV RÜHN

Paris. Happy to be back, in my own country. I feel at home here. And I recognise all the different aromas of my city. How could I ever forget them? A steaming cappuccino on the zinc café counter, the flower stall on the Place des Ternes.

This year, we are blessed with a very Indian summer, and September smiles on me. It's lovely weather for playing football. As for the sexy young women back from their holidays, they look tanned and gorgeous. You miss this when you live in London. On the café terraces down Rue des Abbesses, everybody seems to be competing in their desire to show off, greeting each other with a kiss. Cliché. It's like a scene from a 1960s French movie. Click-clack. Bonjour la France. Hello Paname.

Football. The English Premier League season kicked off in my absence and my favourite team doesn't yet seem to be in fighting form. We've lost 2–0 against our arch-enemies, and as if things weren't bad enough, it all happened 'chez nous'. It's sickening. Never mind, I'm a true fan and the season is just starting. There is still a long way to go and my loyalty is unquestionable. Walking along the streets of the French capital, everything seems so perfect. Luck seems to have struck home. Tomorrow I'm interviewing one of my childhood heroes.

Football again. I'm reminded that I cried twice watching football on TV. Both times The Man was there. Such powerful emotions that they stayed with me for life. The first one, a real drama, occurred in 1982 in Seville's stadium. I was chilling out in the French countryside with my father, André, who, if the truth be told, has never had time for football. I managed to get him to watch the match: France v. Germany, the World Cup semi-final. Yet even André, who usually didn't give a damn, was enraged when the referee stole the match from a whole nation which did not deserve such an unfair outcome. First, that bastard goalkeeper Schumacher assaulted Battiston. No red card was produced. End of normal time. 1–1. The extra time was spent in hell. Giresse then scored a fantastic goal. We thought we had won. In the end, thanks to Rummenigge, the German striker, they levelled the score again. 3–3. We lost on penalty kicks. No justice. Curtain. Tears. I was inconsolable. It would be another sixteen years before it happened again. The tears, that is.

The second time was in 1998. I tried to play it cool, with little success. I was stuck in a corner of Devon with Martin Luther, my seven-year-old son – a fine football player. France against Brazil. The big final. During the anthems, I held my son's hand very tight. The grudging ITV commentators didn't seem to rate 'the Frogs' very highly. They asserted that we did not stand a chance against the reigning world champions. Martin Luther didn't care, least of all because he didn't speak a word of English. He did his best to reassure me: 'Don't worry, Daddy, don't you worry,' he repeated ceaselessly, rendered incredulous by the strangely unheroic attitude of his dad (his hero), who was sweating heavily just before the kick-off. *Allez Les Bleus!* Zidane scored twice; Petit once. 'And one and two and three, zero!' the crowd chanted. A triumphant announcement resounded through the Stade de France's loudspeakers: 'France are the new world champions.' The tears rolled down my face, this time tears of joy. My son held me in his arms and now he was crying, too. 'See, Daddy, I told you so, didn't I?' In-cre-di-ble. Life can be beautiful sometimes.

On the TV screen, a Latin-looking man is standing behind
the French skipper as he receives the cup. A French football
shirt is visible under his expensive suit. A touch of class,
Italian style. He is delighted, as is everybody else. He looks
jubilant as he kisses the damn thing, a trophy which he, more
than most, is entitled to brandish. The Man carried his forty-
something years well, despite being a little stout, a solidness
which lent him a reassuring air. On any other day the whole
of France would have had eyes only for him. He is the president of the World Cup '98 organising committee.

Not so long ago, in the 1980s, he was the greatest footballer in the world. Numéro 10 – one of the only significant
number 10s to share this honour with King Pelé himself. The
others merely had talent, and Johann Cruyff wore the number 14 shirt. The French nation will venerate this man for
ever, and to the rest of the world his many exploits on the
pitch remain unforgettable. The Man's name is reminiscent of
a rare and precious metal: platinum. He is Michel Platini, the
greatest French footballer ever.

3 September 1999. Palais Royal, Paris, FIFA's French headquarters. My Swatch shows me that it is 10.10. I'm ten
minutes early. I step into an old art-deco lift and the latticed
swing doors close with difficulty. It grinds its way up to the
fourth floor. I feel strange, I could be on my way to heaven.
Or perhaps to some kind of hell. But I remain confident. How
can your childhood heroes betray you? After all, the Silver
Surfer has never let me down. Before ringing the bell, I
wonder what Michel Platini is like in reality and relish these
last few minutes before we meet. Images of those spectacular
magic moments replay in my mind's eye in slow motion: the
Stadio Communale, the Parc des Princes, Guadalajara . . .
Platini's free kicks. Platini's passes. Platini's fabulous goals.
Platini's phenomenal vision. The lot. My thoughts wander
around the world's largest stadiums until the creaking of the
lift breaks my reverie. It's going back down, no doubt summoned by some genteel bourgeoise living in this stylish
apartment block, which exudes a rarefied luxury refined over

time. I can't just stand at the door for ever like an idiot or
some door-to-door salesman. I must ring the bell. Now. Come
on, man, get a grip. Ring the bell. I do it.

*You are the greatest French footballer of all time, yet at the
beginning of your career it wasn't always that easy for you.
How come you were never selected to play in the national
youth teams?*
Back then, football scouting wasn't encouraged so much. The
trainers from my region, the Lorraine, who were in charge of
picking teams probably didn't consider me big or strong
enough, or even a good footballer. Subsequently, this was to
give me greater psychological strength. All through my life
I've never nurtured ambitions of success. My goal was to play
good football above all else. For me, the game has always
been a true passion, but now, for the young, the selections are
a matter of pride. For me pride came later, certainly when I
had to win titles for France or with my club. Changes occurred
as I matured, around fifteen or sixteen years old. Remember
that the midfield players of the 1984 French national team
were never called as youth players at any national level, not
even for the under-eighteens. Neither Giresse nor Tigana nor
myself. The qualities required in young players are based on
physique. There's a huge difference between a thirteen-year-
old kid 1.8 metres tall and another measuring only 1.6
metres, whereas at eighteen years old, each will run as fast as
the other. At that age footballing skills and the understanding
of the game become more important; earlier on the prime
concern lies in athletic prowess.

*You have made millions of people dream. Today, which
footballers and which men make you dream?*
Personally, these days, few famous people make me dream,
since most of them are superficial 'products' imposed on us
by the world media. I respect those who live quietly, who
don't constantly spread themselves across the newspapers,
but are true *seigneurs*, like Giovanni Agnelli. To dream is not

easy for me because life has brought me everything and I have never been envious or jealous of others.

Can football unite nations? Or is it just a game?
Football was a game, but now it is so globalised that it has gradually metamorphosed into something more than just a game. It is the only truly universal sport. When you realise that World Cup '98 was followed on TV by around 40 billion spectators, this proves that football events unite nations worldwide. Here, France's victory was a perfect example – white, black, *beur* [Arab], yellow, green: everyone was affected by it.

It must have been fabulous for you to organise World Cup '98.
The most amusing thing is that I went from being a footballer to becoming president of the World Cup '98 organising committee at the age of thirty-eight. If you look back at my entire career, you can see that I initiated numerous things; subsequently others took advantage of the openings I created. I was the first footballer of my generation to play abroad, to do publicity, to appear regularly on TV, and the first to work with the French football authorities. The most interesting thing for me was that my role as president empowered me to decide how to organise this World Cup. I said to myself, hey why don't we try this, set that up, maybe put the tickets at so much. We decided that the tickets would cost 130 francs [*around £13*] because, although pricing them at 140 would, for us, have meant ten francs [*about £1*] more multiplied by two and a half million tickets sold, it would've made a big psychological difference to the public. On the other hand, I didn't deal with the administrative side, because it's a real machine, but on the level of taking initiatives, like going to find funding, putting in place the schedule and everything to do with football itself. We had great fun doing it with co-president Fernand Sastre.

During the final, you wore France's shirt under your suit. Why was that?

I didn't really think about it. On the last day, my work as president was pretty much done, so I became a fan again, a bit nostalgic, remembering that French team which had missed victory at the World Cup by so little a few times in the past, and which coveted it. But before the day of the final, I tried not to be a fan in any visible way.

Obviously I've always supported France, for two reasons. The first is linked to the fact that I adore France and the second that it was better for the organising committee that the French team should go as far as possible thereby uniting the entire country behind it. But on that day, I said to myself, wouldn't it be great to win this World Cup? And we're nearly there. In the end, we did it.

Is friendship between players necessary in order to make great football teams?
Friendship is important, but it isn't an absolute necessity. Within a group the players aren't always friends, but you can't see this on the pitch. Everyone plays the same way with everybody else, because the aim is to win together. Perhaps some are sly, I don't know about that. Personally, when I played, my attitude on the pitch made it impossible to determine which of my team's players I appreciated the most. But at Juventus everyone was my friend anyway.

The influence of your family has been an important factor of your success. What do you think about the young players who are signed up at the age of fifteen for enormous sums of money?
Minors do not have the legal right to sign a contract without their parents' agreement. When I was assessing this problem, I realised that it was often the parents who pushed them. They make a choice for their kids.

In my day, it was different. When I signed my first professional contract, I was getting 300 francs [£30] a month. I wasn't aware of being paid to play – well, not quite. All I wanted was to play football in front of the public. My father didn't realise, either, that you could make a living playing

football. Today all the kids want to be professional footballers, which isn't the same thing. Everything has changed
and business comes first: it's the age of each for himself.
Because of the Bosman ruling, players are free to leave their
clubs when they choose, and club loyalty is disappearing. The
more a player changes clubs, the more he makes money go
round and it always ends the same way: filling the pockets of
those around him. I'm not nostalgic for the past: on the con-
trary, I think that the Bosman ruling is a good thing for
footballers, but its spin-offs are not good at all. The international football authorities are currently studying how to
collaborate more closely with the European Commission without affecting the game itself so that this situation doesn't get
worse. Today, if the chairman of a club or a player's agent
finds himself in a dispute with the football authorities and
turns to the European Commission, he often wins his case.
UEFA doesn't have the power to settle law suits. FIFA is following this closely.

*You were the king of France and Italy made you its prince.
Do you feel more Italian or French?*
I am a citizen of the world, an international man. I feel as
much Finnish or African or Asian as European. Only my heart
is completely French. Otherwise I'd live in Switzerland or somewhere else.

What is your favourite type of football?
Football has greatly evolved over the last few years and the
responsibility of the manager, given the stakes he's up against,
is massive. He would rather use three defending midfielders
with one striker and a number 10 next to him than play three
attacking midfielders. When I was France's manager, I didn't
use a real number 10 because there wasn't a good one around
at the time. I needed results and ensured that my team played
a certain way. I had no other options than to use the players
at my disposal. Usually the manager is under such pressure
that his side's performance is less important than results. His

duty being to win matches, he has to do everything in his power to fulfil this crucial part of his contract. The anomalous thing about football is that if no goals are scored against you then you are sure to get a point, but if your team scores two goals you're not guaranteed a win.

A couple of years ago, when we were discussing the evolution of the game, I made it clear that I thought it best to change the mentality within football before altering the rules. It would be a different game if we were to increase the size of the goals, or if the teams played eight-a-side, or if the throw-ins were taken by foot. Before, the goalkeeper was an individual set apart. Now that rules affecting the goalkeeper have changed he is a player like the others. When his team-mates on the pitch pass him the ball, he can no longer use his hands to catch it. If this rule had existed when I was playing, perhaps I'd have spent less time running to the defender, who'd pass the ball to the goalkeeper, who'd pass it straight back to him, who returned it, and so on. It was frustrating. Today the referee has to give a red card to the last defender if he fouls an opponent heading for the goal. Since we have improved the game, 0–0 scores are practically non-existent, but now it is the elements of football off the pitch that we have to deal with.

Was your best ever goal the one you scored against Holland in 1981?
It wasn't my best ever, but it was the most important one for a whole generation. If we hadn't qualified for the 1982 World Cup in Spain, perhaps that side would not have won the European Championship in 1984 and therefore would not have reached the 1986 World Cup semi-final in Mexico. No, my best one was the one I scored with Juventus against Boca Juniors during the final of the 1985 Super Cup in Tokyo. After a corner, Olgin, their defender, headed the ball out, Bollini retrieved it and kicked it back into the box. The ball landed on my chest, I lobbed two defenders coming towards me and then volleyed it with my left foot into the top corner of the goal. Unfortunately for us, this goal was stupidly disallowed

by some little linesman from Singapore who signalled an off-side position of one of my team-mates who had nothing to do with the action and was busy retying his laces. This was probably my best goal, and it happened during a major football tie: the final of the World Club Cup.

What do you think of English football and the Premier League? If you were still playing would you find it the most attractive?
I had some important contacts in England just before I went to Italy. Tottenham and Arsenal were keen. Although I didn't follow them up, paradoxically, it was the Premier League that I was the most familiar with. Its matches were often shown on French TV. But I thought that too many fixtures were played during the season. Today British football is at a cross-roads somewhere between the continental style of playing and the British 'kick and rush'. The Premier League is made up of so many clubs that its problems lie in the fact that matches are played at an infernal pace.

The mass arrival of foreign players has made the game more technical, but English footballers still have a little trouble finding their form. A new breed is emerging, players like McManaman and Owen, who are not physically big and strong. It's still easier to score in England because the attacker is not marked much and often finds himself alone in front of the goalkeeper. It's different in Italy, where the defences are more compact. The English still use the traditional 4–4–2.

How do the greatest players, such as Pelé or yourself, become men of importance? Does becoming used to pressure and adulation make you more efficient off the pitch than other former players, or is it that doors open more easily?
Of course doors open more easily, but you have to make sure they don't shut again. Having a name, a look, charisma, or being of a certain race is simply not enough – you have to work hard. Beckenbauer, Pelé and myself were lucky enough to succeed in relaunching our careers within the football community. It's good because in France, for example, the legends

of 1958 had almost all quit football because they were better paid as representatives of Adidas or other manufacturers. Kopa and the others left very little to football other than wonderful memories. After their generation there was a void until the great St Etienne side came on the scene. But over the last twenty years many former players have continued to participate in football and the ensuing results have never been so good for this country.

You're not yet fifty and you are already FIFA's number two, and have organised the largest World Cup ever. You still consider yourself first and foremost to be a footballer who has made it. Is success written in your genes?
The truth is, I'm not really FIFA's number two because I wasn't elected. I am special adviser to the president, Sepp Blatter. Together we formed an electoral 'ticket'.

Success . . . I don't think it's written in my genes, it's not as simple as that. I only get involved in projects I'm passionate about, otherwise I wouldn't be able to see them through satisfactorily. During the eighties there were those who pushed me to get involved in clothing, and I even had a label in my name, but it didn't really interest me so I stopped. All that I've done in football has worked out well because I've had the incentive, even if I looked like I didn't care. Some thought I wouldn't stay long on the World Cup '98 organising committee, but I stayed with it for five years and I went to the office every day without being paid a salary.

I make choices. Juventus were very generous to me, and today I'm lucky enough not to have to work. So I do what I like. When you believe in something it's easier to succeed and you do it better. That is why I joined FIFA. As part of this organisation I have the means to make things move forward for the football community.

The midfield you formed with Giresse and Tigana was probably one of the greatest, maybe along with that of Brazil's team in 1970, Tostão, Jairzinho, Rivelino. Do you agree?

There was also that midfield formed by Zico, Cerezo and Falcão in Brazil's 1982 team. If, with Giresse and Tigana, we had won the World Cup in 1982 and 1986, maybe you could say that we were the greatest, but we didn't win. I still think that we were an excellent midfield, though.

It is said that you instigated the arrival of Eric Cantona in England. Is this true, and how would you rate his stay?
It is true, and I think he's done wonderfully for someone who almost stopped playing football. It was one of those great encounters between player and country. He and Manchester United shared a fantastic love affair. Eric, who is an intelligent and sensitive young man, needed to play somewhere where he felt free. In France he became the prisoner of a system, whereas in England, despite the hysterical press, he could show his talent with no restrictions. When he feels free, Eric is world class.

Tell me about Action Michel Platini, the foundation you created which helps to find jobs for former drug addicts.
It still exists; generally it's all going pretty well. We find jobs for around fifty people a year. We are a small structure, with a chairman, a company secretary, a board of directors and a doctor who follows cases, but we don't have 2,000 jobs a year to offer. It's a small-scale effort: it wouldn't support fifty employees. The one issue that occasionally provokes disagreement within the board of directors is the promotion of the organisation, because it is impossible for me to do any publicity. We are not a job centre for ex-addicts. I don't want people coming to see us saying, 'I'm a junkie, please help me,' because we don't have the resources to look after such people.

We collaborate with doctors and once people are cured they can come to see us and we try to help them find a job. We then keep tabs on them in case there are any problems, but it's not that easy. I could call in the press, throw cocktail parties and do only preventative work, but ultimately that wouldn't achieve much. I prefer to deal with reinstatement, which constitutes the most important part of our efforts, since if they don't return to a normal life it's impossible for addicts to overcome their problem.

Is drug-taking more prevalent in football today, or is the press trying to give the sport a bad image?
I don't believe that clubs organise the administration of drugs. I guess it can happen that a player might use a stimulant when he's tired, I don't know. Last year, I was contacted by an Italian public prosecutor who was conducting an inquiry into a drugs case affecting Juventus. Everything is possible, especially when you realise that football is a microcosm of the society around it. Drugs, violence and hypocrisy are endemic and there's no reason why these scourges shouldn't affect football, but I think that we are dealing with isolated cases. Football reaches millions of people. In France there are 2 million licensed players, and with four or five people either directly or indirectly looking after each one, you're talking about approximately 10 million people, in other words one sixth of the population of France.

Juventus elected you best bianconero *player of the century. Would you ever consider becoming president of the club that adores you?*
A difficult one, this. My life comes before any sort of ambition. My children are grown up, ready to lead their own lives, and I'll soon be alone with my wife. At which point I'll have more time on my hands. But, being realistic, there's an infinitesimal chance that I might, one day, become the president of Juventus of Turin. It's best never to say never.

Do you consider Zidane to be your natural successor?
We have the number 10 shirt for Les Bleus in common, but we are different. I adore Zinedine, he's a charming, discreet, intelligent, likeable young man, albeit a little introverted, and I think that currently in football there are very few players

with his style. There's Rui Costa in Italy and, as for England, the last number 10 I saw in action was McAllister. This type of player is vanishing, and I really want things to work out well for Zidane so that managers sign more players like him. Neither Barcelona nor Real Madrid possess a real number 10. As for Rivaldo, the last time he produced a pass was probably when he was in schoolboy football!

He's a goalscorer. It was easier to see football in that way fifteen years ago. Then I could still score goals as a number 10, but today Zidane wouldn't dream of trying his luck on a one-two with Deschamps. His role is more difficult than mine was back then, because I was blessed with team-mates who shared my vision of the game. Between Deschamps – who, as we all know, doesn't exactly move crowds, and who deserves praise for reaching the level he's at, given his abilities – and Zidane there's a fundamental difference.

Michael Owen and Nicolas Anelka are Europe's most expensive young players. Football is discovering stars who are younger and younger. What does the future hold for these kids who already have glory and a fortune?
Money isn't everything. In football you have to win titles. It isn't the player who has been paid the most money who will be remembered, but the one who gained the most honours. A footballer who stays alive in the memory of people ten years after his retirement is the one who will go down in the pages of history.

Now, in France, football is appreciated as it has always been in other countries: Brazil, England, Spain or Italy. English players are always stars at home. Here in France, now that we are world champions and are respected, the infatuation with the game is more pronounced. Yet there is a marked difference between the grass roots and professional football. Certain statistics aren't well received by the public. When a player is valued at 300 million francs, it makes no sense, it's meaningless. I'm concerned that football might suffer a setback because of this inflation. It's a problem FIFA is studying.

It's important to be aware, and it's time to find a solution fast, because everything is far from perfect, it seems.

The French nation wept at Seville in 1982, yet your team was probably the best in the tournament. Will this match remain one of the great scandals in the history of football?
With hindsight, this match remains one of the most pleasurable moments of my life. For me, no book or film or play could ever recapture the way I felt that day. It was so complete, so strong, so fabulous. This match was extraordinary and became even more dramatic when the referee literally stole it from us. He failed to give a penalty and did not send off Schumacher after his aggression on Battiston. The end result apart, this was the most intense moment. It's one of the most beautiful memories of my career. In the heat of the action, I felt a sense of profound injustice after Schumacher's foul, but now I remember that match as one of the most thrilling moments of my life. Incredible.

The ultimate match for you: was it one in which you played or the France–Brazil final at St Denis?
The World Cup final was not especially spectacular; I retain more of the emotional side of it than its technical aspect. On an emotional level we all felt as though we were on the pitch. It was the greatest joy to win at last the trophy that had escaped our generation and its public. The frenzy surrounding this victory wasn't just a response to this particular French team or to one of its players, it was also the result of a long period of frustration and a series of setbacks preceding it.

For five years I played in Italy, so I am infused with Italian culture. After telling the Italian press that the perfect score was 3–3 I was teased: for them the perfect score is 0–0, because this means no mistakes have been made by the defence.

The ultimate match? It's hard to say. I'd prefer to talk more about historic moments: the 3–3 at Seville, the 3–0 of France–

Brazil, the 4–3 of Italy–Germany in Mexico in 1970 remain fabulous encounters. What really excites me is when a player passes the ball spot on, at the right moment, to one of his team-mates. It is increasingly rare in football today, so I get less and less excited. The Champions League final between Manchester United and Bayern Munich at Nou Camp was mediocre for the first hour and a quarter, but metamorphosed into an historic match in the last fifteen minutes, when the Germans hit the woodwork twice and the English scored two goals. That was a thrilling moment.

Why are you still commentating on football matches on TV? For kicks?
I used to do it but then I stopped. Now I'm presenting Michel Denisot's new football programme on Canal Plus. For me, since I'm neither manager nor player any more, TV is a fantastic medium through which I can express my ideas about football. I'm at FIFA for similar reasons, since this allows me to discuss the game.

Without a doubt St Etienne and Marseille are the greatest French clubs of the last twenty years. Yet their successes were followed by major scandals. Could we in France, one day, have clubs like Juventus, Barcelona or even Arsenal?
The scandals involving Olympique Marseille and St Etienne had nothing to do with each other – one was about corruption and the other about a slush fund. Back then slush funds existed everywhere, but all that has changed now that football clubs are monitored. Scandals like that are neither typically French nor typical of football.

During France–Brazil in 1986 in Guadalajara, Zico and yourself each missed a penalty shot. What would go through the minds of two of the world's best players in such a situation?
Zico missed a penalty during the match, whereas I missed mine in a shoot-out. In either case, though, only those who

shoot can miss. At that moment I knew that it was my last
World Cup as a player, and I thought of the team; that it was
a pity for those who love football; that the journalists would
slaughter me. My head was spinning. When Luís Fernandez
took the last penalty and scored the winning goal, everything was forgotten. Never before had I missed a penalty for
France.

*Inter Milan and Real Madrid are made up of stars from all
over the world. If this had been the case during your time,
who would you most have liked to play with? Zico, Socrates,
Maradona, Hoennes, Rummenigge . . . who else?*
I would have liked to play with Johan Cruyff.

*Heysel was one of the greatest tragedies in the history of
football. Could such a nightmare occur today?*
Fortunately not, because tragedies of that kind have brought
about change. FIFA has insisted that stands should be all-
seater, that seats should be numbered and that there should
be no more barriers. That doesn't mean that accidents are a
thing of the past, however.

*You were one of the first players to be individually sponsored.
Today this is normal. Will players end up being owned by
brands rather than by their clubs?*
When a player has a four-year contract with Adidas, he'll
honour it. When he has a contract for the same length of time
with a club, he rarely respects it.

Do you have time to pursue passions other than football?
I have no passion other than football. Three things matter to
me in life: family, friends and having a laugh. I enjoy watching team sports on TV – basketball, handball, volleyball. I
play golf with my mates because it's a good way of getting
fresh air in magnificent green spaces. I also like to play cards,
never for money but for friendship.

In France, politics are ever-present in sport. Is it difficult for you to keep your distance from that?
It isn't difficult, you just say no. Politics are a form of power. I have power without getting involved in politics, so why go and get exhausted for something which isn't my thing? Politics are not a part of my world.

You are so high up in the football hierarchy that I guess it's impossible for you to imagine returning to the grass roots. Don't you miss them?
I can't see myself sitting on the bench any more. I've gone into executive leadership, and it's difficult to do a U-turn. My future lies in the opportunities which occur, as has been the case in the past.

Do you think that the future of football depends on the success of the game in the USA?
I think the future of football lies in women's football, as Sepp Blatter once declared. In the US people have ignored soccer for twenty years and they can continue to do so. Women's football, on the other hand, is on the rise. They have 8 million licensed players, as many as France, Germany and Italy have male players. I've seen women's matches of great quality. And it seems to me that women are becoming more and more interested in football.

Your friend and co-president of the World Cup '98 organising committee, Fernand Sastre, passed away at the beginning of the tournament. How did you handle such an ordeal?
We had known for some months that Fernand was ill and, sadly, we were half-expecting it. Luckily, he didn't suffer. The injustice is that he died just before the World Cup. If God had granted him three more weeks it would have been fantastic. As for the organisation of the World Cup, everything was virtually done three months before it began and there were only a few details left to be sorted out. All the major decisions

had been made, everyone knew what they had to do, the tickets had been sold and the marketing completed. What was so sad was for the two of us to have set off on such an adventure and for me to have ended it alone.

The number 10 shirt is a favourite with French fans, thanks to you. What does this number mean to you?
Number 10 has always represented certain special gifts in a player. He is the playmaker who can also score goals. The number has attained a magical status thanks to Pelé – he was the only real number 10, there have been no others. Actually, he never misses a chance of telling me each time we meet, 'I am *the* number 10.'

Football is a business. Do you consider yourself to be a businessman?
If I was a businessman, I'd be a player's agent or a manager. I'm not in the football business. I'm at FIFA, in contact with federations more than clubs. The football associations, of which there are 203, are 90 per cent amateur. Today, only a minute part of the world of football is professional. The distribution of TV rights, both in England and France, is made between professional clubs, which is normal. Look at showbiz: Celine Dion doesn't give money to singers from the suburbs and I don't see why OM or AC Milan should act any differently.

Do you feel that you missed the great period of Les Verts? Years later, what does St Etienne mean to you?
Les Verts were my idols. I was seventeen and everyone admired this club. Later, when I arrived, I discovered an incredible town filled with warm-hearted people. It may not be the most beautiful city in the world, but the hinterland is beautiful and the people from St Etienne are charming. I still have friends there. The problem with the period when I was playing for the club was that St Etienne had lost its hunger. Most of its players were in decline. There are times when it's important

to know when to stop. The coach, Robert Herbin, didn't really want me to come because the team, until then, had been largely made up of players from its youth academy. It was easier for Herbin to assert his authority over such players. The club had probably realised that its reserves had run dry, so it began to buy outside players: Johnny Rep, Bernard Lacombe, Jacques Zimako and myself. I enjoyed being there and liked the president, Roger Rocher, but neither my arrival nor Rep's were welcomed by everybody. As chairman of Les Verts, Roger Rocher was an extremely important figure in football, but he ended up losing it; he became a megalomaniac. He has always behaved very respectably towards me, though.

Would you be where you are today if you hadn't been advised by Giovanni Agnelli who is, in some ways, something of a spiritual father to you? Tell me about him.
'L'Avoccato' is the one who wanted me to come to Juventus, against the advice of Boniperti and Trappatoni; he was the one who imposed me on the club. Two weeks before I arrived, they were going to keep Liam Brady, and he told them to let him go and that they should sign up Platini. It was hard on them, given that Brady was a player liked by everybody there. Juventus had won only the UEFA Cup, not the European Champions Cup, or the Cup-Winners' Cup, or even the Super Cup. Giovanni Agnelli took great pride in saying that it was thanks to him that Platini had come to the club, and that from then on trophies had piled up.

Two weeks before I ended my playing career, he summoned me to his office and said: 'Michel, is it true that you're stopping? You're not going to another club?'

'No, L'Avocat, I'm stopping for real.'

'You don't want to stay and work with us, or with Fiat?'

'No, I'm going home,' I said and I left.

I've always considered myself to be like a sailor who went a long way away and who would one day return home.

That was the only question Agnelli ever asked me.

The rules of football develop continuously. You've often expounded ideas on this matter. How do you see the near future?
We've sorted out the question of the game and its rules. I like football at the moment because there are more spaces for the attackers and if the referees are any good, you can really play. One of the key problems today is the lack of unity in the decisions they make. In some cases they will book players, and in other similar situations they won't even give a warning. The public often finds it hard to figure out what's going on. The game in itself is fine, but things off the pitch – the agents, the transfers, the shares – it is time to regulate. Professional referees are badly needed but it's not an easy task. Most of them prefer to keep their daytime jobs and receive perks when they travel. Maybe one day FIFA or UEFA will send paid referees to matches.

Are you an ambassador of French sport?
In the position I'm in, I can't think of myself being French, even if it is my nationality: FIFA is an international organisation. It's only when the president of the French Republic asks me to accompany him on an official trip that I become French again.

Your private life is a jealously guarded secret. Do the tabloids no longer pursue you?
The tabloids have never pursued me. My family never wanted to be photographed and neither do I. If they want to photograph me, well then that's their problem, and anyway, for them I'm a has-been. The media are only interested in marginal people or those on holiday in St Tropez – that's where all the photographers club together. It's not my cup of tea. I haven't married a top model; I don't take drugs; I'm not homosexual – I'm your average guy.

What do you think of David Beckham?
David Beckham is an excellent footballer. But his position on

the right side of the midfield being a little restrictive, I can't see there being much room for development. Creative players no longer play in the centre; the men on the side are the important ones nowadays. During the final of the Champions' League, Tony Banks [the former British sports minister] came to me and asked me, 'Michel, what happened during the first half?'

'The strength of United is Giggs on the left and Beckham on the right and Alex Ferguson swapped them over,' was my friendly answer. During the second half, Ferguson changed back the players to their usual positions and everything became much better. But who am I to talk? I'm not Sir Alex.

What is your greatest football memory?
My entire career. There are times when it is difficult for me to appreciate that at the age of three or four, I kicked a football around in my grandparents' Italian café. From there, everything followed.

Epilogue

People should know that football isn't just about what is printed in the newspapers, it's the most beautiful game in the whole world. A game which requires cunning, intelligence and sometimes trickery. I have faith. FIFA gives money to countries throughout the world for the young to play football. I would rather watch young people enjoying themselves on synthetic pitches brought to countries like Liberia than to watch a match on TV between two professional sides. But football has also experienced deviations. In the space of twenty years, the game has made as many mistakes as society has in 100 years. Corruption, slush funds, hooliganism . . . it's essential to bring these issues under control, otherwise it will be the end of football.

10

Zizou Zidane – The World's Best Player

MOUNSI

In the Name of the Father

In the Name of the Son

Prologue

That which is written is written: 'Mektoub!'
'When he came to France before the Algerian war, my father moved in just behind the stadium. In St Denis at that time there were just woodlands, hilly plots and ruined houses. That was where my father lived. My mother showed me a photo of him from those days . . . an old yellowed black and white photo. My father was young back then.'
(*Zidane*)

In the Name of the Father

As it was, as it still is, as it will always be: the seething black
suburb encircling the red belt, and everything that came
before. The endless jumble of housing estates, already built
on the water-sodden ground of a landscape filled with factory
chimneys spreading their deleterious fumes far around them.

In wintertime, the very snow falls from a sky bespeckled
with soot. And the entire region is covered in a crust of piss
and rust.

In the Name of the Son

You arrive, one behind the other, from the underground
tunnel leading to the pitch.
French on the right, Brazilians on the left.
The two captains, Deschamps and Dunga, leading the way.
Watching over you, around the ground, are blue and khaki
silhouettes, helmets, clubs, uniforms, police, soldiers, and
special forces.
Further off are forgers, tricksters, counterfeit money dealers
and football shirt-sellers clearing out their stocks of blue.
At the black market rate, a seat is 10,000 francs.
In the stands, ministers, stars, officials, the president of the
Republic and the prime minister.

In the Name of the Father

Mud, rain, dust, splatterings of tar, stunted, stubby trees brushing the ground. Mean dwellings of recycled steel, chipboard, breezeblocks.

Most foreigners who took root here finished by losing their roots. They worked hard to feed their families. And there, poor among the poor, they toiled at the everlasting vocation of their kind: survival.

In the Name of the Son

You arrive on the pitch to the thunderous acclaim of the
    spectators.
The Brazilians raise their arms in salute.
They sing their national anthem.
Then France, the whole crowd sing as one.
Eighty thousand throats at work.
You! Lips scarcely moving.
The president of the Republic and the prime minister . . . just
    as in 1789.
Karembeu . . . mouth shut.
The nation has waited years for the day of glory.
But you, what are you thinking of at this moment?
Of your boyhood room with the photo of Enzo Francescoli
    on the wall?
Of that pair of Kopas you were given on your twelfth birth-
    day?
Of your earliest professional days at US St Henri?

In the Name of the Father

So it is today, within these slabs of buildings, many an immigrant arrives from the four corners of the world in search of a haven of hope. From street level rise the shrill yells and cries of their children as they play with a black-and-white ball.

There is nothing that can save them from this encircling belt of towers that line the road. Further down still, the capital's ring road vomits traffic from both ends.

In the Name of the Son

The lines break up.
Here you are, greeting the Brazilian players.
You shake hands with each other before lining up for the
    photo.
Photos and cameras.
The world is there.
The whole world.
With
Djorkaeff's Armenia.
Desailly's Ghana.
Laurent Blanc's France.
Thuram's Guadeloupe.
Karembeu's New Caledonia.
Zidane's Algeria . . . and all of you . . .
'The blue-black-white-Arab cockerel'.

In the Name of the Father

Smaïl was born over there. Born hearing the echo of the soft singing of women, with their clear voices and long henna-stained fingers, cradling their delicate infants in their arms and languidly shooing away the tiny flies that danced and buzzed around their heads. He knows the parchment faces of the old Kabyle men, and the old women leaning against walls made of dry stones and adobe.

He remembers their names.

In the Name of the Son

There's a decision to make, the referee tosses a coin then picks
 it off the ground.
The two captains part with a handshake.

In the Name of the Father

Over there, he is everywhere. On the mountain, in every white stone, in every spiny bush, in every tuft of grass, even in the bed of the *wadi*, in the dusty-violet-coloured far-off hills, in the endless skies where the wind still whistles, carrying muffled snatches of the voice of the muezzin as he utters the call to prayer from the *Djemaa*. Algeria: in this land, he is everywhere.

In the Name of the Son

It is nine o'clock in the evening. To the sound of the shouted
   applause of the crowd, the kick-off of the World Cup
   final.
You look up to the stands, then kiss your wedding ring.
The ball rolls right, left, then away, forwards.
The crowd in the stands, painted in blue, exhorts, trumpets,
   shouts.
This way you have of turning back on yourself . . . gliding as
   if on roller skates . . . balletic passing . . . applause, shouts,
   quiet periods . . . runs, accelerations, dummies, dribbles,
   breaks . . . control . . .
This way you have of killing, of enveloping the ball between
   your legs, dancing as you feint with your body . . . and the
   ball that passes from right leg to left.

In the Name of the Father

Yet his presence in St Denis is beyond doubt. There, among
the foreigners wrenched from their soil, like a plant pulled
from the ground but whose tiniest roots still hold fast.

In every one of the men's movements, in every inflexion of
their voices, in every feature of their bodies, a timid pardon
was asked of the world for that small patch of land they were
doomed to inhabit. As the days flowed by, they dwindled, so
small that they might disappear.

From time to time they . . . disappeared . . .

In the Name of the Son

Twenty-seventh minute.
Emmanuel Petit places the ball on the corner spot.
He strikes.
The ball takes flight.
You jump.
You send your header speeding to the post.
The ball slides to the back of the net.
France 1, Brazil 0.
In the stands, on the terraces, everywhere the crowd yells this
    exclamation:
'Zizou! Zizou!'
The diminutive makes a circuit of the stadium.
Your comrades clasp you to them.
You kiss Emmanuel Petit.

In the name of the Father

That day, he suddenly remembered memories so far distant, so long past, that it was like a miasma within him. He saw it like a dream, as if it was not real, as if somebody else had lived it. That day, 12 July 1998, he remembered something far-off, forgotten. His arrival in Seine St Denis.

In the Name of the Son

In the stands, fabrics of many colours are waving.
French flags mix with the red star and crescent of Algeria.
Shouts of joy are heard in every language, from every mouth,
    in every accent.
Once upon a time in the twenty-seventh minute.
Twice upon a time in the forty-fifth minute.
Djorkaeff places the ball on the corner spot.
And the story begins, the legend . . .
France 2, Brazil 0.
In the second half, Emmanuel Petit is six metres from Taffarel.
You are into stoppage time.

One minute to play.
He scores from a pass by Vieira.
France 3, Brazil 0.

In the Name of the Father

Marseilles, the northern suburbs. That night, Smaïl sighed
and closed his eyes. His head gently lolled on to his shoulder.
His breathing forced a great sigh into his pillow. He was
already asleep.

Fragments of images, images without order or logic, passed
through his head, images of things he'd seen in childhood. It
appeared to him that the house was full of visitors shouting
his name.

The images scrolled and whirled through his head. Some
pleased him and so he tried to grab hold of them, but they
passed across his vision and faded away. These images struck
him with the power and the clarity of dreams, and suddenly,
before his eyes he saw the blurred silhouette of Yazid stoop-
ing towards him.

Between his hands he held a trophy.

Smaïl ceaselessly intoned the strange words that seemed
imbued with magic: 'Mabrouk my son! Mabrouk!' Gold
flooded from the ball, from the cup, as if it were the light of a
sun.

In the Name of the Son

The grandstand.
Didier Deschamps leads the way.
He kisses Michel Platini and the president.
They shake your hand.
They present you with medals.
The president of the Republic hands the cup to the captain.
The trophy is passed from hand to hand, from mouth to mouth.
Then you all return to the pitch.
You sprint, you careen, you spin around like whirling
    dervishes.
Champions of the world, you dance to the tune 'I Will
    Survive', now truly your theme song.

In the Name of the Father

In the Name of the Father,
In the Name of the Son,
And so be it.

The ties between father and son are sacred.

'Whatever happens, my father will be with me. What he has taught me is the way of God.' (*Zidane*)

In the Name of the Son

Pouring along the Champs Elysées.
The crowds.
Horns everywhere.
Flags everywhere. On balconies, on cars, in people's hands, in
    trees, in bars.
Your name lights up on the Arc de Triomphe.
Millions are crying 'Zidane, president!'
Everywhere are clutches of men, of women, of children,
    perched on phone boxes, car roofs, newspaper kiosks.
Cheers ring out in all languages, from all mouths, from all
    ages, reaching to the very mountains of Kabyle.
The sounds of ululating in the village while the shadows of
    night fall upon the trees of the Parc Clairefontaine.

11

Oooh, Aaah, Cantona!

IAN RIDLEY

It was Sunday 1 October 1995, the day of Eric Cantona's comeback after eight months out of English football due to that mad moment of kung fuey at Selhurst Park. I was travelling up to Manchester on a train for the game, United against Liverpool, and became engaged in a conversation with a Red Devils' fan who happened to be reading a newspaper article I had written about Cantona's return.

I recognised him. He was Christopher Eccleston, a brilliant British actor. The next day, he said, he was to begin filming on *Jude*, an adaptation of the Thomas Hardy novel *Jude the Obscure*, in which he was to play the hero, and for which he would rightly receive copious plaudits. He should really have been at home learning lines, he added, but he just couldn't miss this day.

I was reminded of the encounter when watching the film *Elizabeth*, in which the developing thespian Cantona played the French ambassador, M. de Foie, to Eccleston's Duke of Norfolk. Reminded, too, of a story told by another actor in the film, Geoffrey Rush, who won an Oscar for his performance in *Shine* and played Sir Francis Walsingham in *Elizabeth*.

Rush, a New Zealander probably more at home with rugby union than football, had not a clue about Cantona's background during the filming. He was aware though that Eccleston seemed in awe of this taciturn Frenchman. One day during a break between takes, Cantona was sitting on the throne specially constructed for the English monarch, for a few moments alone with his thoughts. Eccleston noticed this and dashed off in search of a camera to capture the moment that so perfectly summed up Le Roi of Old Trafford. When he returned, however, Cantona was gone and Eccleston was left frustrated and disappointed. Rush could not understand what the fuss was about.

Cantona would have been flattered. He certainly should have been. Eccleston was the senior, more accomplished actor. But he was reduced to worshipful reverence around his Saturday hero. Footballers have that effect on people. Even celebrities, hugely talented in the creative arts, often slip from the articulate to the tongue-tied when in their presence, simply because these sportsmen have a gift in their feet and physique which their admirers so envy.

The Cantona effect went beyond even that. Before him, there was a dribble of foreign players; after him *le déluge*. Before him, Didier Six had come to play briefly for Aston Villa; after him David Ginola, Frank Leboeuf, Marcel Desailly and Didier Deschamps felt that they, too, could succeed. It is unlikely, however, that any player, French or of other over-seas nationality, has had the same impact either on a club – England's biggest, at that – or on the country's football.

He always spoke so little, and the things he said were so enigmatic. Who can forget the seagulls-and-trawler quota-tion that might have brought him the title of Le Marquis de Sardines? Instead he carried himself with hauteur and a myth, a legend, grew up around him. In France he may have been seen by some as a pretentious country boy, a roguish son of Marseilles, an *idiot savant* as depicted by the French equiva-lent of *Spitting Image*, *Les Guignols de l'Info*. In England, though, he was the mysterious man in black, his swashbuck-ling derring-do on the field stoked by an image of dangerous, brooding silence off it, in line with his preference for heroes like Arthur Rimbaud, Mickey Rourke and Jim Morrison.

It's funny. You see a figure like Cantona – not that there are many – and watch some of his horrible, spiteful tackling. You picture again in the mind's eye the incident that emulated another of his formative influences, Bruce Lee, that January night at Selhurst Park – and no matter what the provocation, no matter how unpleasant the fan who baited him, his action was wrong – and at times you felt distaste. How you miss a character like that now, though. Probably even those who called for him to be kicked out of the English game pine just a little.

It is worth remembering just what English football was like when Cantona first arrived, in January 1992, for a trial with Sheffield Wednesday. The Premier League, and the riches from the satellite television broadcaster Sky which were about to transform the landscape, were still six months away. Grounds were still being rebuilt after the terrible tragedy of Hillsborough. Some reasonable players from overseas had arrived, but there was nowhere near the quality and quantity of these days.

Cantona came not because he really wanted to but because – a fortuitous piece of advice – he was told he would do well to do so. 'The whiff of sulphur,' as one member of a French disciplinary committee put it, had followed him through a career of controversy in France with Auxerre, Marseille, Martigues, Montpellier and Nîmes, and he was an outcast in his own country. Michel Platini, then the national team coach, recommended, after consultation with his anglophile assistant Gérard Houllier, that the English game would be suited to his heart and lungs. As Alfred de Musset once said: 'An artist has no homeland.'

An agent arranged the week's trial with Wednesday. When the then manager, Trevor Francis, asked him to undergo another, as the pitches had been frozen and he had seen him perform only indoors, Cantona refused, his pride stung. He was ready to go home until Leeds United manager Howard Wilkinson heard about it and drove the 40 miles south to persuade him to sign with them.

It was a marriage that would not last. Cantona was a substitute for much of the season in which Leeds won the title, though he played some significant cameos in crucial games. When he was omitted on several occasions the following season, he fell out with Wilkinson, becoming ever more unco-operative. Again he was ready to walk out. It alarmed Gérard Houllier, who had by now succeeded Platini as the French coach. He was worried that, with Cantona unlikely to find a club back in France to take him, a valuable asset might be lost to the national team, and so he phoned Alex Ferguson at Manchester United.

It was a signing, a meant-to-be moment, that became a turning point in United's history. The Leeds managing direc-tor, Bill Fotherby, rang his Manchester United counterpart, Martin Edwards, one day to see if the United full-back Denis Irwin might be available. Ferguson, who had been speaking to Houllier in the previous few days, was in the office. 'Ask him about Cantona,' Ferguson wrote on a notepad. Edwards did, and on Friday 26 November 1992, United spent their best £1 million ever and the rest was to become hysteria.

'I think everybody raised a few eyebrows, including myself,' said the then United captain, Steve Bruce. 'Because I didn't really know about the ability he had. I didn't realise the skills, the balance and the vision he had. As soon as I saw him in training, I knew he would give us another dimension.' Added the man who would play alongside him up front, Mark Hughes – and who was deemed difficult to play with until Cantona came along – 'The team felt right, balanced.'

United had finished runners-up to Leeds when they should have won the title in 1991–2. With Cantona it was imme-diately secured, and for the first time in twenty-six years. *Vive la différence.* 'Without doubt he was the catalyst in us win-ning the Championship,' said Alex Ferguson. 'We had some tremendous young players just emerging, and Eric came at the right time for them. He brought the sense of big-time thinking, the vision and imagination and general play.'

The season of 1993–4 was an immense one for United, thanks to Cantona. Not only did they retain the title, but they did the Double, thought impossible by some in the modern era, by winning the FA Cup as well. Ferguson believed this to be a team that might win him the European Cup at last, but the limitation then on the number of foreign players was too great a hurdle to overcome.

There are two images of that season that stick in this observer's mind to illustrate the good and the bad of Cantona's play and personality. United against Arsenal at Old Trafford was a tight, tense game as usual, its fevered pace and physical intensity almost inducing a headache. It always looked as if one goal would decide it. This duly came from Cantona with a 25-yard cannonball shot from a free kick. 'Ooh, aah, Cantona!' went the chant around the ground, the anthem that was to become the soundtrack to the visual trademark of his turned-up collar. It fitted. It seemed to symbolise the me-against-the-world attitude of some lonesome, world-weary movie hero.

And the other image of that campaign? A downside, in fact, Cantona sitting in the stands of the Nou Camp, serving a suspension for a sending-off, as United were being beaten 4–0 by Barcelona. He was badly missed. 'Cantona is someone you want on your team,' said his team-mate at the time Paul Ince. 'The very fact he's playing, his presence on the field, his awareness of where everyone is on the field, it sets you up. You want that beside you. He can take it all in straight away and he can pick them out in the right positions at the right time. Cantona, man. Respect. Bona fide respect.'

Cantona's importance to United was emphasised around the time of that Selhurst Park disgrace. With Cantona, United had won the Double the previous season, two penalties from him helping them to a 4–0 win over Chelsea in the FA Cup final, in which he became the first Frenchman to play; during his suspension they lost both trophies. With him, they had a certain *je ne sais quoi*. Without him they had a *je ne sais pas*. Then, wouldn't you know it, the following season, 1995–6, they regained the Double with Cantona back in the fold. As they secured the title he scored goals in six games in a row, four of them match-winners. In the Cup final against Liverpool, he scored another against Liverpool in the dying minutes with a flourish that a scriptwriter would have deemed fanciful.

A genius? United's fans thought so, and according to the *Oxford English Dictionary*, they might be right. 'Two opposed spirits or angels working for a person's salvation or damnation,' goes the definition. 'Also, person who powerfully influences one for good or ill. Person having exalted intellectual power, instinctive and extraordinary, imaginative, creative or inventive capacity.'

If there was an area in which Cantona's shortcomings were exposed, it seemed to be in European competition. United went in search of the Holy Grail that was the Champions' Cup, which Ferguson coveted as the fulfilment of his ambition to emulate Sir Matt Busby in 1968. It eluded him season after season, due to the three-foreign-players rule at one point, but also due to the trial-and-error process of accumulating experience and the right men for the job.

During his patchy European career with United, Cantona was sent off at the end of a bad-tempered match against Galatasaray in Istanbul, then suspended for that crucial match in Barcelona. He was also anonymous in Gothenburg when United needed a big performance. In his fifth and what was to prove final season, 1996–7, United were bundled out in the semi-finals by Borussia Dortmund.

I understand that Ferguson, in his anger and sadness at United's exit from the competition, expressed his disappointment at Cantona's performance to him in the dressing room afterwards, to the surprise of the other players. It was almost the first time they had heard the manager so berate his favoured son – whose muscular playing style and disciplinary record probably reminded Ferguson of his own, though he would readily concede that Cantona had much more talent – and it may have been the moment when Cantona, on the cusp of his thirty-first birthday, decided his time was up.

It may also have been why this time – unlike some eighteen months earlier, when Cantona had announced his retirement after the FA prevented him from playing private practice matches during his suspension – Ferguson did not follow him to Paris to dissuade him. 'I think if he is here today, tremendous,' Ferguson had once said. 'But if he is gone tomorrow, we just say: "Good luck, Eric, thanks for playing for us."'

But just as Neil Kinnock paved the way for the modernisation of the Labour Party and Tony Blair's final election as prime minister of England, so it can be said that Cantona's influence on United's eventual capture of the trophy by beating Bayern Munich in 1999 was immense, even decisive.

First, there had been the development of young players as Cantona brought an atmosphere of self-motivated work, of European professionalism, to the club. After training at the Cliff, United's complex in Salford, Cantona would often ask for a goalkeeper to work with for shooting and free-kick practice. Others, including the dead-eye David Beckham, would want to stay on to the point where Ferguson would sometimes have to call them in on a Friday afternoon to stop them tiring themselves out.

Then there was the way he smoothed the path for other strikers. Old Trafford had often been a graveyard for big-money signings, Alan Brazil and Garry Birtles among them. The boot was on the other foot for Cantona, though. 'Eric just swaggered in, stuck out his chest and looked around,' said Ferguson. 'He surveyed everything as though he were asking: "I'm Cantona, how big are you? Are you big enough for me?"' Though in private Cantona may not have thought Andy Cole the most suitable of partners, he brought him along to the point where he was able to become a prolific scorer for United. Shown that it was possible to come in and succeed, Dwight Yorke, in his turn, settled in quickly.

Finally there was the tactical nous. It was Cantona who showed United how to pull teams around and to exploit the gaps with a killer pass. When man-marked, he would sometimes simply stand still. Markers drift around, he reasoned. On edge, they cannot resist moving. Therefore by standing still he created space. From that canny position just behind a striker and in front of the midfield, he taught United to retain possession until a gap appeared. Gérard Houllier called him 'an attack-maker'. Perhaps what was most astonishing about him was the deft touch of such a big man. Alex Ferguson's analysis was simple: 'The best player I have ever had.'

Yet in addition to the question-marks over Europe, there were doubts about him at the highest level. It was a serious sadness of Cantona's career that Aimé Jacquet did not pick him for Euro '96 in England. Cantona knew that consequently he would not be selected for France '98. The then Arsenal manager George Graham described him as 'a cry baby who would let you down at the highest level'. And one suspects that Howard Wilkinson believed something similar after seeing Cantona flounder against Stuttgart in a European Cup tie.

There were doubts about his pace, or rather change of pace. Even Ferguson said that he was a terrible tackler and had to tell him to refrain from trying to tackle because it was getting him into trouble. And at one point, Michel Platini wondered if he was too unselfish, too concerned with making the grand gesture. He revised his opinion after seeing Cantona's ruthlessness in England.

Jacquet's reasons for omitting him emerge perhaps in this quotation: 'Sometimes he lacks the killer instinct in front of goal. There he is a poet, in love with the ball, seeking a gesture for its own sake. He does not use his powerful shot enough, perhaps because he has so many other weapons. Sometimes the game can seem too easy to him and there is a danger, as with all gifted players, that he becomes too static.'

Punctuating it all were those brushes with authority. They ranged from the verbal, such as calling the former French team manager Henri Michel '*un sac à merde*', to the extremely physical, like throwing his boots in the face of his Montpellier team-mate Jean-Claude Lemoult and stamping on Norwich City's John Moncur. Not to mention Selhurst Park, of course.

Then there was the life outside football so untypical of a footballer; the fondness for poetry and art – 'Compared to

Eric, the rest of us are painting by numbers,' Mark Hughes once said – and the love of the cinema. It may have been, though, that sometimes Cantona's image as an intellectual was rather far-fetched. Some colleagues and commentators pointed out that he had been known to quote the wrong philosopher or film-maker. How was Cantona otherwise? Both Lee Chapman and Paul Ince, former close friends at Leeds and Manchester United, have told me that he did not stay in touch with them after he moved on.

It all adds up to a picture of a figure the like of which English and French football will probably never see again. There may be better players, though they will have to be good, and there may be more colourful characters, though that is even more doubtful. It is highly unlikely there will ever be such a combination.

Quite often, senior pros at clubs are nicknamed 'legend' by respectful young apprentices. Few really deserve that accolade. Cantona did. In a way, it was appropriate that Christopher Eccleston didn't get his picture in that fleeting moment. Far more vivid are the stills and movies that run in the imagination. And Cantona had imagination in abundance. It is the best place for him to live on.

12

Frenchy But Chic – David Ginola

SALMAN RUSHDIE

In a game played the week before the Worthington Cup final, Tottenham's French superstar, the gifted David Ginola, scored a goal that was almost a replay of Ricky Villa's famous Cup-winning masterpiece: a labyrinthine solo run past most members of the opposing defence, then an unstoppable shot. Ginola has movie-star good looks and Pat Jennings' hair: tresses long and silky enough to win him a featured role in a L'Oréal-shampoo television commercial. Ginola's skills are even more lustrous than his locks. Ginola can shimmy like your sister Kate. His balance, his feinting, his control of the ball at high speed, his ability to score from 30 yards out, all make him a defender's nightmare. But ever since his early days with Newcastle United, the English team he played for before he came south to Tottenham, two criticisms have been made of him.

First, that he is a 'luxury player'. No term in the football lexicon is more damning. It is a phrase freighted with the profound British mistrust of the artist (and, implicitly, the equally profound British admiration for the artisan). A 'luxury player' has great gifts, but he's lazy. He doesn't run enough, or tackle enough. He's selfish and narcissistic and vain and ought to be taken down a peg or two and reminded that, as the cliché goes, no player is bigger than the game.

Second, that he dives. Diving is a form of gamesmanship,

and to appreciate the skill involved you have to understand the fundamental rule of football: you're meant to play the ball, not the man. Play the man – trip up his legs, take him out at the ankles, slam him across the knees – and it's a foul. A diver pretends to be fouled when he hasn't been. A great diver is like a salmon leaping, twisting, falling. A great dive can last almost as long as the dying of a swan. And it can, of course, influence the referee; it can earn free kicks or penalty kicks; it can get an opponent thrown out of the game. The course of the 1999 Worthington Cup final between Spurs and Leicester would be greatly altered by a dive.

An earlier Spurs star, the great German goalscorer Jürgen Klinsmann, also used to be accused of diving. England fans had booed and howled at Klinsmann when he plunged to the ground during the 1990 World Cup while playing for Germany. But once Klinsmann was traded to Spurs – he was the star of the pre-Ginola era – then the fans understood that this noble spirit was more sinned against than sinning. A similar change of attitude followed Ginola's arrival from Newcastle. Oh, now we saw the subtle pushes with which cynical defenders knocked him off balance, the surreptitious little trips and ankle taps in whose existence we had so vocally disbelieved. Now we understood the tragedy of genius, we saw how grievously Ginola – like Klinsmann before him – had been wronged. Was this just our self-serving fickleness? Certainly not. Reader, it was because the scales fell from our eyes.

As for the other criticism, that Ginola was lazy; that all changed when, midway through the season, Spurs hired a new manager, George Graham, known, when he was an elegant player, as Gentleman George. As a manager he has acquired a less cultured image as the hardest of hard men, whose teams are built on the granite of an impregnable defence.

What would a grim fellow like George Graham make of the blessed butterfly Ginola? It was widely believed that the L'Oréal model would be the first player Graham unloaded after taking charge. Instead, Ginola has blossomed into greatness. The manager has inspired the player to work hard, and the player has, well, inspired the manager the way he inspires us all. 'Do something extraordinary,' Graham now tells Ginola before each game, and it's astonishing how often Ginola obliges.

Oh, there's one more thing about George Graham. First as a player and then as a manager, he made his name, and won a shelf of trophies, at Highbury. Spurs had hired the former manager of its arch-enemy, Arsenal.

How could our old arch-enemy be given control of the Spurs team? The answer lies in the long, depressing tale of Spurs' decline. Boardroom incompetence during the late 1980s had landed the team in financial trouble, and in 1991 its star player – England's moron-genius, the child-man Paul Gascoigne, as famous for bursting into tears during a World Cup game as for his exceptional talent – had to be traded to Lazio in Rome to help pay off the club's debts. The 'sale' was a traumatic event for the fans. Gascoigne was what we thought of as a true Spurs player, fabulously gifted, a 'flair player', an artist. The low point was reached in 1998, when the team's owner, a computer-industry millionaire named Alan Sugar, appointed a Swiss manager. He was named, alas, Christian Gross. Commanding little respect and unable to attract first-rate players, he came close to letting Spurs slip into last place and lose its élite status. Gross was duly sacked. But then Sugar turned to an ex-Gunner, Gentleman George.

George Graham had taken some hard knocks of his own. For while, as the manager of Arsenal, he had led the Gunners to two League Championships and four other major honours in nine years, he had faced accusations of wrongdoing. In 1995 he was found guilty by the Football Association of receiving 'bungs' – under-the-counter cash payments of around £450,000, made as 'sweeteners' during big-money trades of big-name players. Gentleman George lost his job.

But if some Spurs fans mistrusted Graham – and who can blame them? – the speed of the team's improvement shut them up. Tottenham still doesn't have a great team, but getting to

Wembley is the most glamorous event in a club footballer's life. George Graham must take the credit for bringing a little of the glamour back to depressed old White Hart Lane.

Observed on the way to the big game: a man, passing a pub near the stadium, grimacing at the pavement, which was ankle-deep in plastic beer glasses and empty cans. 'That's why the game will never catch on in the States, right there,' he said, a little shamefacedly. A second man chimed in, 'That and the food,' he said. 'The meat pies, the fucking burgers.' The first man was still shaking his head at the rubbish. 'Americans would never leave this mess,' he sighed. 'They wouldn't stand for it.'

A third man, passing, recognised the first, and greeted him gaily, 'You're like bleeding dogshit, mate – you're every-where, you are.'

The three men went off happily towards Wembley.

Inside the stadium, the field was covered in two giant shirts and a pair of giant footballs. As the teams arrived, great flocks of blue and white balloons were released – something plainly learned from studying American sporting occasions. Even so, you'd have to be made of stone not to be affected by the communal excitement of standing together against the world – or against the opposing team, anyhow. The chanting swelled and surged from one end of the grand old stadium to the other. Wembley is to be demolished and a new, third-millennium super-stadium built in its place. This was almost the old lady's last hurrah.

The game began, and it was evident that it wasn't going to be a classic. Leicester looked distinctly second rate, and although Spurs settled first into a rhythm, the team didn't inspire con-fidence. In the twenty-first minute, its captain and star defender, Sol Campbell, completely missed a crucial tackle and Leicester almost scored. My heart was in my mouth, but Ginola gave me things to enjoy: a fast, swerving run past three Leicester players unable to stop him, and a moment of breathtaking ball control; he pulled down an awkwardly high ball with one touch of the outside of his right boot, and passed it away almost instantly – speed, artistry, danger.

No goals in the first half.

In the second, however, high drama. In the sixty-third minute, Tottenham's Justin Edinburgh was crudely brought down by Leicester's blond-thatched Robbie Savage. Irritated by the clumsiness of the tackle, Edinburgh reached out with an open hand and smacked Savage somewhere on the head. Blond hair flew. Then, after an absurdly long pause, Savage suddenly feigned a serious injury. He executed a perfect back-flip and collapsed, writhing, on the ground. In other words, he took a dive.

The referee, having been fooled, promptly showed Edinburgh the dreaded red card. Once a player is shown a red card, not only is he expelled from the game but he can't be substituted and, with Edinburgh now sent off, Spurs were down to ten men against Leicester's eleven. 'Cheat, cheat,' chanted the Spurs fans, and then they booed. The noise made by 35,000 fans booing in unison was unearthly, monstrous; but in our hearts we feared that the day might be lost. And for the next several minutes, as Leicester City charged forward, our fears seemed justified.

The play was one-sided – all Leicester City – but slowly Tottenham regained its confidence. The Tottenham right back, Stephen Carr, started making more and more penetrating runs. Darren Anderton (once nicknamed Sicknote because he got injured so often, but fit at last these days) was also beginning to play well, with his trademark long-legged stride and his dangerous floating crosses. And even though Ginola appeared to be having a quiet game, he was forcing Leicester to use two or even three players to stop him. This meant that in spite of being a man down Spurs started acting like the team with the extra player. The fans sang a rousing chorus of 'Glory, glory, hallelujah'.

Meanwhile Leicester's Savage, clearly rattled by the boos that filled the stadium whenever he touched the ball, was involved in another bit of rough stuff, but got away with it.

The game was into its last five minutes. If there was no result after ninety minutes' play, there would be half an hour of extra time, and if the score was still level, the game would be decided by penalty kicks. (Football fans hate the arbitrariness of the sudden-death penalty shoot-out.)

Four minutes before the end of regulation time, Tottenham's goalkeeper, Ian Walker, ran over to pick up a loose ball and slipped! He missed the ball completely. Amazingly, after Leicester's Tony Cottee rushed over and knocked the ball toward the now undefended Tottenham goal, there wasn't a single Leicester player there to tap it into the net. The first of two terrible goalkeeping mistakes, and Tottenham's moment of danger had passed.

And then, in the last minute, lightning struck. Leicester, settling in for extra time, was caught unprepared by a sudden whipped pass from Les Ferdinand, in midfield, to Steffan Iverson, who was sprinting down the right side of the field before anyone realised what had happened. He cut in toward goal and shot. It wasn't a great shot: it was on target but weak. Somehow, the American goalkeeper, Kasey Keller, failed to hold the ball, and palmed it feebly toward the charging Allan Nielsen. Boom! As the Latin American commentators like to put it: 'Goooooooooaal!!!!'

It was over in an instant, and Tottenham had won 1–0. There were the celebrations – the losers' consolation medals were given to Leicester, the winners' medals and the cup itself to Spurs – and, of course, the jeering: 'You're not singing, you're not singing, you're not singing any more.' The oddly three-handled Worthington Cup was lovingly kissed and triumphantly held high by each Tottenham player in turn. In victory, the players suddenly stopped looking like rich, pampered superstar athletes and became, instead, innocent young men bright with the realisation that they were experiencing a great moment in their lives. Never mind the scrappiness of the game. It's the result that counts.

George Graham is famous as a manager of 'result teams', teams that will somehow grind out what they need without bothering too much about providing entertainment along the way. I can't remember when the term was last applied to a Spurs line-up. It's an Arsenal kind of concept. 'Boring Arsenal' was also 'Lucky Arsenal', because of its habit of stealing games like this one. Well, who's boring and lucky now?

As I left the ground, beaming foolishly, a fellow Spurs fan recognised me and waved cheerily in my direction. 'Gawd bless yer, Salman,' he yelled. I waved back, but I didn't say what I wanted to say: Nah, not Gawd, mate, he doesn't play for our team. Besides, who needs him when you've already got George Graham and David Ginola; when you're leaving Wembley Stadium with a win?

13

The Englishman: Frank Leboeuf Comes to London

WILL BUCKLEY

It was a midweek evening at Stamford Bridge and Toby, Flat Cap, Wol and myself came hazily out of one of the new bars named after an old number 9 – Bentley's, Tambling's, Ossie's, who knows? – cheered not only by another Chelsea victory but by the style in which it had been achieved. There were downsides to the new Chelsea – primarily an influx of Jeremys and Natashas – but the acquisition of Vialli, Di Matteo, Zola and Leboeuf more than compensated. Of the quartet it was the last-named who had made the biggest impression. For decades we had been accustomed to watching old-fashioned, traditional centre halves at Chelsea. This breed was epitomised by Mickey Droy: bearded, 6 foot 4$^1/_2$ and 12 stone 2 when he started playing professionally, 15 stone 5 when he finished, and nicknamed Igor. Mickey played a simple game of football. If possible he would kick the ball into the stand; if that was not possible, he would lump his opponent into the stand. He was not expected to pass the ball, just head it repeatedly.

Frank, on the other hand, was bald, thin as a whippet, regularly passed the ball over 60 yards to someone on his own side and for the first two months of his career was the club's top scorer. An achievement we decided had to be celebrated with a song. When devising lyrics for a football chant it is advisable to follow Sir Tim Rice's example and keep it very, very simple. Complex rhyming patterns are to be avoided as, let's be honest, are words of more than one syllable. Indeed, throughout the 1980s Millwall successfully dispensed with words altogether as they frightened the life out of all and sundry by droning for the entire ninety minutes in a manner reminiscent of, though probably not inspired by, a Gregorian chant. With this in mind we concocted a catchy little number which involved shouting the name 'Frank Leboeuf' over and over again to the tune of 'La Marseillaise'.

It didn't catch on. But no matter, Frank soon had a song: 'He's here, he's there, he's every fucking where, Frank Leboeuf, Frank Leboeuf [and repeat ad nauseam].' Some players go through an entire career without the fans dedicating a song to them; Frank received the accolade within a matter of months. It has been something of a mutual love-in from the moment he arrived.

Prior to that moment, no one in England had heard of the man whom his team-mates in the national side call 'the Englishman'. Leboeuf was picked for the French squad for Euro '96 but didn't get a game. A state of affairs that pleased Ruud Gullit, who used the tournament to launch himself as an evangelist for sexy football. If Leboeuf had played, his price would have definitely gone up; as it was Gullit only paid £2.5 million for him.

Three years on we meet at the flash Chelsea Hotel, which at present appears to have more restaurants than residents. He is impeccably dressed – baggy jumper and jacket, tight trousers – and very relaxed. The first surprise is that he smokes, although somewhat guiltily taking little, mannered drags rather than throaty lungfuls. The second surprise is that he might have become an accountant. 'I left school at fifteen but carried on studying accounts by correspondence course. I used to play for the village where I was born, St-Cyr-sur-Mer, and where my dad was manager. Then I moved to Toulon to play with the reserves in the Second Division. In those days I played striker or midfield.'

It didn't work out. 'My girlfriend was waiting outside and the manager said, "We can't keep you because there is no place. And anyway I think you're too much in love so you don't think enough about football." Beatrice was crying and I was pretty devastated. Football had always been my dream. And it was almost at an end.'

First love was a problem, then drink. 'I joined Hyères, another Second Division club, and left after six months because the chairman wanted us to take our wives on the team coach and drink Pernod before the game to cheer us up. It was not my cup of tea.'

After two failures, he resorted to advertising his services. 'I placed an advert in *Magazine France* to sell myself: "Young player, former Toulon Academie. Looking for clubs in the Premier League, 1st, 2nd or 3rd Division. Can play number 8, 9, or 10."' No shrinking violet, our Frank.

No one called. At this stage, his self-confidence might have taken a dent. Not a bit of it. 'I had no doubts. As long as I can remember I was always sure that I would become a football player. For me it was certain that I would become an international player. It was never a surprise. It became a surprise afterwards,' says Frank.

Eventually someone rang. Mieux responded to the ad, gave him a trial and offered him a one-year contract. 'After we missed the step [promotion] the manager asked me if I wanted to play sweeper. I started in September when we were last, and after four months we were second and had the best defence. So I thought, "Maybe it works,"' he says, with the curious mix of arrogance and self-deprecation he often employs.

Things had at last worked out, but after a year Frank felt it was time to move to a bigger stage. Once again his flair for self-publicity came to the fore. This time, in cahoots with a friend, he made a video advertising his abilities featuring an introduction to camera from the man himself, talking about his ambitions. He went to Laval, stayed three days, and 'did the best training session I've ever done. The manager said,

"OK, see you tomorrow in my office. You have three days to decide."'

In his first year Laval were relegated. 'The team were not very good,' says Frank. 'Nor were the management, who found themselves having to sell me to pay the players. No one wanted me to go but I had to say, "Sorry, chaps, it's good for me and it's good for you as otherwise you won't be paid."'

Next stop, Strasbourg. 'The structure was the best I've ever seen. The dressing room was unbelievable. There was a swimming pool, sauna, long armchairs, wardrobes with our names. We had a good team and I had a good time. I won my first international caps and our two kids were born in Strasbourg.'

Then, out of the blue, came a call from Graham Rix asking, 'Do you want to come to Chelsea?' 'I didn't even know Chelsea was in London, but from the moment I arrived it has been a *coup de foudre*. I said to my wife that it would be a good opportunity to understand and know another culture. Everything has worked very well.' Normally Englishmen go to Paris to fall in love; this Frenchman had come to London.

The main attraction of Chelsea had been Ruud Gullit, but Leboeuf didn't see him for three days. Instead, he was introduced to Dennis Wise and John Spencer. 'I'd thought English people were pretty big and I meet a couple of midgets.' He eventually encountered Gullit on the golf course: 'I was like a kid being introduced to his hero.'

They became friends. 'I became very, very close to Ruud. He would ring me and say, "Your manager has an appointment with you for a nice dinner." And we would spend six hours over our meal.' Gullit's dismissal came as something of a shock. Infuriatingly for Leboeuf, his great pal the dreadlocked one was suddenly sacked after a misunderstanding over whether his wages should be paid gross or net. 'It was a big surprise. A journalist called me and said "Have you heard the rumours from Italy that Ruud's been sacked?" I said, "I've just seen him this morning – that can't be right." After an hour, he rang again and said, "Frank, I tell you, he's been sacked." I switched on the TV and couldn't believe it. I called Rudy up and he was in shock so I went to see him and had to leave by the back door because of the paparazzi. He was devastated. He said, "Frank, I will talk to the chairman and we will resolve it." I said, "What are you saying? You're sacked. It's over." But he couldn't believe it was over. It took time for him to come back to reality.'

This anecdote tells you two things. First, that Gullit was genuinely amazed that he had been fired, although whether this is because he was shabbily treated or because he was so arrogant he couldn't believe such an event would come to pass remains a moot point. Secondly, that Leboeuf is more considerate than a lot of footballers. Not many of them would bother to visit a recently dismissed manager. It's a man's game. Meet the new gaffer, same as the old gaffer. Luckily for Frank, he also happened to be great pals with his next manager, Gianluca Vialli: 'Gianluca is one of my best friends.' Leboeuf has a happy knack of being best mates with the boss.

He also has a talent for being in the right place at the right time. Specifically, sitting on the bench during the World Cup semi-final when Laurent Blanc was sent off. 'Ten minutes before Laurent was sent off, I was having a joke about not playing once again. When he came off I didn't realise what it meant. It was only two minutes before the end that it sank in. After the match everyone was very sad for Laurent, so I couldn't show my happiness. When the journalists asked me how I felt I said I was very sad for Laurent because he deserved to play [in the final]. But let me be happy because I'm playing.'

The final was a triumph for France and for Frank. The French won 3–0 and could have won by more, while Frank had little difficulty handling a clearly unwell Ronaldo. Before the match, he had been more popular in England than in France. After it, he was one of the eleven names that every French football fan will be able to recite for the rest of their lives. 'It's for ever,' says Frank, 'because, like '66 in England, it was the first time. Even if we win again it won't be the same. The atmosphere was amazing: I've never seen French people so close together and emotional. Beforehand, everybody had said that the World Cup would be a nightmare for all the ladies. They'd opened theatres specially and there were special prices in the restaurants while games were going on. It was generally agreed that it would be a good thing for guys not interested in football because there would be so many women on their own. But in fact the women started to follow the tournament, and husbands could watch the matches without any pressure from their wives hoovering between them and the TV.

'To see over a million people in the Champs Elysées the day after was fantastic. I particularly remember one old lady saying on TV that she had kept her flag from the Liberation waiting for the moment she could use it again, and she was even happier to wave it than she had been after the Second World War, because this time no one had died.

'As a football player, you want to set an example. And we were an example for relationships, anti-racism, commitments and ambitions. It was a perfect World Cup. Perfect football-wise and life-wise.'

Thankfully, he is capable of distinguishing between the two. 'There are so many interesting things in the world, but football is football. It's only a job. There are some players who, if there are four games on the television, will sit and watch them all. I wouldn't watch any. It's a job and I don't watch my job when I'm having a rest. Why should I? I don't think a plumber spends his spare time watching live plumbing.'

He reckons he has three years left in the game, and those he intends to spend in England. 'The English players enjoy their lives more than the players in France. They can do more things. In France you're not allowed to go to a restaurant for three days before the game and you have to stay in and go to bed at nine o'clock. I also think London is more cosmopolitan than Paris. I have made American, German and Lebanese friends here. In fact, you almost have to search to see an Englishman.'

After those three years he has no intention of staying in the game. 'I don't fancy being a manager. You are like a puppet.' Instead, the man whose footballing performances can tend to the theatrical – no one falls to the ground with Frank's flourish or brandishes an imaginary yellow card with anything like his conviction – has dreams of Hollywood. 'Being a role model is a big pressure because I can't do everything I want to do. You have to have a good attitude. I hope I have the opportunity to do a movie and I will be a very, very bad person.' Does he see himself as a bad guy? 'Maybe there's a bad guy straining to get out. I have a good face and a bad face. And because acting is fake it allows you to show something else. I'd like to play John Malkovich roles. He's fantastic.' John Malkovich roles? Just like that? Without any training? 'I never say I will. I don't know if I have the capacity and talent,' adds Frank, backtracking swiftly from his rather confident assertion. Which is a shame, because there might have been some great LA conversations.

'Do you want the good news or the bad news?'

'Cut to the chase, Brad.'

'The bad news is that Malkovich has pulled out.'

'And the good?'

'We've got Frank Leboeuf.'

If he doesn't make it as an actor perhaps he will crack it as a model. In his diary in *The Times* he wrote of his catwalk debut: 'I greatly enjoyed it, although the only celebrity I got to mix with afterwards, apart from the other models, was Lionel Ritchie.'

This fortnightly diary is only intermittently entertaining. Nothing like the unintentionally hilarious efforts Bobby Moore used to knock out for *Shoot!* magazine. Take this magnificent sample which appeared twenty years ago under the heading 'A Hobby Takes Your Mind Off the Game':

When my West Ham team-mate Frank Lampard is away from football matches he sometimes turns his attention to . . . matches [Bobby's dot, dot, dot]. The type you strike, that is. You wouldn't really call it a hobby, but Frank collects book matches whenever we're away from home, then tosses them into a bucket on the bar at his house. Frank brings back matches whenever we go abroad – the United States is a good hunting ground for him because it's simple to get a dozen or so different types in one day there – and it's interesting to browse through them sometimes and recall memories of places and events abroad.

Instead of writing about collecting matches from bars, Frank writes about having lunch with the president of France. 'That is Monsieur Chirac to you. Jacques to me. Win a game of football and suddenly you are on first-name terms with world leaders.' Two decades ago the England captain spent his spare time browsing through Frank Lampard's match collection, now a French substitute lunches with the president. Two decades ago Mickey Droy was starting his career at Chelsea, now a man who calls Chirac 'Jacques' is finishing his career there. Football has been transformed. Chelsea FC has been transformed. And a Frenchman called 'the Englishman' has been one of the architects of that transformation.

14

Singing the Blues: Marcel Desailly Plays for Chelsea

CHARLIE HALL

See him run! See the legs stretch as he makes it look so easy. With his compatriot, the haughty and arrogant balded wonder Leboeuf, holding the back line of my Chelsea's defence, nobody's welcome. Watch their first team of fools, the newly promoted Sunderland, send wave upon wave of useless attack crashing and foundering on their defence.

The south-east London sky skids over his head and a sunset sets the day easy to rest. The dog is off the leash, questing and snuffling through brown grass, a couple move warily with their nervous eyes fixed on him. The dog glances at them, sensing their fear, but declines the offer of a game. In the distance shouts come from the Astroturf pitch and a ball smacks against a body. He grins. The dog looks up again.

Burgess Park, where the ominous north Peckham estate begins, where the wind whips across from Camberwell and men like him take big dogs out to play. His dog can rip and tear; there's fear in the eyes of people who see the callous loping hound with shark-dead eyes and dripping jaws. The man stalks the grounds watching Saturday's public clearing in his path.

* * *

Dad took me along to Stamford Bridge with his mates from Fulham. We ate at the new trattoria in South Kensington; spaghetti with a sauce I didn't like. Allowed a glass of red wine that filled my head, then squeezed into the back of dad's E-Type, edging down the Fulham Road through the thickening crowd, all blue and white throbbing with potential menace and lusty singing. Into the West Stand, bang in the middle, nice spot, just behind the Bench Mob, who were already pointing gleefully at the Leicester City fans (whose notorious Baby Squad was still doing 'the business' with our own Headhunters down the North End Road). Peter Osgood (was good and isn't any more), Peter 'the Cat' Bonetti and others, the tattered remains of the old FA Cup winners. Two— one to fucking Leicester and the Shed End asked the Leicester fans if they were all man enough to 'Sing their songs outside', an invitation to the parties which gave English football the reputation that lived with us for many years after that. I sweated with fury and embarrassment as I willed myself to be older, old enough to have a little Stanley knife in my five-button baggies, old enough to sport eleven-hole Docs and Argyll tank top, feather-cut hairdo. It was not to be, and I had to wait six more years to be old enough to take revenge on the Babies on a hot afternoon in Leicester (oh yes, we had 'em on their own turf!).

Would you get a fucking black man in the whole ground then, let alone on the pitch? Not fucking likely, mate, this is Chelsea, and there's enough white boys to do the job, ta very much!

The sky above Peckham glows pink; triumphant. What a fucking day, first match of the season and we stuffed the Makums! Set the pace for the coming season. He loves them, his boys from twenty-eight years of following the Blues through the despair of the eighties and the hope of the nineties. Chelsea are back!

Look there, boy, two lone figures on the grass, an eternal sight for sore eyes. The dad, merciless, tireless trainer playing keep-up with his boy, can't be more than eight or nine years old. Dad in specs, got some skill and his boy. They keep the ball off the ground; knees, thighs, chest, feet, shoulders and heads. That's skill for you. That could be a future Blue there, we need a few more home-grown kids on the pitch. But you can't knock the imports – look at the way those French lads kid around. They got the style only a few of the English ones have. Well, we're all bleedin' European now, aren't we? He was supporting the Blues before most of the players were even born or out of nappies. Back in the days when you wouldn't even entertain the idea of a black man running on to the pitch without a few monkey calls and bananas getting thrown out.

Attendance Centre in Greenwich, 1977. What a fucking laugh that was. All the crew were there after that plonker of a magistrate at Horseferry Road Court sent us along. Told us the only way he could keep us out of trouble, only way he could hit us where it hurt was send us along to Greenwich each Saturday for two hours of hard graft, sweating away while our boys were playing at Stamford Bridge. Course it did hurt, every Saturday afternoon, missing the chance to go to the ground, but they let us out in time for the proper action behind King's Cross or Euston stations, where the rest of the mobs gathered to 'meet' the boys from Man United, Newcastle or the Scouse scum. We spent all afternoon training, it was daft. We got as fit as fucking fleas, primed for battle and of course we'd come in on the rearguard tip when all the Old Bill were waiting for the crowd from west London. Had a right laugh, we did! And all the black cunts at Attendance Centre never knew what they were sent along for, didn't know fuck-all about football, never asked, but some of them were pretty tasty when it came to a meet. All ganja-smoking rastas and edgy south London twats. Scared shitless 'cos it was mainly Chelsea there.

And course, we was all white. Proper firm. Never had to call on the services of our black brothers, we could handle anything that came our way.

Marcel Desailly, tallest man on the pitch. Legs like a super-model. Wouldn't say he's even giving it 100 per cent but he never lets the attack get through, and if that happens there's always another Blue in the way. He'll take the ball off his man and then run with it. More times than not he'll take a few of theirs on, too, turning defence into attack before they've even had time to change direction. His legs are so long that it looks like he's put Dennis Wise's shorts on by mistake. There's aggression, not in the way old Chelsea used to do it, with 'Chopper Harris' intimidation, but with silky-smooth skill that makes Sunday park amateurs out of anyone. He's consummate at the famous Chelsea passing game, supplying the long ball out to Petrescu on the right or Le Saux down the left and now he's got his other boy from Les Bleus, Didier Deschamps, he can squirt the ball through the middle. The team moves with the inevitability of the tide as they surge forward or pour back to cover an attack. But what is it about the arrogance and supreme confidence of these French guys? OK, so I'm calling a Ghanaian French, I know, but they all share something that spills over on to the rest of the team and inevitably into the ground, where we soak it up. It can't just be that winner's medal that Beefy's always banging on about, but maybe it's connected with it. The fact that they beat the best (and beat them straight up, with the skill and style you'd normally associate with the Brazilians). But there's a cele-bration in their movements. A glow that emanates from them and warms their mates and chills opponents because the players who come up against them have to beat the man *and* the legend.

Remember the first black geezers running on to the pitch for Chelsea? Who can say they weren't shocked? When most of the Shed End were hurling abuse at the likes of Fashanu and Barnes we'd gone and brought on cunts like Dublin, and they weren't good enough to warrant the fucking nerve of hiring them when there was still enough white players kept out of the sides. They monkeyed around without a fucking clue.

And all of us were expected to bite our lip and stop our chants. How was that supposed to sit with the loyal fans? What a cheek! When all us supporters were white, losing our jobs to immigrants who took lower wages and fucked up our heritage, made you want to go out in the streets and start a bloody war!

Man and dog go walking through the park. Past the burned shells of TWOCs, cars and motorbikes stolen by the local bravehearts and taken to the road that goes nowhere. This crumbling strip of metalled street which plunges into the middle of Burgess Park, hesitates and then appears to give up. So it ends, puncturing the green, a fitting place for the stolen vehicles to enter the nightly demolition derbies where winners and losers get torched together. And next to the street there's the old iron bridge that crosses nothing and goes nowhere, a relic of days when canals and railways pushed the ground apart. Now it stands alone and pointless, serving merely as park furniture. There's a man standing on it, blowing out his blues on an alto sax, the soundtrack to a soulful afternoon. Below him, in the scrub, a mad black man contorting and trembling in accompaniment.

Rudi was the fucking DON. When we had Hoddle, when he had his bleedin' marbles, he brought the dreadlocked god over and the tide turned. When Matthew Harding was still flying high and he'd come down the Rosie for a jar and jaw before the match and he'd tell us we were fucking SAFE! Chelsea was the best and then we were! Yeah, just like that. And Rudi was the first black geezer who got our respect. When he tore Ajax apart in the first match he played for us we knew the change was on us. And Chelsea, the hardest, nastiest, moodiest, most racist bunch of cunts in the League, was the first team to have a fucking black manager! And if that ain't a turnaround I wanna know what is, mate! Then came the avalanche. All the wops, frogs and more spades that you could shake a spear at. And we was reborn! Celestine

Babayarou jumping somersaults like a flamin' Zulu, and then the Rock, Marcel, the grinning bastard at the back saying, 'Go on, 'ave a fucking go, then, the lot of you!' And last season, after those . . . after that lot in Blue won the Cup and we had two of 'em at the back for us, we lost TWO games in the League that season. And I tell you what, you can have me down as an out-and-out Chelsea white boy, but that geezer's done more for race relations than a thousand Stephen Lawrences ever will do. 'Cos he's ONE OF US.

Man and dog. Old hooligan and his 'Devil Dog'; misunderstood and maligned couple. They swing up through the day's end, up to the Astroturf pitch where a game is ending. A gaggle of shouting boys running around, can't be more than ten years old, none of them. He pauses to watch the play, always keen to cast his professional eye over the action, for ever ready to be entertained by the beautiful game. His knee aches, smashed by a Gooner's baseball bat in '84. Can't even kick a ball without a sharp twinge, let alone kick a head! He twines his fingers through the chain-link fence and leans, watching. There's the usual crowd, mostly the athletic Nigerian and Ghanaian kids, but a handful of white 'uns too.

Up at the far end the goalie scuffs the ball away and it runs to the right. Everyone's yelling, no discipline, all enthusiasm, vitality, getting the ball. A black kid picks up the ball, he runs effortlessly round his man, ball at his feet without looking. Then another opponent is left and suddenly defence turns into attack. He turns, jinks and moves through the centre, brushing people away and in a moment it's just him and the goalie.

With the ball in the netting the boy turns back, haughty finger in the air, blue oversized shirt flapping as he runs. Royal blue shirt, could've been Chelsea, could've been Les Bleus, doesn't matter. Two teams whose racist reputations were shattered by the arrival of players such as Marcel 'the Rock' Desailly.

The tide is turning.

15

The Young Guns – Petit and Vieira

BEN RICHARDS

Kate McEwan lay on her bed staring at the ceiling and smoking a cigarette she did not want. She was tired, she was bored, she was miserable, she felt ugly, her life was a mess. She had not left her flat for days. The psoriasis that she had hoped might have gone away for ever had returned to torment her – red blotches like burns all over her arms. She knew that people were looking at her with smug pity and she would glare, sick with envy, at smooth unblemished arms, wondering if their owners could ever be aware of how lucky they were.

She rolled into the foetal position, staring despondently at her bedside table. There was the alarm clock, the empty wine glass, the novel which she had been enjoying but had not looked at for some days, her bracelets and rings, a Wispa Gold wrapper, the little figurines of Emmanuel Petit and Patrick Vieira that her boyfriend Mark had put in her Christmas stocking last year because they were her favourite players.

'Cunt,' she said out loud, because of course he was her ex-boyfriend now and she did not want to remember the nice things that he had done. Better to remember his pomposity, especially his infuriating superiority over the fact that he had introduced her to Highbury, something he never tired of bringing up. She might love it passionately now, but she could never compensate for the fact that (among other things):

a) She had never stood on the North Bank.

b) She had not attended the 1987 Littlewoods Cup final, which was one of his favourite-ever games.

c) She did not remember Gus Caesar or Perry Groves.

'It wasn't always Vieira and Petit, you know.' That was one of his favourite sayings as he regaled her with the appalling midfields of the late George Graham years.

'Selley, McGoldrick, Jensen, Hillier.'

He said the names as if they were tropical diseases.

Frankly, Kate didn't give a fuck about standing on the North Bank, or the midfielders who had preceded Vieira and Petit. She was far more concerned about the fact that it would not *always* be Vieira and Petit. What if one of them left? What if one or both suffered a frightening loss of form? Besides, Mark might have introduced her to Highbury, but hadn't she corrected some of his misconceptions about the geography of the female body and taught him the importance of keeping his fingernails clean?

'That's the problem with men,' her friend Gemma had sighed on hearing about the break-up. 'They just can't commit to anything.'

Kate had stared at her. The problem had been quite the reverse in her case. Mark had been desperate for commitment, had become infuriated when she responded to all his nagging pleas for commitment with a simple 'why?'

'I'm not being difficult,' she had said, although she knew that she was. 'Just tell me why we should get married.'

'Because it's what people do,' he had replied. 'When they love each other. Maybe you don't love me enough.'

Maybe she didn't.

She remembered the patronising way he now didn't attend certain matches. He liked saying that they were just for tourists, lightweights and arrivistes. He had earned the right to be a bit more choosy. It really bugged her when she had assumed that they would be going to see Preston North End in the third round of the Littlewoods Cup and he would look at her with pitying disdain. She had had to resort to childish retaliations, asking if it was only Arsenal who had a majority of nerdy thirty-something fans with receding hairlines, little round glasses and 1970s replica shirts. Mark hated references to his receding hairline; he would rub the top of his head and nervously adjust his little round glasses.

'If you won't make a proper commitment,' he had finally said, 'then I think we might as well call it a day.'

'OK,' she had said.

She was not depressed now just because of his absence. It really wasn't only that. She was depressed in general, opened papers and could not be bothered to read them, saw the names of certain columnists and felt sick, turned on the TV and stared beyond it. She would sometimes think about football and even grow depressed that when Petit was not injured Vieira would get himself suspended. Would they never form their formidable midfield axis again? Was this a trivial thing to find depressing? It made her even more annoyed to have to admit to being depressed because she despised depression and had frequently ridiculed it as a concept, just as she had once ridiculed football.

'Why do you have to ridicule everything?' Mark had asked her once.

'Because I get bored,' she had replied honestly.

She stretched out and reached for the little figures of Vieira and Petit. They did not particularly resemble the players in question: about the only thing that was right about them was that Petit was white and Vieira black. Ebony and ivory, chalk and cheese, opposites in appearance that still went together like fish and chips, Bogart and Bacall. She rolled on to her back again and put one on each breast, making them jump up and down on her nipples as if they had just scored.

She had once seen both men at a ceremony for the Double-winning team. Her friend Maggie was married to an Islington councillor who had not wanted to go. Petit had been wearing a leather jacket, had stopped to sign his autograph for her, had smiled and then moved on. Vieira had looked shy and elegant. She had proudly stuck their autographs in her toilet.

Why hadn't they recognised her beauty, humour and intelligence and invited her to wait for them in the bar afterwards? She could have asked them so many things. Did they ever tease Dennis Bergkamp about his fear of flying? What did they really think of Anelka's departure? Had Petit ever considered desisting from the sarcastic clapping of linesmen in order to avoid unnecessary bookings? Had Vieira ever had the concept of turning the other cheek properly explained to him? She could have commiserated with Manu for the death of his brother, told him about the death of her own beloved brother in a stupid and unnecessary car crash five years previously.

The light was fading. She inspected her arms for the twentieth time: the red blotches on her arm seemed even bigger now. The phone would never ring, nobody would ever love her as she deserved to be loved. A tear of self-pity squeezed from her eye and tracked down her cheek. She looked at the two silly figurines and put them back on each breast, closing her eyes . . .

'But why are you crying, *ma petite?*' Manu had a concerned expression on his face.

Kate was startled, but decided that it would be prudent to suspend her disbelief at having a pair of Lilliputian French footballers chatting to her from each breast. She explained a little about Mark and his departure. Manu wrinkled his nose. 'This man, he sounds as if he has all the charm and sexual prowess of—'

'Nigel Winterburn,' Patrick interjected, and both men laughed and high-fived each other across Kate's cleavage. She giggled guiltily because she had always found Nigel Winterburn endearing, especially when he got overexcited and ran along the touchline windmilling his arms at the crowd or tried desperately to get the ball back on to his left foot.

'It's not just that,' Kate explained. 'Sometimes everything just seems so dull and pointless.'

'Everybody gets depressed,' Manu pointed out. 'Remember, Patrick, after your little incident with Neil Ruddock . . .'

'Yes, or the time you got sent off and sulked about going back to France,' Patrick responded cheerfully.

'At least they put banners up for me saying "Please don't go,"' Manu snapped, tossing his ponytail.

'I'm sure they'd do the same for Patrick,' Kate interjected quickly. Manu was obviously a little highly strung.

'He gets jealous sometimes.' Patrick smiled. 'Because I have a better song than him. "Vieira . . . woo-oo, Vieira . . . woo-oo." They sing that more even than "Walking in a Bergkamp Wonderland".'

Kate was surprised that Patrick was so calm. She had half-expected that he would be the more lairy of the two. Was there an element of racism in this assumption? Probably not, she thought. He could hardly complain if people thought that of him. Spitting at other players and chinning coppers in the tunnel was not particularly conducive to the image of a gentle and cerebral person. But then Manu, in spite of his golden looks, was hardly an angel.

'You have very comfortable breasts,' Manu observed.

'Thank you,' Kate said modestly, remembering Manu's very un-English declaration about his admiration for this aspect of Englishwomen. Mark had snorted with derisory contempt and called him sexist and puerile. This was a bit rich coming from Mark, who was always staring at women's breasts and then refusing to admit to it when Kate teased him.

Kate told Manu and Patrick that she would certainly miss their departure from Highbury more than she currently missed Mark. Patrick frowned.

'Perhaps. But one must always be careful about comparisons between football and life. Besides, I think football as a meta-phor for life or relationships is rather an overworked concept.'

'He wants to be the intellectual of the team,' Manu said, raising his eyebrows.

'But I could never take Tony's place,' retorted Patrick, and they both laughed again, making rather unkind jokes about playing the piano and *Far From the Madding Crowd*. Kate was about to ask sarcastically whether they would have preferred him to be reading Baudrillard or Deleuze but didn't want to upset them. Besides, it was unfair to hold all the French to account for the horrors of postmodernism.

'Which one of us would you miss the most?' Manu asked suddenly.

This was a terrible question. Which would she miss the most? It was like who would you stay friends with when a couple split up. She would certainly miss Manu's mournful eyes but immediately decided to discount such girlish considerations. She thought about what she didn't like about them. Neither of them scored enough for her liking and neither was particularly threatening in the air. She thought that their on-field manner was a little pathetic sometimes. Vieira also had a worrying tendency to squander possession in dangerous areas. But then there was the glory of his long legs powering through a defence on one of those loping runs, or Manu curling the ball over the defence to drop perfectly for an attacker's foot. Vieira would lose possession and then win it back. There was the way that both of them would throw themselves rather elegantly into a well-timed sliding tackle. She thought that probably Manu was a more imaginative player than Vieira, but Vieira's loss would probably be worse for the team. She also suspected that Vieira's commitment to Arsenal might be slightly greater and that Manu might start bleating about going to Lazio after being dumped out of the Champions' League.

'I would like you both to stay there for ever. I think you complement each other perfectly. Things sometimes seem quite fragile. Blink and you're gone.'

She remembered a sunny day in May. Anelka's low shot to seal the Double. They had travelled in a taxi back to Islington, Kate's tanned psoriasis-free arm hanging from the open window. They had sat up laughing half the night with tequila slammers and a gram of coke.

'Well.' Manu stood up and stretched. 'It is perhaps wise to accustom oneself to uncertainty. There will always be replacements.'

Vieira stood up too. He smiled at her and she thought what a nice face he had.

'Don't embrace unhappiness, Kate. Don't give in to illness.'

'It's not easy,' she murmured.

'It's not easy,' Manu agreed. 'But think of our brothers. How much they wanted to live. What do a few patches on your arm really mean in the larger scheme of things? You are beautiful anyway, you have fantastic breasts. *N'est-ce pas*, Patrick? You are clever and funny and maybe a little tactless sometimes, but at least you are not boring.'

'It's not just a mood swing,' Kate protested. 'Depression is an illness.'

'There are people who are really depressed,' Patrick said. 'You are miserable now, but you are not one of those people who is truly ill with depression. You were made to be happy. Deep down you have a sunny disposition. To be ill and depressed is terrible. You must do your utmost to avoid it. At the moment you are not trying hard enough. We might leave Arsenal but that stuff will also leave your arms. It has in the past, it will again. It is good that you have split up with your boyfriend. That was going nowhere. Phone your friends, open the curtains.'

'There are highs as well as lows,' Manu said. 'Remember the World Cup, that last goal.'

And they both looked at each other with a little sadness, a little nostalgia, before running up to her shoulders and leaping up to give her a kiss on each cheek.

'Don't go,' Kate protested, but they just laughed.

'Blink and we're gone,' Manu called.

'Blink and we're gone,' Patrick echoed.

They slid down her arms, legs splayed like kids on a helter-skelter.

Kate opened her eyes. Her hands were sore and she realised that she had been clenching the figurines of two French footballers so tightly that there were red weals on her hands. But when she held her arms up to the light streaming in through the curtains, she saw that her psoriasis was fading. It had gone down so much that it was scarcely visible. She got up and put on a short-sleeved T-shirt for the first time in weeks. Then she went out to buy the paper and a pint of milk.

'Haven't seen you for a while,' the newsagent smiled pleasantly.

'I've been unwell,' Kate said, her eye caught by a headline which read:

LAZIO IN SHOCK BID FOR PETIT

She smiled as she remembered their farewell cry.

Blink and we're gone.

She would read the paper over a cup of tea. There was probably nothing in it anyway.

16

The Lady Loves Fabien Barthez

PAQUITA PAQUIN

As the world champions suddenly find themselves adored by women across the land, so they also find that they are worth an awful lot more money. The player who benefited most from this leap in footballers' fortunes in the post-World Cup world could well have been a member of the victorious team – except that he just missed out on selection. The striker Nicolas Anelka is still a youngster, the embodiment of a brighter future, but in the year after the World Cup, the price of his transfer to Real Madrid – a very tortuous affair – reached dizzying heights.

Never before have the French put such a high price on sporting heads. Following a trend much in evidence in the USA, players are becoming the ubiquitous darlings of the advertising world, and no longer only for sports-orientated brands. A year and a half before the World Cup, some of the players were approached by the Marilyn modelling agency, since the demand was already there, and negotiations went on before and during the World Cup. But it was only once victory was theirs that members of the winning team were asked to lend their image as massively popular players to massively popular brands: Danone, Leader Price and McDonald's. Rather than a film star or top model, these brands want to invest in a footballing hero. And with the impact of their message increased tenfold, the value of the players' contracts soars ever higher. These men are desirable because their appeal is at its height. Even better, they come from a variety of backgrounds, and owe their fame to unremitting hard work and individual flair: the guys who finally gave France its victory have become such big stars that when representing a brand, their achievement has far more impact than that of somebody who is a mere good-looker. When Christian Dior chose Zinedine Zidane's smile to personify his perfume for men, the impact went even further. The players' image and its inherent charm has won over the worlds of luxury goods and fashion, usually seen as impregnable. From now on, everything is possible.

Before each match of the 1998 World Cup, Laurent Blanc planted a kiss on the top of Fabien Barthez's bald head to bring luck to the French team. It was not meant to be a mocking gesture, and no one took it as such: instead, it turned Barthez into the team's mascot. The goalkeeper was the symbol of a boundless and priceless confidence, on which a certain American fast-food brand was nonetheless canny enough to hang a price tag. If Fabien Barthez himself is the incarnation of luck, his game leaves nothing to chance. As a goalkeeper, the way he moves inspires great respect. He'll turn aside balls that have the most tortuous of trajectories, but that doesn't mean you'll see him indulging in acrobatic feats spreadeagled between the posts. Barthez rarely gets down on the ground: he is more likely to get right out of the goalmouth into the path of the ball, his instincts telling him where it is likely to go and calculating his position to the millimetre. A goalkeeper who dared to leave his goal to meet the ball in mid-air was just what was needed to rev up the rest of the team and kindle the passion of French supporters into the crescendo that climaxed in the events of 12 July 1998.

Barthez is a character who makes hearts beat faster, particularly those of the new-style female supporters. And he's the only player not to have had an official other half in the guests' stand from which the team's partners cheered them on. It is tempting to see his flaunting of his celibate status as a deliberate defiance of convention. You'd have thought that, at a pinch, he could have invented a kindred spirit so he wouldn't stand out from the crowd. But that would be to misread this hard-working lad from the Ariège, who is certainly incapable of acting out such a farce. The sexual inclinations of our national goalie were the subject of endless speculation right up to the day when the warrior laid down his arms. A party organised on 22 July by fifteen friends finished up at le Pigeonnier nightclub, where the revellers met up with a few top model acquaintances (the girls had opened the pre-match entertainment at the World Cup final with a catwalk show in homage to Yves Saint Laurent). That night was to set the seal on the romantic idyll we now all know about. It was love at first sight, which blossomed the next day on the big blue when the lovebirds went for spin after spin on a jet ski from a secluded Ramatuelle beach. They got off to a flying start.

That summer, every detail of the lives and loves of the new world champions filled the media. And although everyone enjoyed seeing photos of Dugarry in his restaurant or Zidane and his family on the beach, Fabien Barthez's love affair was the scoop, a sort of apotheosis: the meeting of two stars under the sun of St Tropez. You couldn't honestly say that he is the best-looking guy in the team, but he is fantasy material. Well built, fearless, perceptive – he's got what it takes.

So ten days after the victory, the bachelor falls in love – and not with just anybody: with Linda Evangelista, no less, one of the most successful top models of the eighties and nineties, an era when models were the subject of more adulation and media attention than princesses or actresses. With her highly individual look, less banal than that of Claudia Schiffer or Cindy Crawford, Linda has inspired leading designers and photographers such as Steven Meisel, Peter Lindbergh and Paolo Roversi. At the end of the seventies she was already modelling, although, with the flowing hair she then sported, she didn't make much of a mark. But in 1988, with the help of some colleagues working at *Vogue*, Linda struck out with a second career, this time with phenomenal success. A new-look short hairstyle concocted by Julien d'Ys brought out the light colour of her eyes and lent her a youthful air. It was just like starting all over again. Linda soon found herself gracing endless magazine covers and all the podiums that count. And most importantly, each season she succeeded in keeping herself centre stage by changing the shade of her hair colour or going for daring innovations in the cut.

Her capacity for sustaining a long-lasting career with brilliance and intelligence also owed something to the director of the Elite (Europe) modelling agency, Gérald Marie, who became her husband and so quite naturally kept the best contracts for his wife. But Linda's talent belongs to her and her alone, and with the experience of a successful renaissance behind her, she cannily uses surprise as her trump card and effortlessly comes up with a new look to match events in the fashion world. With her hair always kept above shoulder length, now tousled, now dead straight, one minute intricately styled, the next in a sensible bob, and colour that changes with the seasons, from brown to auburn, auburn to red, then blonde, Linda is the face that launched a thousand styles. And coincidentally enough, Fabien Barthez's hair(less) style also has its followers.

You could well ask what Linda, a woman who has succeeded in all she has turned her hand to, would aspire to at the tail end of an unusually long-lasting career. A relationship in which, consciously or not, she is ready to invest her all. For each of the two lovers, the summer of 1998 marked a turning point. Their liaison took them from the pages of the sports and fashion trade press to the gossip columns of the celebrity magazines: not a very glamorous step. Their affair and subsequent engagement as recounted by the paparazzi downgraded their image. People started to see the couple as a bit naff, even though as individuals they are outstanding professionals. The footballer's TV interviews are now subjected to close scrutiny as people ask themselves how such a down-to-earth bloke managed to seduce Miss Sophistication herself. But although Linda Evangelista may well be the epitome of haute couture, luxury and beauty, she's not a Parisian but a Canadian, with her feet firmly on the ground. She has had enough experience of the fashion world, with its empty values and hypocrisy, to be able to appreciate the candour, good sense and accent you could cut with a knife (maybe not really such a problem for a Canadian) of Fabien Barthez.

And Fabien Barthez himself is not without sophistication. It lies in the beauty of his game. He symbolises the modern goalkeeper. When he was still a lad, he followed in the footsteps of his talented rugby-playing father and acquired from the sport great power and accurate clearances with his hands (up to 15 or 20 metres beyond the centre circle) as well as with his feet. He has a perfect geometric shape: a chunky torso with muscular arms.

Temperamentally, he is just as stable. If he makes a mistake early on in a match, he doesn't brood on it for the rest of the game: OK, he's slipped up, but now he concentrates on what comes next. Right from the beginning of his career he has shown himself to be an unusually cool customer. Twenty-two is pretty young for a responsible position whose usual incumbents tend to be around the age of thirty or thirty-five.

In 1992, the year before Olympique Marseille won the European Champions Cup, OM president Bernard Tapie followed the advice of his coach Raymond Goethals and had Barthez transferred to the club from Toulouse on one of the biggest contracts in France at the time: 10 million francs. During a match in Glasgow against Rangers he could well have been taken apart: the Scots, who play a very physical game, were waiting to catch the youngster out. But Barthez stood his ground and, challenged by the centre back, Richard Gough, charged off his line foot first to make an historic save that demonstrated enormous skill and courage. He could not have been blamed had he been reduced to a quivering wreck, but instead he marked out his territory and earned the respect of everyone.

Barthez is still one of the best-paid goalkeepers in the world: his current club, Monaco, has made the right moves and matched the highly advantageous offers made to him by Manchester United. Barthez has stayed loyal: Monaco suits him. In fact his fidelity has been exemplary. He has never played for a non-French team, sticking with OM even in their worst times, when the team dropped down to Division 2 after serious management problems. Today Barthez declares that he would be quite happy to play out the rest of his career at Monaco.

Rock stars, pop stars, actors and top sportsmen make the girls dream. And they are the dream husbands of a whole generation of models drawn to the adventurous allure of these young millionaires who owe their fortunes to entertainment or sport rather than to industry or finance. The only fly in the ointment is the media. A certain type of magazine, constantly on the lookout for the slightest sign of the break-up that they see as the inevitable result of such a whirlwind romance, keeps close tabs on the Barthez–Evangelista couple. But the more the relationship is cemented, the more the celebrity press has to whistle for their story. We know nothing about the expected marriage in Ariège, nor when Evangelista, who has just lost a baby after six months of pregnancy, will decide to try for a second Barthez heir. The union needs no comment; the image of the two protagonists speaks for itself. The meeting of the two stars, one of whom had just reached his zenith at the Stade de France, was perfectly timed. The child born of that meeting will be the magical creation of two souls who would never have let themselves dream the family dream without a highly successful career behind them.

17

A Geordie Conquers the Heart of the South of France: Chris Waddle Plays for OM

OLIVIA BLAIR

English football never truly appreciated Chris Waddle. It had nothing to do with that penalty miss at Italia '90. It was just that Waddle was a maverick and an entertainer, and English football and maverick entertainers have traditionally made unwelcome bedfellows. Frankly, the English never knew what to make of the lanky, long-haired winger with the round shoulders and shuffling, clumsy gait; the player who once said that 'football was about kissing the ball and loving it, not smacking it about'. Jack Charlton bluntly called him 'a load of rubbish', while Michel Platini described him as 'an artist'.

Vive la différence.

Platini and the French knew exactly what to make of him. When Waddle crossed the Channel in the summer of 1989 to sign for Olympique Marseille – at £4.25 million, then the third most expensive player in the world – he became an almost instant hero. He was no longer just a bad haircut, as some of his English detractors would have it, but (depending on which newspaper you read or where your interests lay) Le Dribbleur Fou, Le Magicien, or Chris 'Magic' Waddle. The latter was what the OM fans dubbed him; it was also the title of a video dedicated to Waddle whose opening lines described him as 'the king of swaying hips, the magician of the round ball'.

The fans loved him, not just for his ability on the ball, but because he was one of them. They loved his attempts to speak French in an accent that was at times unintelligible, even in its native Geordie. They loved it that he played with a smile on his face. And they loved him for being, on and off the pitch, 'the heart and soul of the OM party', as integral to OM as fish to the local bouillabaisse.

Club president Bernard Tapie may eventually have fallen out of love with the player he brought from a run-down council estate in Gateshead, via Tow Law Town, Newcastle United and Tottenham Hotspur – on buying Trevor Steven from Rangers in 1991 he said: 'I'm fed up with dribbling showmen like Waddle, he can stay out of the way on the wing' – but the fans remained loyal. They fondly compared him to Roger Magnusson, the Swedish winger who, two decades earlier, had been such a favourite with the Marseille crowd, and even now, a decade on, there is still 'Waddle Reviens!' graffiti daubed over the Stade Vélodrome.

I was at Wimbledon, thinking about tennis, not football, when my mobile phone rang. The call brought me back to reality. It was the agent Dennis Roach. 'Someone's bought you,' he told me straight out. It was a surprise, to say the least. I knew that a club – I didn't know which one – had made Spurs an offer which had been rejected. Whoever it was must have put together a package that had forced the club to change its mind.

I was shocked. I'd always wanted to play abroad, and I'd been advised by both Glenn Hoddle and Mark Hateley (both of whom had played in France) to take the chance if it came along. But at twenty-eight, and having just signed a new seven-year contract at Spurs, I thought that chance had passed me by. Besides, I loved it at Spurs. The club had just signed Gary Lineker from Barcelona and with Gazza in the team too, I was looking forward to the new season. This unexpected turn of events just wouldn't sink in. All I could think of were the practicalities, so all I said was: 'Well, I can't go anywhere until I know who it is.'

It was then that the OM president, Bernard Tapie, came on the line. I knew who Tapie was, and I also knew enough about Marseille and their players to believe I could improve my game there. I wouldn't have gone to a mid-table French club; it really had to be either Marseille or Monaco. Tapie started talking. He was very charming, really upbeat – and extremely persuasive. He told me – convinced me, really – that Marseille were going places, and that he wanted me along for the ride. I put the phone down and my mate said: 'Who was that?'

I replied: 'Bernard Tapie.'

'Well, what did he want?'

'Nothing much,' I said. 'He's just bought me.'

That was that. It was very strange and very simple. Just a question of flying to Marseilles, having a look around the club and getting a medical. Fait accompli in a couple of days.

It wasn't long, however, before I started wondering whether I'd made the biggest mistake of my life. Those first few months in France were hell. I was so unhappy that I even asked my agent to find out if Spurs would buy me back; I reckoned that they must be being paid in instalments and I thought that perhaps they could just refund Marseille the initial payment. I was that desperate. Fortunately, I was persuaded to stick it out, but it was a tough time. The problem was that Marseille were only bothered about what I did on the pitch. Beyond that, they couldn't care less. They had no idea how unsettled I was. I couldn't speak a word of French, and after staying with Jean-Pierre Papin and his wife for the first few days, my wife Lorna and I had to live in a run-down hotel, which wasn't easy with a small baby. I didn't even have a car. Top footballers might be well paid, but we're only human and these problems made life very difficult. It's not like England, where you get three months in a decent hotel and the club looks after you. Marseille's attitude was that I had signed my contract and I had to get on with it.

To make matters worse, the French League kicked off on the Friday, just two days after I arrived. I was obviously unfit after six weeks off and the coach, Gérard Gili, made it clear he thought I was out of condition. In those early days he really pushed me during training, which was far harder than in England, where players usually train for only two hours in the morning four days a week. In France it's mornings and afternoons, and every day of the week.

Despite being off the pace I made my debut in that opening-day 4–1 victory away to Lyon, coming on for Papin at half-time when OM were 2–0 up, but it was physically draining and I told the lads afterwards that it was going to be a few months before they saw the best of me. Needless to say, that didn't wash with the press, who were on my back from the start. I'd asked them to give me three months to prove my worth and they gave me three games. They wrote that I was a waste of money and not up to the job. So I told them they wrote shit, which they seemed to understand. I was so angry I refused to talk to them for the first year. They would come into the dressing room after a match (which I found strange, as English dressing rooms are strictly players only) but they wouldn't approach me because they knew I'd give them nothing. After a while I did talk to them, but on my own terms.

Things started to come right for me after we moved into our new house in Aix-en-Provence one Wednesday in September. That Friday, I scored a goal in the League against Paris St Germain that changed everything. It's still clear in my mind. I remember beating the offside trap, bringing the ball down, flicking it on and back-heeling it into the net. I'd already scored a couple against our rivals, Bordeaux, in the League, and one in the home leg of the European Cup quarter-final against CSKA Sofia, but that PSG goal was the one that set me off.

Settled off the pitch, I was starting to enjoy life on it, too. I was well aware of the pedigree of French clubs because they'd always done well against English clubs in Europe, and I knew how they liked to play the game. The football was slower and more technical, and OM had a great system: effectively 5–2–2–1, with me and Abidé Pelé playing on the right and left respectively behind Papin. I had time to think about my game, time that I never had in England playing 4–4–2 at 100 miles an hour. It was a breath of fresh air for me not to have to chase the ball. I remember in one of my first games I chased the defender back and he coolly played a one-two around me and came away with the ball. Nine times out of ten an English defender would have booted that ball away. I was told not to chase back, but just to find space up front. At last I had the freedom I'd always craved on the pitch.

It helped that I had so many quality players around me. They all seemed so comfortable on the ball (which explained why so many of them had converted from left winger to left back, or from midfield to sweeper). They could all pass the ball well and had sweet first touches. In England it was so often a case of 'Don't pass it to him, he can't handle it.' I never heard that in France.

It didn't take me long to get to know my team-mates, although strangely, none of them ever talked to me in English, even though I knew some of them spoke it. I think they were frightened of making a mistake. They're like that, the French; when they come out on to the pitch they're full of it, totally dominant, yet they're shy people at heart. The club did their bit eventually by sorting me out some French lessons, but I've never been one for studying. I knew that the only way I was going to understand, and make myself understood, was by listening to the other players and asking for what I wanted in shops and restaurants. I'm a firm believer in 'when in Rome . . .', and I made a real effort to fit in. There was only one thing I really missed. When we came back to the dressing room after a game the fridge was always stocked with bottles of water, so after I while I asked, 'Any chance of a beer?' They were horrified. 'We don't drink that,' they said. But a few weeks later the fridge was full of Guinness and lager. Not that any of them were big drinkers, although quite a few smoked heavily.

Oh, and I must have missed burgers, too, because I persuaded Jean-Pierre to sneak out with me for the odd one. If Tapie had found out we'd have been in big trouble. But food wasn't a problem. Marseilles is a hot city and you really don't want to eat a lot. We ate salads, veal and pasta, everything dictated by the club dietician. We even took our own chefs to European games, which wasn't the norm in those days. That side of things was all handled very professionally. Yet in some respects the club was amateurish. Incredibly, we had to wash our own training kits and clean our boots (that didn't change until Franz Beckenbauer took over). Not only that, but the dressing rooms were old and the lockers were horrible. But if you lost a game they would immediately haul you in for medical checks and scans. No examination was too thorough. You'd always hear Tapie shouting the odds after a defeat, demanding that so-and-so should be checked over. They were constantly striving to get our bodies into peak condition, but our individual comforts mattered little.

Tapie was a larger-than-life character. You could feel the atmosphere change whenever he appeared. We used to joke that he did everything bar drive the bus. He certainly dominated the club's coaches: Gili, Raymond Goethals, then Franz Beckenbauer, who replaced Goethals for the start of the 1990–91 season. The first two, certainly, were more or less puppets, firmly under Tapie's thumb. The press used to call Goethals – whom I christened Elvis because of his jet-black, swept-back hair – 'Le Sorcier', claiming he was a master tactician, but the reality was that he was blessed with a group of world-class players who needed little coaching. The England lads used to ask me what I was learning in France when I went back home, and I would tell them in all seriousness that the players ran the training sessions themselves. Five-a-sides, set pieces – we'd all have our say, pinging the ball around for sheer enjoyment. Goethals' main quality was that he was easygoing, kept it simple and retained the players' interest. But it was still Tapie who called the shots. He could be heavy-handed, but there's no doubt he did know a bit about tactics.

I had my run-ins with Tapie, but I still respected him. I remember going with the two strikers Francescoli and Vercruysse to complain to Goethals that we three were constantly rotated in team selections. Word got back to Tapie. His attitude was: 'We pay you to play as you're told.' I told him he was wrong, but he made it quite clear that there would be only one winner in that argument. Afterwards, however, he came and sat next to me on the coach and apologised. 'If the other players see you beating me in an argument,' he said, 'they will think that maybe they can get away with it, too.' He just didn't want the other players to see him being humiliated. He was a very powerful man and you didn't want to get on the wrong side of him, but he took care of those he liked. The rumour was that Beckenbauer got the sack because Papin and he didn't get on, and Papin was one of Tapie's golden boys. Certainly Beckenbauer was a big personality himself and therefore a threat to Tapie. But Tapie's main characteristic was that he was obsessed with winning and nothing we did was good enough for him. Nevertheless, he was a good guy to be around as he had so much energy. Unfortunately, he used football as a political tool and ultimately paid the price for it.

People ask me whether I missed the atmosphere in English grounds because French crowds are so much smaller. I didn't, because OM is the Manchester United of France and we always had a full house at home and drew huge gates away. If the kick-off was 8 pm at the Vélodrome the fans would be in their seats by 6 pm, and their support was well organised. They always had red and yellow cards or pictures of players to hold up, and that chant of 'Allez l'OM' always made the hairs on the back of my neck stand up. I was never going to miss English crowds given the way the French fans took to me. There was a ripple of excitement whenever I got the ball, and that is what every footballer craves. I was a novelty to them because French football had never really had any personality players before. They loved it when I pulled my shirt over my head after scoring, and they loved it that I always signed autographs if I was warming up near them. They liked the way I played with a smile on my face, and the way I would try little tricks and nutmegs, anything to excite them. Sometimes I did it just because they wanted to see it. I wanted to make defenders look stupid, not because I didn't respect them, but because I enjoyed it. I remember pretending to sleep on the ball when we were playing Metz. The wall wouldn't go back 10 yards and the ref was taking ages to control it, so I just lay down and put my hands behind my head as if I was sleeping. The crowd loved it, but the ref didn't. He ran over and booked me, and got some stick after that.

But I think they also appreciated the way I behaved. I kept my feet on the ground. I wasn't big-headed or arrogant. I tried to absorb their culture and live as they did and they respected that. Going back for Papin's testimonial in front of a crowd of 60,000 and getting more applause than Jean-Pierre meant a great deal to me.

Looking back, being level-headed paid off because in many respects I lived the life of a pop star in Marseilles. OK, so I was popular on the pitch – Marseille sold about 20,000 shirts with 'Waddle' on the back during the two years I was there – but it was mayhem off the pitch, too. 'Waddlemania', they called it. There was Chris Waddle wine and Chris Waddle jeans and kids with Chris Waddle haircuts. At signing sessions I remember having to escape via a back door to dodge the crowds. I'd get free meals at restaurants, and never paid any of the parking tickets I received (which must have been at least eighty). Instead, I'd get asked to sign them as souvenirs. Once I was caught speeding on my way to the club and when I told the officer that I was late for training he just hopped into his car, put his siren on and off we went, me following him in convoy. It was farcical. I remember thinking that it couldn't get any bigger than this.

Of course, the downside was losing to Red Star Belgrade in

the final of the 1991 European Cup, which was Tapie's personal Holy Grail. We really thought our name was on that cup – the record I made with Basile Boli, 'We've Got A Feeling', said as much – and we put out our best team, but they used spoiling tactics and beat us on penalties. Everyone was really down after that. We had a meeting and Tapie said that anyone who wanted to could leave. I'd always fancied Italy and thought I might be worth a year in Serie A, but when I went to see Tapie about a move he asked me to give him another year.

We never reached the same heights again. The next year we went out of the European Cup to Sparta Prague in the second round and our season fell apart. We did win the League again, but forfeited the Cup after the tragedy at Bastia when the stand collapsed. They had erected a temporary stand to pack all the fans in and the disaster brought football back down to earth. Literally.

My last game for OM was against Cannes at home, and although we had a walk on the pitch to applaud the fans I didn't really get a decent chance to say goodbye. I actually wanted to stay in France, and Monaco were interested, but I think Tapie wanted me out of sight and out of mind. He certainly wasn't going to sell me to our big rivals, or to an Italian club, for that matter. In the end I went back home and to Sheffield Wednesday.

Looking back, I'd say my time in Marseilles changed my life. I was a better footballer for being involved in three French Championship triumphs, a French Cup final and a European Cup final and semi-final. And I was a better person, too. I had a broader outlook. I learned enough French to be able to do match commentaries on the radio. In fact, I felt so at home in France that I could have settled there for good. But in the end it worked out better to return to England. I wouldn't have changed it for the world, but you move on. *C'est la vie.*

18

Emerald-Green Aliens

TAM DEAN BURN

I am on my way up from London to Edinburgh to interview Franck Sauzée, the French international and European Cup-winner with Marseille, now playing for my beloved Hibernian. I am first stopping off at my mate's in Dalston because he's got a big Hibs book collection and I want to have a scan for French connections through our illustrious if chequered history. I buy the Scottish tabloid paper the *Daily Record* for news about tonight's match against St Johnstone in the Scottish Premier League, of which there is little, but I am mighty cheered to find that Gilles Rousset, the French goal-keeper with our Edinburgh rivals, Hearts, was sent off last night. Even better, when I turn to the front of the paper which many, especially Celtic fans, call the *Daily Hun* for its bias towards all things Glasgow Rangers, and open it at page 3, the headline blazes: 'E.T. IS A HIBEE'. There's a full-page article with colour photos of Steven Spielberg's cute little alien in a Hibs strip. One of the series of TV commercials that British Telecom have made featuring E.T. has him watching Hibs' Trinidad and Tobago star midfielder Russell Latapy putting a penalty past the aforementioned Rousset, pulling the emerald-green strip over his head and whizzing round the room. Better still, Hearts fans are up in arms and threatening to boycott BT. Result or what! When I show this to my mate, Irvine Welsh, he wonders if it is maybe a consequence of his story

'The Rosewell Incident' in which Hibs casuals team up with alien forces to take on the earth's leaders. His first foray into science fiction becomes fact!

I arrive at our ground, Easter Road, for the match and I feel like an alien. The seats are numbered, there's no smoking allowed and I have women sitting either side of me. Not that I'm complaining on that score, but it just feels weird. The woman to my right has short hair and a hard face and I jump to the conclusion that she is a tough lesbian. To my left there are two blonde honeys who seem to be with the very fat guy next to them. Things seem really out of kilter as the sense memories of so much of my youth flood in but are dammed up by all these factors and the way the rest of the stadium looks these days. Gone are the huge terraces which held 65,000 for the really big games, like the 1964 one when we beat Real Madrid 2–0 and Di Stefano and Puskas were in the team. A crowd of 45,000 saw Hibs narrowly knocked out of the first European Cup in 1955 in the semi-final against Stade de Reims, in which the great Raymond Kopa was outshone by Hibs' greatest-ever player, Gordon Smith, as Irvine's books tell me. This was one of the French connections I found, with UEFA Cup ties in the late seventies against Sochaux and Racing Strasbourg, us winning the former but losing the latter.

I half-wish this was a book about Italian football, so that I could boast about our glorious game against Napoli in 1968 when we turned round a 4–1 defeat in Italy by putting five past Dino Zoff at Easter Road. But I also remember leaner years when there was vast space on those terraces, especially the game when Hibs' full-back, Joe Davis, punted the ball way above the skyline dominated by Edinburgh's inner-city mountain, Arthur's Seat, and it came down to land on my younger brother Russell's head, sending him flying down the terracing. I can't remember anything about the match, but it must have been a pretty dull affair because loads of fans came round from behind the goals to see if he was all right. Taking part in the first European Cup is only one example of the

avant-garde nature of Hibernian FC: we were also the first
team in Britain to get floodlights, undersoil heating and to
have commercial sponsors' names on our strips. OK, so maybe
the last one is not something to be particularly proud of.

All these thoughts evaporate as the teams take the field,
but my heart soon sinks as I see that Franck Sauzée is sitting
on the bench. What's going on? My ever closely hovering
paranoia offers the thought that the Hibs manager, Alex
McLeish, has heard he is being interviewed tomorrow by
someone up from London and so needs taking down a peg
or two. It quickly becomes clear that Hibs are struggling
without Franck as the ball seems alien to them, with mis-
judged passes galore. St Johnstone go and score. Sauzée
comes on after twenty minutes and this appears to be a panic
measure. The word soon spreads round that Paul Hartley
has been taken off with a hamstring injury, which is pretty
pathetic, because that is due to a lack of a proper warm-up.
Unfortunately Franck doesn't make any difference. He is off
his game as much as the rest of them.

The 'dike' next to me seems to be in her element, though,
as she is your type of fan who loves a good moan. She especially seems to have it in for Hibs' Finnish centre forward,
Mixu Paatelainen, but I find it strange that she berates him by
his first name: 'GIT OAFF MIXU YA FAT BASTARD!' We strike up
a bit of banter but I can't take it beyond sympathetic little
smiles with the blonde beauty to my left. The match ends 1–0
to St Johnstone, pissing me off. They come from Perth, the
town where I spent seven miserable months in my first theatre
job feeling like a total alien while my brother Russell and
my pals were really cooking as the legendary punk band Fire
Engines. I phone Russell after the game and have to laugh
when he tells me the highlight of the radio commentary: it
was said that Franck Sauzée has been caught in possession
more times than Keith Richards!

Next day I am back at Easter Road to meet Sauzée and it's
all a bit daunting. I am more than ten years older than him
but somehow football players always seem more grown up

than you. Could it be that the sense memories are most strongly reinforced when you are young, so they bring out the kid in you? Also this role of interviewer feels alien. On the pitch Sauzée cuts a pretty imposing figure with his incredible blistering shots and looks that remind me of the American actor Ted Danson, but he turns out to be a warm, open guy with a light voice. His command of English is something that has only really developed during his seven months with Hibs and I find myself compensating by becoming more staccato and talking too much. My knowledge of French football is limited so I can't really get into detail about his earlier experience, but we cover a lot of ground in forty-five minutes. Franck tells me what he thinks are the reasons why French football has really taken off in the last twenty years or so.

First, it is that every team possesses a centre for bringing on young players, coached by older ones, and that managers bring them into the first team at a young age. They are the sort of youth academies that teams in Britain are only now getting together. Secondly, he says that St Etienne reaching the European Cup final against Bayern Munich in Glasgow in 1976 was a landmark occasion and Marseille winning the European Cup in 1993 (Sauzée played in midfield in that team) encouraged French football clubs to feel that they could beat the best. Also that Michel Platini had given France an enormous boost of confidence, having won so many honours before he became France's manager. These days, almost all the best French players play outside their own country, because of the level of taxation in France and the great experience they gain in the other top leagues in Europe. The best to him is the Italian Serie A, where he played for a year with Atalanta de Bergame following Marseille's triumph.

Christov Rühn, the editor of this book, was intrigued to hear that Sauzée, a champion with his beloved Marseille, had gone to what to him was a little-known Scottish team. Franck said that talking to ex-French international goakeeper Gilles Rousset about his experience with Hearts had convinced him that it was a worthwhile move. There is an enormous enthusiasm for the game in Scotland, and Edinburgh is one of the great capitals of Europe. The transfer would give him the opportunity to develop his English and Alex McLeish had persuaded him with his plans to restore Hibs as a great European side.

We discussed the similarities of Marseilles and Leith, the home of Hibs; both ports, they have long been places frequented by a wide range of nationalities who came through work, unlike the tourists who visit Edinburgh and might enjoy the place but rarely engage with the local people. I have also found this to be the case when travelling abroad. I have got inside cities much more when I have been there to work than on holiday.

The fact that both Marseilles and Leith are historically made up to a large extent of poor folk is another common factor. The teams are an essential part of the community and have been an escape from the grinding poverty, especially so with Hibs' origins, formed by and for the ghettoised Irish Catholic immigrant community of Edinburgh in 1875. As Alan Lugton states in his invaluable and definitive early history of the club, *The Making of Hibernian* (which stretches to three thick hardback volumes yet has only covered up to 1946!), 'The Edinburgh-Irish were treated as the city's underclass and Hibernian had to struggle against a wall of bigotry'.

Many will be aware of the rivalry between Glasgow Celtic and Rangers which stems from the opposing sides of the Irish conflict they traditionally support, but the Edinburgh Irish were in a much more isolated and weaker position in the society of the capital. Over the years the Catholic element has been superseded by the sense of Hibs being Leith's team, rather than Edinburgh's, but the affinity with the Irish struggle for freedom from Britain remains. This has been shown most recently in the competition to design a new club badge, in which most of the proposed designs have restored the original Irish harp. Despite going to Protestant schools (the religious divide still remains in Scottish education), I learned many Irish rebel songs on the Easter Road terraces and am still so glad to have had the good fortune to be on the side of justice in the Irish struggle through being a Hibs supporter. Indeed, the man Alan Lugton rightly describes as the most remarkable Hibs supporter ever was James Connolly, one of the leaders of the Easter Rising in Dublin in 1916. Lugton says this was Europe's first expression of people-power in a social and national revolution, but I reckon the French might argue with that. Connolly's position as Edinburgh's finest son has been ignored by its civic leaders, but there is a little plaque at the place of his birth in the city's Cowgate, heart of the Little Ireland ghetto:

To the memory of James Connolly
Born 6th June 1868 at 107 Cowgate
Renowned International Trade Union
and working class Leader
Founder of the Irish Socialist Republican Party
Member of Provisional Government of
Irish Republic
Executed 12 May 1916 at Kilmainham Jail, Dublin

A personal resonance for me about all this rings on from the weekend that combined the first legal James Connolly march through Edinburgh with my first experience of Ecstasy at the legendary Edinburgh techno club Sativa. Connolly's plaque had recently been painted over after lying defaced for months by loyalist bigots, i.e. anti-Catholic supporters of British rule in Ireland, so I put all this into a song for the Edinburgh music collective, the East Coast Project:

. . . past the plaque, the plaque that was under attack from the enemy within,
*   James Connolly's plaque, now painted black, calling me back to the march that weekend that changed my life.*
*   He said: 'The great only appear great because we're on our knees.*
*   Well I've been on my feet since then . . . dancing.'*

Now have I got you thinking?

What's all this to do with big Franck Sauzée? Well, I didn't get up and sing for him or give him a lesson in Irish politics, but much of what he told me did seem socialistic in content, even if he didn't term it as such. He said that despite the higher taxes in France, he believed in the social security system to help the poor and that although he loved his country, solidarity between people was more important. He equated this with football, saying that solidarity between players on the pitch is vital. He is glad that borders are coming down across Europe and that football is at the forefront of this. He hopes that the rise of Le Pen and the National Front is over with their loss of control of the town of Toulon and believes that people now have their eyes open to such dangerous nationalism.

Big Franck's on the side of the aliens.

We finish up by sharing understanding about being separated from our children on a day-to-day basis and then a beautiful look comes over his face as he describes how speechless he was when he went to see St Etienne play as a kid from his little village, Aubenas. Finally, he vows to me that Hibs will be much improved when we tackle Aberdeen at home on the coming Saturday. I fucking hope so – Aberdeen are bottom of the League and have yet to win away from home this season.

So here I am, back at the holy ground on Saturday afternoon and immediately more at home on the terracing side. It might be seated but the seats are not numbered. I can also smoke to my heart's content and my lungs' consternation. There are plenty of girls around and there is something so sexy about seeing them with Hibs scarves. This and other thoughts I am able to share with Brian, fellow Hibee and pal from way back. A slight shudder runs through me as I remember how we used to come to games when I moved away from my mum and dad's in Clermiston into Brian's flat and my Clerie pals ignored me, then gossiped that I'd been seen with some 'auld poof' at the match. But this was because moving into a flat before marriage was totally alien at the time and I was the first in my whole extended family to do so.

Shake off the maudlin self-indulgence, Tam, the cabbage and ribs are on the park, they are shooting down the famous Easter Road slope and we are free to move down near the Aberdeen goals.

Immediately it's clear that there is going to be no repeat of Wednesday night and Franck Sauzée comes very close to giving this story the perfect ending with some ferocious shots that bring out the best in the former Hibs and Scotland keeper Jim Leighton.

Franck doesn't get on the scoresheet but Hibs win 2–0, playing some classy fitba' and sending me back to London happy to be on the same side as Kaiser Sauzée, James Connolly and E.T.

19

Black Star: The Unforgettable Roger Milla

ARNAUD RAMSAY

If elections were based on nothing more than simple popularity, Roger Milla would be president of the Republic of Cameroon. Even today, at the age of forty-seven, he is a living god of the style of football he epitomises: the immoderate flamboyance that is African football. When he tries to make it across the concourse of an African airport he misses his plane, slowed down by the people's overwhelming desire to touch him, to feel his presence, to tear his clothes and bracelets from him. Out of pure love and gratitude.

According to Milla, 'Football is a way for a small country to become large.' It's a statement of certainty, leavened with empiricism. After all, it was Milla himself who created this phenomenon and introduced Cameroon to the world. It was in Italy, during the 1990 World Cup. You need to cast your mind back and immerse yourself in the spirit of the times to understand the euphoria Cameroon generated.

In 1990 Roger Milla was semi-retired from the glorious game and living a tranquil life under the beneficent sun of the island of Reunion. Our attacking hero was defending the colours of St Pierroise, a top-division amateur club where fellow footballing legend Jean-Pierre Papin had recently played out his last footballing days. Milla was unhurriedly preparing for his coaching certificate. Basically, he was on holiday.

Meanwhile, in keeping with their unfortunate tradition, his national team were riven by internal conflicts, and during a tour of China the squad broke up. Cameroon were on the point of implosion. The remedy remained the same: once again an SOS went out to Super Roger. The call started in the press, was taken up by the public and the issue was settled when the president of the Republic added his voice to the demands. Milla was recalled to the squad, to the irritation of a number of its members. He was thirty-eight years old and far from match-fit.

The opening game: shock horror! Cameroon beat Maradona's Argentina, the defending champions, by 1–0. Milla was on the field for only eight minutes. Six days later, on 14 June, it was Romania's turn to face the Untameable Lions. Milla's studs finally appeared on the pitch at Bari during the sixtieth minute. In the next ten he scored twice. Then, without a trace of smugness, his face lit up by a dazzling grin, he let drop a few laconic words: 'I've proved that I've still got some life left in me.'

In their next match Cameroon were taken apart by the USSR (4–0). So what? They were already through to the next round. The time to shake off their lethargy was against Colombia in the last sixteen. With the score 0–0 at the end of normal time, Milla had already been cantering around the pitch for thirty minutes. In extra time he again scored twice. His second goal seared itself into the minds of all who saw it: he stole the ball from the feet of Higuita, the idiosyncratic Colombian goalkeeper, who had moved way outside his area in a vain attempt at a passing move. 'He tried to dribble the ball past me. He should have known: you don't dribble Milla. I'm the one who's paid to get the ball past goalies.'

The incorrigible Milla took off like a kid to celebrate his goal. In pure joy he ran to the corner flag and engaged it in a devilish belly dance. The crowd went crazy. They adored Milla. Or Miller, as the caption on Italian TV called him. Miller, as in Albert-Roger Miller, the real name of the genius whose talents sent his comrades – a diverse mixture of ethnicities gathered under the wing of this Central African country nestling on the Gulf of Guinea – into the quarter-finals of the World Cup. Unique.

In front of 55,205 spectators on 1 July, at the San Paolo stadium in Naples, Cameroon took part in an Homeric confrontation against England, the most awesome match in the whole competition. In spite of being comprehensively outplayed, England, captained by goalkeeper Peter Shilton, struck in the twenty-sixth minute with a David Platt header from a cross by defender Stuart Pearce. Milla replaced Maobang at half-time, and the tone of the game changed instantly. The atmosphere became even more electric. Fifteen minutes later the sorcerer, on the receiving end of a perfect pass from Omam-Biyik, was brought down by Gascoigne inside the area. The penalty was converted by Kunde. Five minutes later, Milla, once again in the thick of things, set up a scoring pass for Ekeke. Milla confesses: 'Despite myself, I can't help thinking that if I'd taken the penalty and scored our second goal I could have ended up as the top goalscorer of the competition. No matter, I prefer to play for the team.'

Seven minutes from the end of normal time and Cameroon are holding out for victory. The euphoria evaporates in the eighty-third minute when, inside the penalty area, Massing fouls Lineker, who scores from the spot. During injury time, after picking up a Gascoigne pass, Lineker was again flattened inside the area, this time by Nkono, and with the same result. Cameroon didn't deserve such a cruel fate, especially since Makanaky, Milla and Omam-Biyik all had the chance to swing the outcome in their favour. 'It's true, we should have killed the game off earlier on. But only if we had not played like Africans. We were too keen on the fancy stuff. But that's the way it goes in football.'

Germany went on to win the competition. Franz Beckenbauer, their coach, told Milla that he feared having to play the Untameable Lions. Our sainted hero adds: 'Of course we were disappointed, especially when we watched a recording of the game three days later and saw how many chances we'd squandered and how dubious the England penalties were. But in all honesty, nobody expected us to get so far. From our very first victories the people of Cameroon were mad with joy. If we'd beaten England, and I've wonderful memories of that spectacular game, then I'm sure there would have been rioting.'

There you have the art of seeing the bright side of a defeat, however valiant it may be. As it was, their elimination not-withstanding, the country went wild on their return. Milla himself was a World Cup veteran. He had already distin-guished himself back in the 1982 World Cup in Spain. In the pool games his team drew with Peru, Poland and Italy, the eventual winners. Prior to the competition, after watching Cameroon perform in Libya, the Italian coach declared, 'All I noticed were the rabbits scampering around the pitch.' During the competition itself Milla was unjustly denied both a goal and a penalty. The result: Cameroon were eliminated from the tournament on goal difference despite remaining unbeaten. This setback did nothing to discourage Milla in his quest for pleasure. Throughout his life, the joy of playing football would for ever keep him running fluently. And the entire footballing world will be for ever grateful . . .

In 1994, he re-signed with Tonnerre of Yaoundé, ending up as top scorer in the Championship, and was still in roaring form for the World Cup in the USA. He scored in the match against Russia, a 6–1 defeat for Cameroon, the only bright spot in a pathetic opening phase. At the age of forty-two years, one month and eight days, he became the oldest goalscorer in the World Cup finals.

Roger Milla is still playing, dribbling, shooting and ham-mering home the goals today. For love of the game. These days he makes his public appearances at high-profile events, turning out for the Black Stars, a dazzling team of top African players. Their most recent fixtures were in South Africa, where they played against the prisoners in a Soweto jail, and in

Ghana, a testimonial game for Marcel Desailly in the country of his birth. The sound of the applause that greets his loping gait, the smell of camphor in the changing room where he gets together with his friends: these are what inspire him.

Milla writes his own destiny with the tips of his studs. A grandiose destiny, to be a star – and the final chapter remains unwritten. The opening one is set in the alleys of Makak, a neighbourhood in Yaoundé, capital of Cameroon.

A few cloths tied together form a makeshift ball. Despite the uneven bounce, the young Milla is soon teasing it into action with ease, his skill matched only by his delight. Papa Mooh Germain is proud of his son. Papa works on the railway. His ceaseless shuttling journeys lead him to settle in the town of Douala, where, in 1971, Roger begins his playing career with Léopard of Douala. The following year, aged twenty, he signs for five seasons with Tonnerre Kalara Club of Yaoundé. The club is a national institution, and their new attacking thoroughbred helps to keep their trophy cupboard full: champions of Cameroon, winners of the Cameroon Cup and the African Cup of Cups.

The year 1976 sees him winning, for the first time, the African Golden Ball to go with the commendation he earned the year before. The recipient of the Golden Ball, awarded to the best player, is chosen by a panel of pan-African journalists under the aegis of the leading magazine *France Football*. Milla went on to win the award a second time in 1990, after his World Cup performance in Italy.

You'd think that the end of the line was in sight. Wrong. Following the World Cup miracle, offers came rushing in, from Australia, Mexico, Austria. 'Everyone wanted a slice of Roger Milla,' he says. But he preferred to amuse himself crisscrossing the world in the guise of a VIP representative of football. You might have spotted him, for example, at Peter Shilton's testimonial game, at Pelé's fiftieth birthday, or in Belgium, recording the album *Saga Africa*, which featured a track named 'Sandy' after his daughter. 'But I've never chased after money. I've never earned a monthly salary higher than

50,000 francs. My real wealth is my family. I've always been
exploited. I didn't have the career that I deserved. Without
being big-headed, I'm one of the best centre forwards in the
world.' So why was there such a shortfall between his mone-
tary worth and his status? 'He's a great character. As great
a player as Johan Cruyff. His game is fluid, intelligent, his
acceleration electrifying. But he may have been badly advised.'
So says Claude le Roy, currently coach with RC Strasbourg,
and coach of the Cameroon team during the period when
Milla and his team-mates won the 1988 African Nations
Cup.

It's not something to which the man who describes himself
as an unpaid ambassador of football will admit. There's only
a trace of somewhat frustrated nostalgia when he allows himself to reminisce about his time in the French Championship.
His success, over and above futile polemics, made him one of
the pathfinding African players in the French First Division.
The year 1977 found this child of the sun shivering in the
northern chill of Valenciennes. When he signed his contract,
his bosses promised him a fabulous salary, with villa to
match, and top-ranking status. The reality did not quite match
up to these promises: a cramped studio, salary to match and,
although he scored goals that came out of nowhere, he played
mostly in the Third Division. He couldn't take any more
and left, citing no particular reason but simply stating his
inescapable fate: 'Black players are the lowest of the low in
French football.'

Following two seasons with USVA, where he was accused
of being too individualistic – something he denies – he made
his way to Monaco. There Milla enjoyed a French Cup-
winning season, a feat he repeated with Bastia the following
year. He followed this up with four seasons in Corsica, and
then the darling of the terraces joined St Etienne, helping it
to achieve promotion to the First Division. He ended his
French footballing years with Montpellier from 1986 to 1989.
Adored by the public, he became close to club president Louis
Nicollin who, like Milla, saw friendship as one of the most

precious assets life can offer. A jovial, self-taught man, stout and kind-looking, he had made his fortune in refuse collection. 'He's the only one who didn't rip me off, who gave me a helping hand when I needed it. He recognised my worth,' maintains Milla. 'I adore him. We're two of a kind, he's my brother.'

Their paths were to cross again: Nicollin put him in charge of the top-division team – a responsibility he shared with Mama Ouattara, a former Ivory Coast international – as well as giving him control of recruiting players, from under-fifteens to professionals. Milla was also generous with his advice to young African players, such as the Montpellier midfielder Marcel Mahouvé contracted by Roma. His life revolved around football.

And he had no hesitation in continuing to make his presence felt on the field. Seemingly inexhaustible, and with his enthusiasm for the game unabated, on the eve of the World Cup in 1994 Milla took on a final, if improbable, challenge: to spread his fame to the Indonesian Championship.

In Jakarta he scored twenty-three times in as many games for Pelita Jaya, who were to be crowned champions of this South-East Asian island state, and his presence gave a boost to the average gate. The following season, on loan to Pusam Samarinda, he adopted the role of co-trainer. He takes great pride in having stayed in shape. 'I haven't changed. The scales have stayed at 73 kilos for my height of 1.76 metres. It's all about respecting yourself and your partners.' His body hasn't changed since 1972 when he first turned out for Cameroon, whose strip he has worn between 150 and 200 times. With Cameroonian records as unreliable as they are, this phenomenon is impossible to verify. But those figures would make him a world record-holder for the number of international appearances made.

So now, at forty-seven, what is there left for Milla to set his sights on? He doesn't know. He journeys through the world of football at his own pace, following his desires. Happily settled at Montpellier, he no doubt has a few regrets about his

unsuccessful attempt to take charge of the affairs of his
national side. For three years he was the administrative director of the Untameable Lions. Not his thing. 'And on top of it
all, it was tribal war. We didn't have any resources, no infrastructure, nor any proper management. I even had to pay for
the balls out of my own pocket. So now they can get on with
it.' He doesn't hide his bitterness. He would have liked to
have given even more to his country. But as it is his influence
is felt further afield than Cameroon alone. It extends to all
African countries, north, west, east and south; to a continent
where football has the mysterious 'power to heal wounds',
according to Nelson Mandela. Sure, George Weah, the Liberian
player for AC Milan, currently on loan to Chelsea, is Africa's
emperor and big brother, but Milla is Africa's god. A humble
and accessible god. And the fact that 18 per cent of players
in the French Championship are now of African origin
compared to 2.2 per cent in 1970*, is thanks in good part to
Roger Milla: a marvellous, mythical man.

---

*It is also worth noting that since the arrival of the remarkable Zimbabwean
Bruce Grobelaar at Liverpool, the English Premier League has followed suit,
recruiting talent from Nigeria, South Africa, Ghana and Jamaica, among other
countries.

20

Anelka: The Unknown Soldier

Q

Credits roll: The Unknown Soldier.
Music: Latin.

Episode 1

It was sunny in Madrid; a fabulous condition. Didier Anelka
was at the wheel of his Mercedes. The city was slowly waking
up from its siesta, but he'd been up for hours. He was aware
of the beauty that surrounded him.

The fountains spouting powerful jets of water into, around
and above exotic works of art. The modern constructions,
blending in with the refined, mature creations of a time gone
by. Everything was in harmony. Banks, hotels, apartment buildings, corporate office blocks, shops dripping with designer
labels sat side by side without prejudice. They happily lined
either side of Paseo de la Castellana, one of the main arteries
of the city centre.

Didier pressed a code into his mobile phone and listened to
his messages.

He felt good about himself. Victory was never exhausting.
With the help of his brother Claude, and the same *joie
de vivre* Toussaint l'Ouverture had used in fighting Napoleon,
the black knights in shining armour had fought the hard,
dirty battles and won the tricky terrain that had taken their

younger brother Nicolas to Paris St Germain, Arsenal and valiantly on to Real Madrid.

Didier liked to be discreet in his business and personal life. Only the tightly knit group of people around the table when the deals were struck and his immediate family knew the exact business details and the tough reality behind the fearsome reputation of the Anelka brothers.

Didier pulled over to the side of the road and opened a package emblazoned with British stamps and airmail stickers. There was a tape and a letter.

Dear Didier,

Hope all is well. The information contained on the tape was recorded from a radio interview. You guys are still causing a storm over here.

Best wishes

Q

Didier pushed the tape into his player, fired up his engine and hit the road.

MAN

Nicolas Anelka was greedy, a mercenary. He broke a contract and said he would never kick another ball for Arsenal. It was his brothers' fault. They are to blame.

Didier turned up the volume.

WOMAN

He is right to keep his money in the family. The British do. Why should he let his brothers go hungry? Why should he let his brothers go homeless? He's a smart young man. At least he can trust them.

MAN
*Leaving Arsenal the way he did is going to
haunt him for the rest of his life. He's a miserable kid with millions. I have no sympathy for
him.*

WOMAN
*The minute a black man starts to make money
in England you guys get paranoid. Going back
to that contract issue. What about George
Michael?*

MAN
This is football, not the music industry.

WOMAN
*They go together. In Brazil, Jamaica, Africa,
they dance, whistle and play the drums while
the game is going on. It is only in England where
they don't dance on the terraces. All they do is
Nazi salutes, sing provocative songs and fight
in the streets, especially when they go abroad.*

MAN
What has this got to do with Anelka?

The Mercedes stopped at a traffic light.

WOMAN
*You guys didn't say George Michael was greedy
when he broke his contract with Sony. He said
he was unhappy, that he'd never sing another
note for the company.*

Didier's eyes surveyed the elegantly dressed patrons of Madrid.
They walked at an easy, comfortable pace.

MAN
OK, *what if the British club refused to pay him? What would he do then? He would go to court to get his money, wouldn't he? It goes both ways.*

WOMAN
Exactly. So say Arsenal approached him when he was under contract to Paris St Germain and signed him. Then the bottom line is that he can do what they did to him. Don't you agree? The Artist Formerly Known as Prince felt the same way, he scribbled 'SLAVE' on his face. Is this what you wanted Anelka to do?

MAN
We're wiping racism out of the game.

WOMAN
You can't get it out of the boardroom.

The lights changed to green.

WOMAN (continues)
George Michael and Anelka are both artists: one does it with his voice, the other with his feet. It was David Geffen who came to George's rescue, saying that the world would lose an enormous talent if it was denied his voice, and the same goes for Anelka.

Didier's Mercedes moved off at a gentle pace. He had a warm, soft side but he could also be dangerous. He had been labelled '*the protagonist*' by the media. He took the role in his stride. He was growing happier by the day; he knew what direction he was going in, what he had to do and how he was going to do it.

MAN

You think his brothers did the right thing? I suppose you're right. I wouldn't complain if my brothers got me a few million quid.

WOMAN

David Geffen spoke to Sony and brokered the deal that eventually took George to Dreamworks. The Anelka brothers did the same and it took Nicolas to Spain. It would be a crime if the difference was because of the colour of their skin. Arsenal made an astronomical profit over a short period of time. They were really happy on the inside but the board members couldn't show that emotion on the surface – it isn't a British thing to do.

MAN

So you reckon they just complained and made a fuss in public?

WOMAN

Yeah. All through the negotiations they were holding out for more money.

MAN

Why?

WOMAN

Anelka was young and still hadn't reached his full potential. How much would he have been worth in another two years? He wanted to be paid now.

MAN

He'd just signed a new contract.

WOMAN

*He is a footballer with a hip-hop philosophy,
not one with a colonial or ghetto mentality.
The black English footballers understood
Anelka's feelings, but they don't have the strength
to break the chains, so they keep suffering and
smiling. Anything can happen in football – the
next tackle could be his last. But now there is
money in his account if, God forbid, that rainy
day ever arrives.*

Didier took the tape out. The mention of rain depressed him. It reminded him of London. He had relocated to Madrid with Nicolas. They'd met the King of Spain and felt well treated in the country, better than in France. Claude was in Paris with the rest of the family. He was developing other business interests.

Didier's job was to protect his younger brother.

Nicolas was the Unknown Soldier.

The media were kept away from the superstar so that he could concentrate on what he did best, which was playing football. The mystery surrounding him would continue to grow.

However, there was only one problem with the end of this fairy tale.

Nicolas had not scored a goal for Real Madrid. So the swords were drawn and the golden calf was getting closer to the slaughterhouse.

Nicolas had arrived from Arsenal with great expectations, but he found himself either sitting on the bench or lying injured on the treatment table. He was now a young man under a tremendous amount of pressure, living a nightmare existence.

The British press were laughing and taking digs at him.

The Spanish fans were unsure of his loyalty.

There had been reports in the press that Nicolas was on his way to Lazio. That he wanted to play for them. That he felt the Real Madrid team were not good enough. The courtesans said that Nicolas had sent word to his fans in Italy and that they were now eagerly awaiting his arrival.

The heavens shifted and the game switched overnight.

Real Madrid were said to be fed up with their troubled star and they wanted to cut their losses. They wanted to loan Nicolas out to Juventus or swap him with another high-profile warrior.

Rumour upon rumour built up, a match was lit and the bonfire of lies caught fire.

By day, a counter-attack came from behind the hills.

Nicolas refused to be loaned out. If Real Madrid were saying they did not want him, then they should sell him. He would refuse to play for the club.

The tapas bars and courtyards were filled with whispers and gossip.

'Nicolas is committing suicide.'

'He has done it once before with Arsenal, he could do it again.'

'Not to a club as great as ours. A country as bold as ours?'

'What other country would take him? Italy? If he fails there, he has to go home back to France, defeated.'

Events were reaching a climax. Everybody was having sleep-less nights waiting for the next strike. Would it come by air or by ground?

Were the Anelka brothers manipulating the press and nego-tiating another big payday?

The night drew in. The campfires were burning. Trumpets sounded, alerting the weary troops that things had taken a turn for the worse. John Toshack, the coach who had brought Nicolas to the club, had been beheaded. Nicolas had lost his one and only ally.

Some quarters of the press levelled the blame at Nicolas. They wanted his head on a stake as well. He was a disruptive influence, bad luck. The Real Madrid team had been split in half on his arrival. Some players were for Nicolas, others were against him.

The people of Madrid were captivated by the drama.

Would the golden calf survive and become a hero? Or would he fall, break in half and meet his bloody death?

Episode 2

Didier Anelka's Mercedes glided past the colossal Estadio Santiago Bernabeu, the home of Real Madrid.

He was midway through a conversation on his mobile phone with Q. They had spoken on a number of occasions. There was an easy flow of words and a good rapport between them.

Didier's tone was soft, his manner polite, his English good, his sentences measured. A Spanish word pirouetted off his tongue and danced into the conversation.

'I'm sorry,' said Didier, laughing. 'I'm thinking in Spanish now.'

'So quickly?' asked Q, surprised.

'Yes. It gets even worse if I am speaking in French. We have to adjust. This is our home now. We like it here and are making our life here.' Didier's voice was proud. 'We have friends, so we must learn the language. I find it easier than English. Nicolas likes Spanish.' His voice dropped a little. 'We spend so much time at the club that there is a joke going around that the president of Real Madrid is going to give me an office there.'

'What kind of music does Nicolas like?'

'African, Rap, R'n'B. You know he likes the female bands,' replied Didier.

'And you?'

'The same, music from Cameroon plus Caribbean.'

'What kind of music do you have in your car now?'

'Zouk,' said Didier, turning up the volume slightly.

'Are you from Africa?'

'We are from Martinique,' said Didier, with more pleasure than he would have thought possible. 'Oh, and I love salsa music and dancing to it.'

'You do?'

'Yeah.'

'I'll make you a tape. I'll put some African salsa on it.'

'That would be nice.'

'Why did Nicolas join Puma?'

'It is better to be a king in a brand.' He was listening intently to every intonation in Q's voice.

'So he is following Pelé, Cruyff and Maradona. But if Nicolas doesn't perform on the pitch it could make it harder to get more lucrative endorsement deals.'

Didier asked Q gently, 'Do you know why we chose Puma?'

There was a long pause.

Didier continued. 'They had the right philosophy. They said there were all these big mountains, Nike, Adidas, and they were a small mountain.' His voice had a poetic lilt. 'When the snow fell on Puma, it was not white but that fresh, blue colour that glowed, that lit up and stood out from the rest. We have just shot some commercials with them. They are great.' He allowed himself a smile. 'Nicolas is very happy with them.' Didier's voice became cold. 'If people are jealous and envious of us, then we are doing things right.'

'I'm thinking of coming to Madrid on Friday.'

'Good. We can meet. I'll make sure Nicolas has time,' he said in his exquisitely polite voice.

'No, it is OK. I'm coming to see you.'

'Call me when you arrive.'

Episode 3

'Georgia, it's Q. I've got a meeting with Didier Anelka. Can you arrange everything? Make sure it is a good hotel. The first question Didier is going to ask me is, "Q, where are you staying?"'

Georgia's tone was relaxed. 'I have a contact in Spain, Enrique Perez de Guzman. I'll get on the phone and e-mail you the details.'

Episode 4

Dear Q,

Here are the details.

Hotel Residencia Galiano
c. Galiano no. 6
Plaza Colon
Madrid
tel: 91 319 2000
fax : 91 3199 914

Enrique says it is a safe, charming place. Fifteen rooms.
Quiet, discreet, great furniture.

Georgia

Episode 5

The plane landed under the cover of darkness. Q breezed
through customs, exited the airport and jumped into a taxi. It
was 12.30 on Saturday night.

Episode 6

The taxi slowed down as it reached a barrier across the street.
Armed government officials approached the car.

They peered into the back seat.

The hotel was made of black marble. The word 'Galiano'
was constructed from silver metal and jutted out over the
entrance.

This was a high-security part of town, the Ministerio de las
Administraciones Públicas was at the end of the road.

Episode 7

It was a bright Sunday afternoon.

Didier and Q were enjoying their telephone conversation.
Didier told Q that his parents were in town. They had travelled from Paris and they were going to watch Nicolas play
against Real Sociedad.

This was going to be the most important game of Nicolas's
life. His parents understood that, and they had come to give

him moral support. Their presence in the stadium would lift their son above the crowd.

It was a make-or-break game and Nicolas knew it. The fans had been waiting for his first goal. Now they were fed up. Today they wanted the goal or his blood.

How was Nicolas ever going to get into the French national team for Euro 2000 if he couldn't score goals for his club side?

Had he lost his touch?

Was he worth the money?

Was he suffering from stress?

Was the team good enough to play with him?

Had his brothers ruined his career?

There was only one person who could answer all these questions and that was Nicolas.

Could the Unknown Soldier win his most important battle in front of his parents?

Didier and Q arranged to meet after the match at the Euro-building Hotel. It was a stone's throw from the stadium.

Episode 8

Q glanced at his ticket for the match with pride. He felt as if he were on his way to a pop concert.

Episode 9

Estadio Santiago Bernabeu was packed. The atmosphere was electric. Nicolas Anelka was the primary focus. He was wearing the number 19 shirt.

The referee blew the whistle.

Episode 10

Didier and Q sat next to each other in the very luxurious surroundings of the Eurobuilding Hotel. It had been the Anelka brothers' home for months. They had recently moved into new properties.

Didier took off his Puma jacket and placed it over his body like a blanket as he eased himself back into the seat.

He was relaxed, comfortable, warm and enjoying Q's company. They were now talking eye to eye. Q was on his turf
and Didier felt safe in that knowledge.

Georgia was sitting opposite them. She was the translator.

Q was speaking in French, which Didier had requested
because he found it easier to understand than English.

Every now and then Q's sentences broke down. Georgia
quickly picked them up, assembled them and delivered them
in pristine condition to Didier. When all the information had
been received, he glanced back at Q.

'I think Nicolas played very well,' said Q in French. 'He
didn't score, but from my point of view he scored a greater
goal today,' said Q in English.

'What do you mean?' asked Didier. 'Everyone is waiting
for Nicolas's first goal.'

'On the left-hand side. Number 3 for Real Madrid. He has
a bad first touch. He overlaps with number 11 and likes to
shoot from everywhere. From too far outside the box. He should
slip it to Nicolas.'

'You are talking about Roberto Carlos.' Didier's tone was
stern.

'The Brazilian player?'

'Yes.'

'I don't care,' Q said confidently. 'I don't care if the crowd
applauds if he gets a red card. I don't care how much of a hero
he was. I paid for my ticket, so I can say what I want. If I had
got a free ticket then I would shut my mouth.'

'You have got a point there.'

'They were all just numbers to me. I don't know who they
are. He is too old, too slow. But I'll come back to him. I think
Nicolas is a good team player. He was linking up with his
team-mates, passing early, losing his marker and running into
the spaces in the box. But they didn't pass to him. It must be
so frustrating for him. At Arsenal he was surrounded by a
good team.'

Didier nodded his head in agreement. 'There they played
modern football. You know, one or two touches. It is a fast

game. Nicolas likes to play that way, use his pace. He has good technique and vision,' he said earnestly. 'Here the Spanish game is all about building it up from the back. Every player likes to take two, three, four touches of the ball. The game is slower.'

'So it breaks down. He is worth the money. The new coach, when he arrives, must see that. Anyone who has played football can see what is happening on the field.'

Didier was immediately curious. 'Tell me.'

Q slid Didier's teacup across the table towards him. He pulled Georgia's glass of water forward and pushed his orange juice to the side.

'There is a triangle. Players number 7, 10 and 11, they play as a unit. 7 and 10 are on the right. They pass to each other.' Q placed a finger on the glass of orange juice. 'Number 10 thinks he is the star of the team and he wants to let everybody know that.'

Didier did not hesitate. 'He is our friend.' His face froze into a hard mask. His eyes narrowed. He was not so charming now. 'We spend a lot of time together.'

Q said coolly, 'I can't see that on the pitch.' He was now watching Didier as intently as he dared. 'I saw him shake hands with number 7 during the game. I'm an outsider. I'm just watching the game, the drama, the personalities, the skills. 7 and 10 were at the club before Nicolas. They play for each other. They want him to fail, to be dropped. Number 10 thinks he is the playmaker.'

'Number 15 is.' Didier sat up slightly. He was listening very carefully. His seductive-looking mobile phone was lying on the wooden table in front of them. It rang, wanting attention. He switched it off.

Q shook his head. 'The whole team, every time they get the ball, they are looking for number 10. On the right-hand side Nicolas never gets the ball. So he moves over to the left, goes deep. Now number 11.' Q moved the teacup to the left. He looked straight into Didier's eyes. 'Nicolas has to run into midfield sometimes as far as the halfway line to get the ball from him. He gets it, plays a one-two with number 11, who then runs up the field.' Q pushed the glass of water forward. 'And knocks it to number 7.' Q picked up Didier's saucer and placed it in the formation on the table. 'Sometimes he kicks it over Nicolas's head,' he said, touching the saucer. 'To number 7. Who is now in the centre forward role. So now Nicolas is out of position. When numbers 7 and 10 get the ball, who do they look for? Number 11, not Nicolas. So you see Nicolas is in a difficult situation.'

Q put the cup on to the saucer and pushed it towards Didier. 'The image you get in the press is that it is all about money, that he has no passion for the game,' said Q casually. 'What I saw today is a young man who wants to play. Maybe he was playing for his parents, but either way he was playing. If you ask me, I don't think he is ruthless enough.'

'I have told Nicolas that if he is not happy with the quality of the balls he is getting he should say so.' Didier's tone was mellow.

'You are a businessman,' said Q forcefully. 'You have to be ruthless in the boardroom. Nicolas has to do that on the pitch. He is not a selfish player. There were times when he got into the box and could have shot, but he slipped the ball to another player and waited for the return. But it never came. He passes to them but they don't pass to him. He wants to play with them but they want him to look bad. Instead of raising their game to his standard they are trying to drag him down. The good thing is the fans can see he is trying. They love him, they want him to score. It is as if they are waiting for a new baby to be born. When he came off, they booed and some of them got up and left the stadium.'

Didier raised the cup to his lips and took a sip of tea, his good-natured eyes alertly watching Q. 'Claude told Nicolas that whatever he does he must remember that football is an individual sport.'

Q sighed. 'Nicolas is on his own out there. He has to be more ruthless on the pitch if he is going to score in that team, playing the way they do. It is going to have to be an individual goal. Or he is going to have to stay in his central position like

Ronaldo and say he is not moving and let number 7 drop deeper. The fans can see what is happening.' Q was positive. 'Nicolas is really trying, really working hard. He has a marker from the other side on him, who he is trying to lose, and his own team is making him play out of position. He is dangerous in the box, not outside it. But the fact that he is dropping deep means he wants to play. When he was taken off, he showed a lot of character. He didn't complain. He sat on the bench and watched the game. Today was a turning point for Nicolas, he played well and won a lot of hearts. Tell the Unknown Soldier to be more ruthless. Watch the video of the game. You'll see Nicolas's runs and what I mean about 7, 10 and 11.'

Didier said in his cool, reasonable voice, 'When number 11 scored the goal the whole team hugged each other. I have never seen that before.' He smiled. 'I think things are changing.'

'Yes, but number 11 scored from a cross, from number 10, I think. Nicolas is the star, the one we have all come to see. In a Hollywood movie the star is the one who carries the film. Nicolas has to develop another side of his game, he has to pick it up and dictate it, even if it means scoring from the halfway line. You know, a friend told me once that it is silly giving a ball to a guy who cannot juggle. You are being cruel. Right now, unless the team changes and plays with Nicolas, it is silly for him to expect them to see his runs. He has to go it alone. Then they will change.'

'Do you want to meet Nicolas?' asked Didier sincerely. His voice was quiet, the voice he used for those he trusted.

'No. Let him enjoy his time with your parents. I'm sorry, I should let you go and see your parents. You know, the funny thing is that the English papers go all around the world. So anything Nicolas did there was known, talked about. In England we hear nothing about Spanish teams. But I am sure the rest of the continent and world knows what is happening.'

'Don't worry about that,' said Didier, picking up his mobile phone. 'Like you, we are using the Internet. The site is nearly ready: www.nicolasanelka.net,' he said with a grin.

'Nicolas is now the king of Madrid. He scored a big goal today. This match was the turning point, now the goals will come.'

'Yes.' Didier switched on his phone. 'We have time and things will get better. We like Spain, we shall do well here. Give me a call before you leave tomorrow.'

Episode 11

Q rang Didier Anelka's mobile phone.

'Didier, it is Q.'

'Hi, Q.'

'I'm going to the airport now.'

'It was very nice meeting you. I hope that one day we can meet . . .' Didier paused.

Q finished off the sentence. 'Again.'

'Yes,' replied Didier. 'Again. Say hello to your mother. I hope you have a nice flight back to London. I am sorry you are going to miss the lovely weather in Madrid.'

Q looked towards the hotel window. The sun was shining. 'What are you going to do today?'

'I am going to school,' said Didier. 'For my Spanish lesson. Then I am going to spend the afternoon with my parents and my brother. We will go for a walk.'

To be continued . . .

Fade to black.

IV

Les Coaches

21

The French Evolutionary: Arsène Wenger

AMY LAWRENCE

Imagine being voted World Player of the Year. Imagine the sense of achievement, the dizzying feeling of reaching the absolute pinnacle of a sport which fascinates every race known to man. Imagine attending a beautiful, baroque awards ceremony in Milan where a zillion pounds' worth of football icons wear dapper suits on their backs and dazzling women on their arms, the cameras roll, and the honour is yours. In 1995, when George Weah strolled up to collect the highest accolade the biggest game on earth bestows upon an individual, imagine the peculiar vibration in the air when he confessed he didn't want it.

International football's glitterati looked at one another and shifted uncomfortably in their seats. The Liberian gently explained that somebody else deserved it more than he. More squirming in the stalls and suspicious glances. He insisted upon giving the award to his mentor, his father figure, the man who made him. He beckoned a tall, lean, unassuming Frenchman, who had flown over from his post in Japan, on to the stage in order to present the trophy. Weah believed this was the only way he could express his thanks to Arsène Wenger.

The watching legends and hangers-on clapped benevolently to disguise the general bafflement. Most of them had no idea why this guy up there cautiously cradling the prize and squinting under the spotlight was so special. Wenger looked humbled, flabbergasted, awkward, blinking bashfully behind his spectacles.

Outside France, where Wenger had developed Weah, his own ideas and an entire football club at Monaco, and Japan, where he became a legend for his work at Grampus Eight, he was not what you would call an influential voice in the football world.

Nowadays he's probably just as famous as Weah. It is necessary to spend time with a publicly recognised person to appreciate quite how weird fame is. This business of strangers randomly professing anything on the emotional spectrum from love to hate takes some getting used to. For someone who shies from celebrity, Wenger copes remarkably well. In fact he is amazingly pleasant to strangers. It would be typical of him to notice that the bizarre dynamic when admirer meets admired can make the well-wisher feel even more uneasy than he does. So he will make a joke or throw in some gratitude of his own. And as if by magic, anxiety is soothed by a mood of effortless warmth.

It is in his nature to take what he calls a 'tolerant view' of other people. The roots of this can be found in his childhood in Alsace. Being born near the border with Germany and educated by a French system opened his mind from a young age. 'When you have only one cultural influence you think that is the only right way of doing things, but I have always lived with the fact that the truth is not really one unique way,' he opines in those wise tones to which you feel it would be stupid not to listen.

The young Arsène, when he wasn't observing and absorbing what was going on around him, was obsessed with playing football. Contented as he was chasing a ball round the streets and turning out for his village team, he wanted more. 'During my youth I never had any coaching, and the first time I met a coach I felt straight away that he made me improve,' he recalls. Then he smiles to himself and arches an eyebrow. 'He must have been good.'

Most kids would simply feel pleased with themselves to have mastered a new trick. The ever-curious Arsène, however, asked himself how it happened. Why? It was a simple enough equation: aspiring player plus coach's advice equals better player. Analysing the nature of his improvement left him even more intoxicated by the game, and the seeds of his fascination with coaching were sown. By his mid-twenties he was a coaching instructor, teaching men far older than himself how to run a team. Considering how dearly he craved a life in football, he chose his niche well: his playing career, culminating in a handful of appearances at centre back in Strasbourg's first team, never quite took off.

After two decades as a professional coach, Wenger has come to the conclusion that the greatest coach in the world is the game itself. His reasons are mind-bogglingly scientific. 'Football has many billion different situations but there are some analogical ones. When a player makes a mistake he tells his brain: "I have made a mistake – why?" He works out what he should have done instead and stores it in his memory. So if he meets an almost identical situation his memory opens the door and tells him: "You have met this situation before and you lost the ball, so this time you have to change it." It's basically called experience, and using it is the sign of a big player.' As he spells it out, the intellectual thrill of the theory animates him so much he is almost up and out of his cosy chair.

Softly, softly, slowly perceiving and perusing, Wenger refined his ideas as he ascended the coaching hierarchy. First with the Strasbourg youth team, then as assistant manager at Cannes before taking full control of Nancy. Before long, Monaco – an unusual club, funded by its royal supporters in the opulent principality, and home to deliberately minimalist crowds so as not to disturb the Rolexed residents – were alerted to this blossoming talent and offered him a three-year contract. He didn't sign. He wasn't convinced he was cut out for big-time management and felt it prudent to give himself a trial period. 'I thought if I wasn't good enough I could go back to what I'd been doing before. I was just happy teaching football, being involved on a daily basis. It was not my obsession at all to be in the spotlight.' A few months later, though, the contract was sealed.

As it happens, Wenger became the longest-serving manager in the club's history in an era during which Monaco were transformed. In his first season they claimed the French Championship. From that moment, the rivalry with Olympique Marseille, the giants from along the Riviera, kicked in hard. It was a bruising collision course, especially from Monaco's point of view, because their heavyweight opponents put lead in their gloves. Marseille, to put it bluntly, were corrupt. Their interpretation of fair play was poisoned by greed and dishonesty and games were later proved to have been bought. 'We had a very difficult time because we fought against people who didn't use regular methods,' says Wenger. 'You cannot accept corruption because it is killing sport – look at how it has killed boxing. I am sure we would have won more trophies in normal circumstances, and it makes me sad because Monaco will never get those titles back.'

The antidote to that frustration came in Europe, where his team arrived as a new force on the continental stage, sailing to a succession of semi-finals and a Cup-Winners' Cup final. Not bad going for a team which had never before negotiated the first round. Wenger's acquisition of renowned gems like Jürgen Klinsmann and Glenn Hoddle, coupled with the rough diamonds he polished like George Weah, Lilian Thuram and Emmanuel Petit, began to turn heads outside his native France. Bayern Munich soon came calling. Monaco urged him to stay and he reluctantly agreed to one more year at the Stade Louis II. To have left them in the lurch without a replacement would have pricked at his sense of responsibility.

Mistake. Five games into the new season (three defeats and a couple of draws), he was fired. His only regret is that he did not leave in the first place. He is not a fan of the last year of a contract: 'If the club feels it has no future with you, at the first bad period you are out.' Whatever the circumstances,

Wenger's marriage to Monaco had reached its seven year itch. 'It's a difficult job, because there are no supporters, and after seven years of pushing the team I was quite exhausted,' he sighs.

As options go, switching from the establishment of Bayern Munich to the unknown of Nagoya represents an alarming quantum leap. For Grampus Eight, aware that the evolution of the J-League depended on importing experienced figureheads, Wenger was the chosen one. They invited him to Japan for a one-week voyage of discovery and he promised the club's officials that he would give them an answer two weeks later. At the eleventh hour he was still undecided. He had promised to contact them before midnight, but as he walked to the phone in his Mediterranean apartment he was still mentally flipping a coin. Call made, he returned to his girl-friend, Annie. 'What did you do?' she asked.

'I said yes.'

His decision owed much to that multicultural intrigue he has carried with him since his childhood in Alsace. 'I didn't want to stay in France. At all. I wanted to do something else, to extend myself. If I was going to face a challenge, I thought I may as well face an entire challenge, not half of one. Football-wise it was a huge step because it was looked upon as a regression for me. But to go to a club at the bottom of the League would show me what I was made of, because I was used to working with stars at Monaco. As a human being, I thought, I cannot become weaker, only stronger. People in France wondered what I was doing going to Japan, just making money or taking it easy,' he says, with a shake of the head as subtle as it is loaded.

The football experience was one to cherish as once again he transformed an ordinary team into winners and was immediately named Japan's manager of the year. The personal experience was something else. Isolated from family and friends, ensconced in an alien culture with little distraction from the drive for success, his obsession for the game naturally intensified. Away from football he sometimes felt low. 'You feel that impossibility to touch back to your roots. That looks endless when you can't do it,' he remembers, staring into the middle distance. 'What you miss in Europe slowly drifts away.'

He nearly stayed for ever. After a couple of years in which he became increasingly submerged in the Japanese spirit, he reached a turning point. His girlfriend was pregnant and he had to decide whether to return or to bring his family to Asia. A timely invitation from his friend David Dein, vice-chairman of Arsenal Football Club, tipped the balance in favour of the West.

Returning to Europe, he brought with him profound impressions of Japanese culture. There are not many countries in the world where you could be enlightened by life in a hotel lobby. Wenger, passing the time before a match, regularly found himself transfixed by people around him going about their day. Girls arranged flowers as if it was the most sensitive of art forms, cleaners picked up paper from the ground as if it was an endangered species. 'You learn to respect the dedication of everybody to what they do. You think you are doing your job well, and then when you see them work you think you are a small man. They treat a leaf from a tree like a human being. With respect. It's an amazing experience.'

From respect to resistance in one fell swoop. 'Arsène who?' scoffed the English newspaper headlines with snotty condescension when his name emerged for the situation vacant at Arsenal. They had expected a familiar name like Johan Cruyff or Bobby Robson. What, they wondered, could a Frenchman working in Japan possibly offer English football? Generously, they gave him a small benefit of the doubt merely because Glenn Hoddle gave him a positive reference and they had heard of him, at least. *Bienvenu*, Monsieur Wenger. *Bonne chance*.

If Japan had been a culture shock, suddenly this urbane, open-minded, multicultural individual was confronted with an island mentality perhaps even more forbidding. To be frank, a frightening number of Englishmen don't like foreigners and aren't very subtle about it. They are blinkered by an illusion that the English way is the only way. Wenger, rather than shrinking from this xenophobic attitude, endeavoured to understand it. 'This phenomenon is more emphatic on an island because historically people lived in a more isolated way. England has a strong identity based on a pure culture, so, of course, they sometimes mistrust foreign influences. They think it might kill what makes their identity. It's understandable. I was not upset by people wondering who I was – that is absolutely normal.'

What wasn't normal, though, were the methods used to undermine him. He had been in London only a few weeks when a poisonous rumour campaign spread malicious allegations about his private life. Before long the swirling whispers threatened to turn into a cyclone, and with speculation about his likely resignation sweeping like wildfire and the media vultures circling Highbury's marble halls, Wenger knew he had to defeat this ill wind before it engulfed him and his new club. With unimaginably cool composure, he dared his detractors to tell him what skeletons were supposed to be in his cupboard. Print it. Say it. Try it. Anything false, and we go straight to court.

His tactics were both brilliant and brave. The rumour-mongers, unsurprisingly, fell silent. The only shame was that they escaped any kind of punishment for the hurt they caused.

Many observers who had been ready to bid Wenger *bon voyage* were forced to have a rethink. They couldn't help but respect his dignity. As time passed they became more and more impressed with the man, his manners and his management. The impact he had on his club was mesmerising to watch. People were drawn to the new adventure evident in a team traditionally nicknamed 'Boring, boring Arsenal' and intrigued by the sophisticated approach which would shake the very foundations of English football. Perceptions of club and boss were virtually turned upside down.

In his first season back on European soil he took the opportunity to visit the game's showpiece, the European Cup final,
in Amsterdam. He was running late, so David Dein found
himself filling in a hotel form on behalf of his manager. 'Name:
Arsène Wenger. Address: c/o Arsenal Football Club. Profession:
Miracle worker.' Dein didn't have to wait too long to see that
he had not excessively exaggerated.

The reincarnation of Arsenal was sudden and sensational.
Wenger introduced a modern regime of stretching exercises,
specialist diets and vitamin supplements designed to help the
players scale new physical peaks. He employed masseurs and
men to manipulate spines. It wasn't rocket science, but it
had veterans playing like souped-up teenagers. Steve Bould
reckoned it added two years on to his career. Paul Merson
famously symbolised the Wenger effect by saying that he gave
the team 'unbelievable belief'.

Remember what he was up against. At that time, for an
English footballer to even consider eating broccoli was out-
landish. But hardened British players responded to Wenger
because he didn't storm in and bombard them with orders.
He listened, got to know everybody and built bridges across
which to transport his ideas. The bonds he develops with his
players tend to have more of the human touch than most
of the working relationships found at football clubs. For
example, when Arsenal reached the FA Cup final and the
boys wanted to pop open champagne on the coach back to
London, Wenger requested that they wait until they were
back because Tony Adams, a recovering alcoholic, also deserved
an enjoyable ride home.

The second phase of Arsenal's French revolution took
the form of signings hand-picked by Wenger to strengthen
specific weaknesses in the team. Forming a midfield axis
with Patrick Vieira, whom he prised from the shadows at AC
Milan, and Emmanuel Petit, whom he had raised at Monaco,
was a masterstroke. He made it sound so logical: one is right-
footed, the other left; one prefers short prompts, the other
long passes. Beneath his reasoning, though, lies the heart of a

gambler. Other key signings, like Marc Overmars and Kanu, arrived with fitness question-marks and represented significant risks. On both occasions, though, his hunch paid off, and with interest.

To become the first foreign manager to win the Championship in a country inherently sceptical of outsiders was a phenomenal achievement. Two weeks later, Wenger doubled the joy by leading his team to victory in the FA Cup final. The summer of 1998 was one long smile. As the first coach in the history of French football to make a major success of himself abroad, he went home to watch his compatriots win the World Cup. And there, in the twenty-two, were Lilian Thuram and Thierry Henry, prodigies from his Monaco days, and Patrick Vieira and Manu Petit, so crucial to his success at Arsenal. 'When they combined to finish like that for the third goal it was amazing,' he beams.

'It was a massive victory for France. France has a mixed history, and the most recent is a history of losing. Also, the country was exploding a little bit with different tribes of immigrants. The feeling was that the country would go bankrupt and die with so many of them, then suddenly you win the World Cup with a team made up predominantly of immigrants. It changed the whole political process. It gave the country the feeling they could win with different people from different countries mixed together.' Back in England, the morning after France–Brazil, one newspaper printed a front-page photograph of Petit and Vieira embracing under the headline: 'ARSENAL WON THE WORLD CUP!'

Wenger says he is a winning animal. 'You feel you have more chance of winning if you concentrate every part of your energy on how to win,' he muses. 'If you lose a day by not concentrating on it, you feel guilty. The years and the years and the years teach you that every small detail can make you win or lose. It is like somebody who takes drugs. He just thinks of taking drugs and slowly forgets his own life.'

A high-level football manager can seldom afford to switch off. So, when an old friend recommends a young African striker playing in the Cameroonian league, Wenger phones every Monday for six months to check on the boy's progress before taking him on. That's what he did with George Weah.

Wenger concedes that his life has improved since he started to appreciate how to relax. So clever is he at guarding his privacy that quite how he relaxes nobody knows for sure. Because he was once seen walking his dog on Totteridge Common, it is assumed that dog-walking tops his list of hobbies. Because he is French, it is supposed that he enjoys wine. Because he is seldom out with his wife and daughter, it is wondered whether they even exist. The voyeurs desperate for an insight into the person behind the professional remain frustrated. They merely imagine him studying a mountain of football videos.

The game holds Wenger in endless thrall. The chase for the winning fix never ceases. The complexities to be unravelled never ease. Doesn't he ever enjoy a moment when the simple beauty of the game transcends all those complications? 'That's a miracle,' he replies, in wonder. 'It happens when you feel your team is a really happy unit playing the game, enjoying it, not distracted by any selfishness or anxiety. It might happen if the team is 3–0 up and everybody is up behind them; they express themselves, they respect the game. That's it. Sometimes it lasts a minute or two. It's so short. But you would battle for ever to experience it again.'

22

The Right Man: Aimé Jacquet

PHILIPPE TOURNON

Aimé Jacquet wouldn't like it. He'd protest, he'd certainly complain, but that wouldn't alter the facts: on 12 July 1998 his name went down in French history books.

Because he is the man who gave French football its first World Championship, it is thanks to him that a tremendous wave of joy suddenly washed over the country. It is he who brought the entire population out on to the streets, in the largest cities and the tiniest hamlets. Aimé Jacquet swelled French hearts, shook the French from their easy platitudes and their smugness, to the extent that he precipitated a fraternal multiethnic celebration on the streets that left extremists of all hues speechless. But it is also due to the man himself, his life's journey, his values, his way of living which, through the prism of this astounding sporting triumph, fired everybody's imagination and drew the veil from their eyes.

As a result the World Cup-winning coach was deluged by torrent upon torrent of affection, recognition and devotion, all the more impassioned since a few months earlier there had been nothing but suspicion, scepticism and derision for the man France's only daily sports paper, viscerally opposed to him, grudgingly tried to pass off as, at best, a 'plodder'.

And then, suddenly, the true worth of Jacquet's achievements throughout his tenure as national coach – through discipline, dogged perseverance, efficiency and hard work –

was revealed and acknowledged. Suddenly there it was, illuminated by the light of this World Cup victory, the magisterial professional skills and moral uprightness of an outstanding technician whom nothing or nobody could distract from the route he had mapped out.

Many were to regret that they had not from the start had faith in the man whose first name seemed suddenly so apt – '*aimé*' means 'loved'. Indeed, in the thousands of letters, faxes and messages which streamed into the headquarters of the French Football Federation and the training centre at Clairefontaine all through the summer of 1998, there was one word that often appeared alongside the 'thank yous' and the 'well dones': 'sorry'.

Sorry to have doubted. Sorry not to have understood what was being created. Sorry . . . It was perhaps this contrition that most moved the boss of Les Bleus after all he had had to endure during the previous four years. Four years during which results were overwhelmingly in his favour – three defeats in fifty-three matches, and a semi-final at Euro '96 in England – and during which all the voices that counted, spearheaded by that of Michel Platini, tirelessly reiterated their confidence in the coach, the man and his methods.

His track record, and the trophies he had gathered as both player and club coach, should have been enough to spare Aimé Jacquet all these accusations, the perverse questioning of his working methods and of the technical validity of his approach. Judge for yourself: his playing career boasted five French Championships (1964, 1967, 1968, 1969, 1970), two French Cups (1968, 1970), two caps for France A, all in the green strip of St Etienne. His successes as director of football with the Girondins of Bordeaux were almost as impressive: three First Division Championships (1984, 1985, 1987), two French Cups (1986, 1987), and a place in Europe every year without fail (including two appearances in the Champions Cup semi-finals) during his nine-year tenure in the Gironde.

Yet results past and present, the unfailing support of those who really matter within French national football, all of this was apparently an irrelevance to a small handful of journalists from the Paris press who had never warmed to Jacquet. These commentators praised, or more often damned, Les Bleus' coach entirely according to their own whims, fantasies or pet theories of the moment.

For the record: Aimé Jacquet inherited and scrupulously adhered to a number of extremely simple values and virtues, from his rural upbringing, from his parents, butchers in Sail-sous-Couzan, a small town in the Monts du Forez area of central France, and from the time spent in the world of 'fraternity and solidarity' in the factory where he worked for a few years as a machine-tool operator before opting for football and St Etienne – against the advice of his parents. They were: honesty, humility, respect for others and hard work.

These were also the very things, so integral to the man and to his approach, that were shamefully twisted and mis-represented as he worked with the national team. However much he was at pains to explain and justify his approach, it elicited only sour commentaries and derision which increased in intensity as the months went by, so much so that there was a risk that as Les Bleus went into their 'home' World Cup, it would be amid an atmosphere of incredible hostility.

'I thought, obviously naïvely,' Jacquet explains, 'that from January 1998 the knives would be put away and that a sort of peace of the brave would reign. I hoped that, away from the unfounded and sterile polemics, every French man and woman would get behind the French team before the tournament began. In reality, what happened was that Les Bleus were forced to prove themselves on the pitch. To prove that they truly were the talented performers, hungry for victory, that I'd been telling people about for ages. It was only then that the disinformation was seen for what it was and the French finally got squarely behind their team.'

Although his methods proved to be justified, and many months have now gone by, for Aimé Jacquet this dis-information is still a bitter pill to swallow; something that perhaps one day he will forget, but will never forgive. 'They wanted to destroy me, to blacken my name. As there was no way to validly attack the coach or the results, instead they went for the man. They tried to paint me as an unskilled bumpkin, not up to the job. It's contemptible.'

Jacquet's knock-out win was not for himself, but 'for football, footballers and for the backroom staff'. To listen to him you would think that his only merit was to have been in the right place to carry on the work previously entrusted, with varying degrees of success, to Georges Boulogne, Michel Hidalgo, Henri Michel and Gérard Houllier – all natural leaders of a tightly focused national technical strategy which is often cited as a model, and which, over the course of the last thirty years, has made French football among the best in the world.

'I carried out my task well.' That is all the coach of the world champions has to say these days. He continues to astound by his simplicity, his modesty and his genuineness. At peace once again, he now holds the eminent post of national technical director, a position that allows him to put back into grassroots and élite football everything the game taught him throughout his career as a player with St Etienne and as a conspicuously successful coach with Lyon and Bordeaux.

You could easily imagine there being over a hundred Aimé Jacquet stadiums in France today. His image and his fame could have earned him a substantial sum from advertising contracts. He refused them all. He involves himself with only two causes which are especially close to his heart. The first project is to aid elderly people in hospital, working with a foundation led by Bernadette Chirac, wife of the president of the French Republic. 'We don't have the right to leave 100,000 elderly people sidelined. The elderly are our memory and our wisdom. It's not acceptable for them to end their days isolated, uncared for. It's a question of dignity, our dignity as well as theirs.' His almost pathological discretion prevents him from adding that his wife, too, is heavily committed to this cause: Martine Jacquet has worked for many years assisting elderly people in difficulty.

The second is vocational training, from which he himself benefited, and which opened up to him the road to the factory and to a blue-collar world he has never forgotten. 'It's rubbish to require all youngsters to continue with their traditional studies up to the *baccalauréat**. First of all, because not everybody is capable of reaching the standard, and also because many skills that are in high demand can be learned very early through training and apprenticeships. We need to boost the image of vocational training and stop youngsters from thinking that it's just going to lead them to working in a garage.' He is incorrigible!

When you hear Aimé Jacquet speak it is little wonder that the whole French nation, with the shocking pre-World Cup misapprehensions now firmly in the past, can't help but fall in love with a man who is so out of step with the times, but at the same time so close to the deep-seated character of the French people: a man who has given them so much pleasure.

---

*The French school-leaving certificate required for university entrance.

23

From Teaching to Coaching: Gérard Houllier

ANDY THOMPSON

For forty years the philosophy of Liverpool Football Club – their raison d'être, their public image, the whole idea of the 'Liverpool way' – was synonymous with one man: Bill Shankly. Paisley, Fagan, Dalglish, Souness and Evans all won trophies, but they were still cast as disciples of the great man. Despite the very public schism between Shankly and the club following his resignation back in 1974, his presence towered over the club, partially obscured by the continued achievements of his successors in the seventies and eighties but ever more apparent through the mediocrity of the nineties.

It didn't help that as Liverpool's fortunes dwindled, both Souness and Evans took to publicly invoking the Shankly spirit to try to ward off the evil magic of teams who were quite simply better organised and better motivated, which, ironically, had been the greatest strengths of Shankly's Liverpool. Just as Drake's drum would beat itself should the nation be in peril, Liverpool seemed to be enveloped in this unshakeable faith that no matter what, they were still Shankly's children; that Liverpool's place on high was assured for ever.

Like Leeds post-Revie and Manchester United post-Busby. The whole process took longer at Liverpool, but the inexorable decline of the most successful team in the land was much more than a rumour by the time, in 1998, the Liverpool board finally looked outward rather than upward for salvation.

To many, in hiring Frenchman Gérard Houllier they looked far further outward than suited the very British persona of what had remained, in the north at least, a very British game. In appointing a French manager, Liverpool didn't so much buck a trend as tear their traditional fabric asunder. And that's a lot of traditional fabric. London had foreign managers, but these were the very teams that Shankly himself famously described as 'Drury Lane fan dancers'. Besides the fact that for every Arsène Wenger there was a Christian Gross waiting in the wings, it just wasn't the Liverpool way.

That no one seemed to have heard of Gérard Houllier only made matters worse. If Liverpool were going to go down the continental road, then surely a foreign coach of international standing was a must for a club like theirs? The fact that they got one, the fact that Liverpool were now under the direction of the man who had masterminded the infrastructure behind the most unlikely of recent World Cup victories, completely escaped England's allegedly football-mad public.

Mainly because England's allegedly football-mad public, the perfect microcosm of British society as a whole, has this unique way of not knowing things. Especially foreign things. Football, from boardroom level through to the supporters and the media, seems to suffer from a benign jingoism; abroad has always been dealt with on a strictly need-to-know basis. People rejoiced in Ossie's 'Tottingham' and Jan's Scouse accent because they constituted a comforting confirmation that Johnny Foreigner, deep down, wanted to walk like us, talk like us.

Which made the whole nineties concept of them piling over here trying to teach us to play football less than welcome. Except that they're not. Especially not Gérard Houllier. Maybe his original experience of Liverpool, as a school-teacher thirty years previously, left its mark, but his simple assessment of his role is respectful of Liverpool's strong tradition, despite the obvious need to move on from the tunnel vision of the last decade. 'I came here to work and not to give lessons. I came to be part of the life of the club and of the town, and to give my best.'

It's a down-to-earth and straight-down-the line approach that is echoed in the refreshingly unreverential way in which Houllier has set about managing the club that has overawed so many, both inside and out. Best of all, Gérard Houllier hardly ever mentions Shankly. For the first time since December 1959, Liverpool have a man unconcerned with what has gone before. He is aware of Liverpool's history. Shankly, Paisley and the Liverpool greats are in no way about to be airbrushed out of the picture in the manner of Stalin, but Houllier has successfully drawn a line under the past by singlemindedly looking to the future.

Given the nature of Houllier's appointment, his unfamiliarity with the club and the town and their unfamiliarity with him, he could have been forgiven for making the obvious links with the club's glorious past to ease him into the job. That he taught in Liverpool for a year is well documented, but Gérard Houllier has never used that to invent some sort of spurious Gallic–Scouse bond. Resolutely his own man, he openly admits that his biggest influence as a coach was his first coach's brother-in-law, not Bill Shankly. Hardly the stuff of the traditional Liverpool folklore in which the Anfield secret was passed by word of mouth from generation to generation, Beowulf style.

Liverpool's current manager has little time for any comparisons with former managers and no truck with the idea that his time on Merseyside, and on the Kop, in the late sixties has given him some sort of mystical connection with Liverpool's favourite son. 'As a manager you have to be true to yourself. I don't manage like Walter Smith, I don't manage like George Graham, I don't manage like Arsène Wenger. My experience and my knowledge is my own. The way Bill Shankly did things, what he said and the decisions he made, appealed to me, but I wouldn't say that they inspired me.'

The way in which Houllier has gone about inspiring the club is something he has achieved, initially at least, despite

Liverpool. For having got their man, having successfully gained the services of the technical director of the world champions, Liverpool then proceeded to make him a co-manager. It was a decision that baffled and amused a nation and embarrassed loyal supporters who deserved better – and there was no more loyal a supporter than Roy Evans.

It wasn't working out with Evans at the helm; it just wasn't happening for him or the team, and he had to go. It was that simple. Except that the Liverpool board, consolidating their comical ineptitude in the painful, drawn-out departure of Graeme Souness, managed to create an even more painful and drawn-out departure for Roy Evans. Co-managers? It was like trying to make a footballer a better player by giving him an extra leg. The goings-on at Liverpool were becoming pure theatre: the 'Drury Lane fan dancers' tag seemed to have boomeranged its way back to Anfield.

That Gérard Houllier's still-brief tenure at Liverpool has successfully reversed the club's slide both on and off the field is testimony not only to his own self-belief but also to a new-found belief in him among players and supporters alike. Any manager will be judged ultimately on results, but Houllier's changes go far, far deeper than the creation of a greater resolve on the field of play. Houllier himself says that the role of the modern manager 'has far less to do with tactics' than ever before, and this is supported by a tangible feeling of excitement in Liverpool itself that has been absent for years. Liverpool, above all other cities in England, is football mad. Something big is happening. The whingers and the boo-boys who have tarnished Liverpool's fanatical support in recent seasons have gone back to watching Everton or whatever. The local radio phone-ins can no longer rouse the rabble to spout their ill-thought-out comments about Houllier's incompatibility with the club. 'Evolution not revolution' has been his only piece of memorable rhetoric, but it has so much more reson-ance than the carping of all the empty vessels who delight in taking cheap shots at easy targets.

Houllier's capable handling of the various slings and arrows

of the English game is testimony not only to his self-belief
but also to an open-armed welcome of a true test of his
managerial ability. In an age in which the pressures of high-
level football management far exceed the manager's traditional
role, Houllier has adapted to the new multifaceted nature of
the job with ease, relishing the mental challenges of piloting
a multimillion-pound business. There are those who lament
the passing of the halcyon days when the manager simply
managed, but Houllier isn't one of them: 'Every manager
would acknowledge that it was easier to manage then. But
because it's different now, because it is more complicated, you
can turn it the other way round – it's more exciting. From an
intellectual point of view, and from a psychological point of
view, it's better to be confronted by these problems than to
have a situation where you ask a player to do something and
he just does it.'

So how did Liverpool get someone like Gérard Houllier to
fight their corner? What prompted a man at the pinnacle of
his triumph in his own country to uproot and move abroad?
Back in 1969, Houllier actively chose Liverpool ahead of
England's capital and its other more celebrated centres of
learning. Then as now, he came to Liverpool for its football,
but his return wasn't prompted by anything so romantic as
a sense of destiny, more by an acknowledgement that he
had reached the top of the game in France and that his next
challenge would have to be elsewhere.

'I was fifty; I could have kept my position [as technical
director] until I was sixty and then retired, but I wanted to go
back into team management; as technical director I was in
charge of several teams, but I wanted to deal with a side on
a daily basis, even with all the problems that entails. Even
though I was in the top position I needed to reactivate what
I came into football for, and I knew it had to be outside
France.'

The desire to rediscover the game's more visceral thrills and
to prove oneself once more is a common one in football; the
type who makes a good manager is also the type who just

can't resist a challenge. But the vaulting ambition that has characterised so many of the finest players and managers has all too often ended in a nasty fall from grace, and the bruising English game has taken perverse enjoyment in battering more than its fair share of reputations. Especially foreign ones. Yet it was here that Gérard Houllier, who had nothing to prove to anyone, chose to come. 'I was aware that English football had not always been that kind to foreigners, players and coaches, but as a manager you are always in a no-win situation; you are always going to get a lot of stick from everywhere.'

And giving out stick is what the English seem to do best, nowhere more so than in the nation's media. Although Houllier has not been the victim of the kind of tabloid persecution that blighted the early part of Arsène Wenger's tenure at Arsenal, the English press, or the tabloids at least, haven't really taken to Houllier in the same way as they have to Vialli at Chelsea. But then, Houllier hasn't really taken to them, either, and he is under no illusions as to the peculiar merits of the dreaded back-page exclusive: 'I wouldn't say I was surprised by the English media, but they go on to a point that I had not imagined. There is so much competition between the papers themselves that they're trying to find stories all the time. Five tabloids and five broadsheets every day, and the weekends . . . you don't get that in France, and in France they respect your privacy. Here it's all about stories. They're more concerned about parties and whether players have a drink than the way they play and the tactical approach. Maybe that's where Glenn Hoddle was unfortunate and perhaps not wary enough.'

It all sounds like the voice of experience, but in fact Houllier has largely avoided the wrath of the popular press. Save for the three pages' worth of sour grapes that Paul Ince saw fit to commend to column inches, Houllier has largely been left in peace to get on with his job.

Maybe the tabloid hacks just don't have anything to write about. Houllier, in much the same way as his friend Wenger, is hardly the rent-a-quote kind of football boss the English press like to deal with. He just doesn't play the game. No gimmick, no catchphrase, no temper tantrums on TV. Every response to a question is considered, measured and articulate (and delivered in someone else's language). Not your average Frenchman – at least not in the eyes of your average tabloid reader. Your average Frenchman should be phlegmatic in the Vieira sense, not in the self-possessed, composed one. Gérard Houllier doesn't even look very French. Michel Platini, Dominique Rocheteau, they look how the French are supposed to look, but Houllier's faintly bookish air comes almost as a disappointment to a nation schooled in stereotypes.

If anything, it's a quality that endears Houllier to Liverpool fans, who have long viewed most of the press with suspicion and the *Sun* and the *Star* with outright hatred and contempt. Having endured the almost constant courting of the media by Graeme Souness and then the inability of Roy Evans to cope with the worst excesses of the nation's sports hacks, it's something of a relief to have a man with as much media savvy as Houllier at the helm. Neither courting popularity with journalists nor running scared of loaded questions, Houllier plots a lone course that strikes a chord with the passionately independent city of Liverpool.

There is one comparison to be made with the current manager and Bill Shankly: the way in which they have both harnessed this intense local spirit and channelled its energy through the team. Their methodology is completely different, but the end result is the same. If you want to see it, just look to the pitch and Houllier's side. Players like Stephen Gerrard are visibly upset when losing even the most humdrum of League games. For Gérard Houllier to be able to nurture and channel such a fierce pride and will to succeed in an age of such professional cynicism is a gift indeed. The Liverpool way still exists, but it no longer leads downwards.

V

Les Scandales

24

Scandal on the Canebière

AVI ASSOULY

No matter whether you're in Peking, London, Tokyo, Tel Aviv, Amsterdam or New York, the moment Marseilles is mentioned it is an instant cue for both broad grins and the appearance in conversation of those two mythical letters: OM. Football is suddenly the most important subject in the world to whoever it is you are talking to. You'd be forgiven for believing that when it comes to Marseilles, no matter how beautiful and attractive its sea, sun, the Canebière avenue, Notre Dame de la Garde and Old Port, none of them count when compared to how the club that bears the city's name is doing. There's an old story told in Marseilles that when the city was founded 2,600 years ago, the first building to be raised was the Stade Vélodrome, and the rest of the city was constructed around it.

Olympique Marseille! We've talked endlessly about this legendary club for a century now. The thousands of supporters, the famous coaches, and the dozens of presidents who have all contributed to the greatness of the club that is OM. These days, the *enfant terrible* of French football is the biggest club in France, thanks to its history, its titles and, especially, its turnover. It was the first club to launch its own TV channel (OMTV), its magazine sells 100,000 copies, its 40,000 season ticket-holders descend on the Stade Vélodrome for every match so that they can celebrate, for ninety minutes, an event whose secrets are known only to supporters of OM.

The club is nine-times winner of the French Championship (they were stripped of their tenth title because of scandal on the Canebière) and ten-times holder of the French Cup. It has reached the finals of many a European competition, but most famously and most magnificently, the finals of the greatest European competition of them all: the Champions Cup, which was brought home triumphantly on 26 May 1993 after OM beat the great Italian side AC Milan in Munich.

OM is the only French club to have pulled off this feat, and it's a safe bet that it'll be the only French side entitled to add the words 'Champions of Europe' to its visiting cards. Sadly, though, the euphoria of 26 May 1993 was to be short-lived. That summer the dazzlingly white Olympian strip, so great to wear and so fashionable; that shimmering insignia fashioned of gold and of light, was to tarnish, and the club was to darken the hearts of the whole of Marseilles. The club that had reached Paradise suddenly found the gates of Hell opening to consume it.

That night in Munich saw OM write a golden page in the history of French football. With their 1–0 victory, thanks to a Basile Boli header, OM became the first French club to lift a European trophy, the greatest of them all: the Champions Cup. OM was ecstatic, and readied itself to take on the world in the forthcoming Intercontinental Cup in Tokyo. The club felt themselves to be on the brink of a golden era. Who now could stop Bernard Tapie's OM?

The law, that's who.

The story of the scandal on the Canebière is a dramatic one for the club, for its president, for the players and for all the supporters. The relentless steamroller of the legal system was to destroy everything. The Valenciennes–OM affair became the talk of the summer of 1993 – the talk of the year, in fact.

Six days before their epiphany in Munich, OM had played an unimportant League game at Valenciennes. Can there ever have been a less glamorous end-of-season match than this ill-fated meeting? Valenciennes, lying seventeenth in the League and in danger of relegation, pitted against the Championship leaders who six days later were to defend French national honour in the final of the Champions Cup. It all began that night at a Nungesser ground packed to the rafters. The northern club's fans were keen to see the stars from OM in action, and 18,102 spectators had filed into the venerable stadium. Down on the pitch the Valenciennes Juniors team proudly took to the field, each bearing a giant letter held aloft to spell out the phrase '*Tout Valenciennes avec OM à Munich*' (All Valenciennes supports OM at Munich). It was a festive occasion, and there was no clue that the greatest scandal of the last twenty years was about to unfold.

Come the kick-off, tension was at fever pitch. Valenciennes needed points to avoid relegation; OM didn't want to lose, either – neither the match itself nor any player to an injury that might jeopardise their chances in the forthcoming final. As a result the game was far from pretty, and, in keeping with the pattern of play, striker Allen Boksic opened the scoring for OM. When the whistle blew for half-time, the twenty-two protagonists made their way back to the changing rooms. After the requisite fifteen minutes, the players had still not reappeared. Murmurs began to swirl around the ground. It seemed that the referee was locked in a summit meeting with the home team. After much discussion, the game was resumed and there was no further score. It was a 1–0 victory for OM.

Down in the corridors leading to the changing rooms a player made his way towards the microphones, but wasn't intending to venture any comments on how the game had gone. Instead he spoke of corruption. The guy was tall, thin, blond and self-assured. He was the Valenciennes sweeper Jacques Glassmann. 'They wanted to buy us off,' he announced to the assembled media. 'I was offered 200,000 francs if I didn't try too hard, and I'm not the only one: approaches were also made to Jorge Burruchaga and Christophe Robert.' Those few words popped the lid off a huge can of worms.

The law was to take its course.

It transpired that Jean-Pierre Bernès, at the time OM's managing director, had asked an OM player, Jean-Jacques Eydelie, to approach the three Valenciennes players to get them to withdraw from their side on match day. But in every sordid business there's always somebody who upsets the applecart, and in this case the wagon-flipper went by the name of Glassmann. The next day the daily sports paper *L'Equipe* was already headlining the story and pointing a hypothetical finger at the Marseilles club's bosses. As far as the National Football League was concerned, there was a rather big 'if' to the allegations. 'Let's wait for the Champions Cup final to be played,' said its president Noël le Graët. 'But if there has been any attempt to alter the course of the League results, I can assure you that Marseille will not be appearing in Europe next season. I promise you that I will spare no efforts to get to the bottom of this affair.' Le Graët was indeed to go all the way. A complaint was filed against a person or persons unknown at the office of the public prosecutor at the Valenciennes District Court. In the meantime, President Le Graët travelled to Munich to share in OM's joy. He even went down to the changing room to congratulate the OM players.

The Marseille players returned home in triumph and the Stade Vélodrome was opened to the public the following day. All the conquering heroes were on show. Three days later, OM played host to Paris St Germain in a Championship decider. OM won the match 3–1, one of the goals again coming from the unstoppable Boli.

Then the committee of inquiry began its work. The law also swung into action. The public prosecutor, Eric de Montgolfier, named an examining magistrate, one Bernard Beffy.

The new season was imminent. The Marseille squad were gathered at their pre-season camp at Font-Romeu. Up in the Pyrenees, at an altitude of over 1,000 metres, the air was pure but the ambience was bizarre. At 2.05 pm on 1 July, the players were just sitting down to eat, when suddenly the dining hall was swamped by twenty police officers. 'We're here on the orders of the examining magistrate to conduct inquiries. We'll give you twenty minutes to finish your meal, and then all the players who were in the Champions Cup-winning squad [around a dozen were present] will have to come with us.' Such were the orders given to club vice-president Jean-Louis Levreau. The players trooped off in pairs, following the police officers, just like petty criminals. Being European champions doesn't buy you preferential treatment. The police and the legal system wanted to discover all there was to know; they were hunting for the smallest clues, the tiniest pieces of information. It was raining at Font-Romeu, but it was only later that we were to learn that the club was being spattered with the ill tidings of scandal. In Paris, prosecutor Eric de Montgolfier appeared on the eight o'clock evening news to explain his actions. In essence he declared, 'I'll scare them out of their silence.' It was certainly true that right from the beginning of the affair one could sense a desire to 'get' OM president Bernard Tapie who, in the worlds of business, sport, and politics, was a man who provoked jealousy.

Television, the medium that he knew best, was also to turn against Tapie because of his repeated denials and the relentless way he tried to use it as a platform. His image was distorted, debased, deformed, demonised. But however much he voiced his outrage, Tapie was a hot item and the media weren't about to let him off the hook. Neither was the law.

The new League season kicked off and the club began to run short of cash. The law was moving at its own pace. The first interrogations took place. Christophe Robert, the Valenciennes midfielder who had been arrested a week earlier, on 24 June, admitted freely that he had indeed received money and volunteered details. Investigators found 250,000 francs in an envelope hidden in his aunt's garden. His wife Marie-Claire, who had picked up the money from the OM players' hotel, also confessed all. Both were charged and released on bail. The Valenciennes–OM affair was taking off, and from now on the number of people charged would snowball.

On 27 June, OM's Jean-Jacques Eydelie was charged with offering bribes and was remanded in custody. The noose was tightening around the club. Still the saga continued: it was hard to believe that what we were hearing was true. In Marseilles, the supporters claimed a conspiracy, pointing the finger at the president of the National Football League. Some of them went so far as to threaten to travel up to Paris and blow up the offices of the French Football Federation. 'They're out to get OM! It's because the club's too strong,' was the sort of thing you overheard down on the Canebière. However, Judge Beffy was unmoved and his investigations continued. The results were electrifying.

The first day of July saw the Argentine striker Jorge Burruchaga, a member of the World Cup-winning Argentina side, charged with receiving bribes. He was allowed to remain at liberty. The system that 'little judge' Beffy was operating soon became apparent. It was a pretty tough approach. He began by bringing charges against the 'artist' footballers, who were pretty fragile. After a day spent in the hands of expert police officers, they would crack. One by one, they confessed. The grip around the neck of Tapie's inner circle was tightening. Finally, it closed around the chief protagonist, the president of OM himself.

At the end of the week, after the interviews with the OM players, Tapie was hit closer to home. His managing director, Jean-Pierre Bernès, was charged with offering bribes, but for the time being was not taken into custody. In the corridors of the Palais de Justice in Valenciennes word was put about that it was now only a question of time. According to a source close to the judge, Bernès was the small fry who would lead the authorities to the big fish. There was a new series of witness hearings and a new investigation was opened: an affair within The Affair. A file was sent to the public prosecutor's department as a result of statements made by Valenciennes coach Boro Primorac. The new investigation centred on the suborning of a witness. Primorac stated to the investigators that 'Bernard Tapie, the president of OM, put it to me that I carry the can for this business in return for a pay-off and the post of coach at Martigues [a Second Division club some 40 kilometres from Marseilles]. I met him on 17 June at his office in Paris.'

It is 12 July. In his detention cell at Valenciennes, Jean-Jacques Eydelie cracks. He writes a letter to the judge. The envelope bears the words: 'Very urgent, very important, personal'. In his letter Eydelie asks the judge to interview him again to hear the important revelations he intends to make.

We were to discover a few months later that while the OM player had been languishing in detention, the police had been leaning on his wife. The results were immediate. Eydelie, understandably enough, didn't want his family put under such pressure, so he cracked and admitted everything. In the office of Judge Beffy, the clerk set his machine rolling and the confession was recorded. 'In reality, I did attempt to bribe three Valenciennes players – Burruchaga, Robert and Glassmann – acting on the instructions of OM managing director Jean-Pierre Bernès'. Eydelie signed the statement and Judge Beffy grinned broadly. The magistrate confided to a close friend that he was almost happy: 'The dénouement is at hand. I've got him, he's going to fall!' Clearly the 'he' in question was Bernard Tapie. The wheels of justice, despite grinding along at their customary slow pace, had managed to unearth the weakness in the evidence and to get at the truth. On 21 July, at the Petit Palais de Justice in Valenciennes, a large room was requisitioned to confront their witnesses with each other. Jean-Pierre Bernès, accused in Eydelie's testimony, didn't flinch: he denied all the accusations. He was set free the next day. However, five days later, Bernès resigned. One by one, Tapie's intimates were recanting. The umbrella was being furled and Tapie was due for a soaking; worse, in fact, a drowning. The next ally to retract was Jack Mellick, the former socialist minister who had flown to Tapie's aid with a cast-iron alibi. He had declared that he had met Tapie on the same day, at the same time and at the same place where the main witness, Valenciennes coach Boro Primorac, claimed to have been talking to him. Better still, Corinne Krajewski, Jack Mellick's parliamentary secretary, who had supplied a *vrai-faux* testimony backing her boss's tale, had sent an urgent letter to the judge. 'What Mellick says concerning where he was and when, is true,' she wrote.

The meticulous police investigation continued, in close collaboration with the examining magistrate. They next turned up in Marseilles, at the OM offices at 441 Avenue du Prado. The search began early in the morning. Files were seized, everybody was questioned. They moved from office to office, and demanded that the safes were opened. The press had been tipped off, and were kicking their heels outside the building. It was discovered that Beffy, the examining magistrate himself, was also present at the scene. At around 9.30 pm the dustbins that had been left outside the club's headquarters were carried back inside. 'Incredible, but true,' exclaimed a journalist from the TV channel France 3, 'they're even rummaging through the dustbins.' No stone was to be left unturned.

28 December 1994: Bernard Tapie and Jean-Pierre Bernès are summoned to appear before the Valenciennes Criminal Court on a matter of offering bribes.

10 February 1995: Bernard Tapie is further charged with attempting to suborn a witness, and is placed under court supervision pending trial. The battle has only just begun.

13 March 1995: The trial at Valenciennes finally gets underway. Jean-Pierre Bernès has changed his lawyer and his tune. Assisted by Maître Gilbert Collard, his new advocate, he offers up a new rationale for what took place. From here on in, Bernès owns up. He admits the attempted bribery, but swears that the enterprise was carried out 'at the behest of President Tapie'. The examining magistrate sends out flurries of demands to the police to make further inquiries and to take sworn statements. He works night and day.

Corinne Krajewski, Mellick's parliamentary secretary, changes her original testimony.

18 March 1995: The former socialist minister Jack Mellick is in turn arrested and held in custody. He, too, retracts his earlier statements. He now swears that he never saw Bernard Tapie. The statements that the prosecutors have been hoping for are in the bag. Tapie is going to fall. Jack Mellick would be given a six-month suspended sentence and two years' ineligibility for public office for the crime of having suborned Corinne Krajewski.

15 May 1995: Mellick appeals.

The entire French and international press trumpet what had now become inevitable.

In the criminal court

The Bosses
Bernard Tapie is sentenced to two years in prison, with one year suspended.
Jean-Pierre Bernès receives a two-year suspended sentence.
The Players
Jean-Jacques Eydelie receives a one-year suspended sentence and a 10,000 franc fine.
Jorge Burruchaga and Christophe and Marie-Christine Robert are sentenced to six months suspended, and fined 5,000 francs each.

23 October 1995: The final *coup de théâtre*. Bernard Tapie confesses that he did in fact meet Boro Primorac on 17 June 1993 at his Paris office. Thus the final piece of the puzzle falls into place. One month later, the Court of Appeal at Douai finally condemns Tapie to two years in prison, with sixteen months suspended, plus ineligibility for public office for three years and a fine of 20,000 francs. In the end Jean-Pierre Bernès is also sentenced to eighteen months suspended and a fine of 15,000 francs.

20 January 1997: The Court of Appeal at Douai rejects Tapie's request to remain at liberty on the eve of the hearing of his appeal. From here on in, matters move quickly. Tapie himself wants to get it over with.

3 February 1997: Tapie turns himself in so his appeal can be heard.

4 February 1997: The appeal is rejected and Tapie remains incarcerated at the Prison de la Santé in Paris.

21 February 1997: To allow easier family access, Bernard Tapie is transferred to the prison at Luynes, near Aix-en-Provence, where he will serve his eight-month term. Confined within the four walls of his cell, he writes his book *Librement* (Freely), which will be published by Plon. In it he tells his side of the story.

Epilogue

Speaking to *L'Equipe* two days after the match at Valenciennes, Tapie had referred to a possible departure from the OM presidency, but only if one condition, one wish, could be met: 'I want to be the first president of OM to leave a happy man.' Sadly, it was not to be the case.

Olympique Marseille, too, were punished and barred from competing in the Champions Cup in 1994. This was to cost them revenues of between 350 and 450 million francs. At the time Tapie declared – and you can't argue with him – 'Forcing OM out of Europe is the same as killing off the club.' OM were also demoted to the Second Division for two seasons. The loss to the club and to its millions of sympathisers was enormous. The heartbroken people of Marseilles were shattered by the actions of the French footballing authorities in bringing to a sickening halt the exploits of the finest club in Europe.

However, the whole business throws up a number of unresolved issues. Was the blanket media coverage accorded to the affair due to the personality of the OM president? If it had been anybody else but Tapie, would the case have aroused such ferocious interest? The answer is clear – it would not. Bernard Tapie's success in politics, business and, of course, sport were beginning to rub too many people up the wrong way. Once he himself had provided the rope with which he would be hanged, his disappearance from these worlds as a result of the goings-on at Valenciennes would hardly occasion any great outpourings of grief.

And then there was OM itself. Champions of France for the fifth consecutive year, champions of Europe, soaring through the rarefied heights of success with insolent regularity; invincible, irreplaceable, leaving slim pickings for the other clubs. Clearly for some it would be very convenient if the club were to be forcibly removed from the top echelon of French football. And here's some food for thought. If, as we now know to be the case, three members of the Valenciennes team had been approached, and money had been passed to some of them with the aim of assuring a Marseille victory, did anyone else know that there were compromised players in the team that day? And why wait until half-time – and especially until OM scored – before making a complaint?

One thing is certain: if, on that night of 20 May 1993, the two teams had played out a goalless draw, we'd have never heard anything of the Valenciennes–OM affair, nor of the 250,000 francs unearthed a month later in somebody's auntie's garden in Périgueux, a sum of money that pales into insignificance compared to the stakes involved in a European competition.

But history teaches us that great clubs never die. By late 1999, OM had carried their battle on into the second stage of the Champions League, and in the preliminary stage the team led by Robert Pires beat the defending champions, David Beckham's Manchester United, at the Stade Vélodrome. Yet another feat already inscribed in the annals of the club's history. The processes of evolution and revolution continue apace during the club's centenary year. Roland Courbis has resigned, to be replaced by OM's fifty-ninth coach: Bernard Casoni, who was wearing OM's white strip on that famous day in 1993 against AC Milan.

Bernard Tapie, the leading player in this extended soap opera, is once more getting himself talked about. But that's just the type of man he is. Tapie has become an actor, and has already featured in two films directed by the renowned Claude Lelouch. Every night at the Théâtre de Paris, 1,200 ticket-holders pack out the venue to cheer OM's former president in the role of McMurphy in *One Flew Over the Cuckoo's Nest*, the play by Dale Wessermann. The Parisian critics are amazed: Tapie, in the leading role, proves himself to be a fine performer. Jack Nicholson had better look to his laurels!

There's more still to the man. Every morning, from 8.30 to 9 am, Tapie the workaholic keeps a date with Radio Monte Carlo listeners for his daily programme *Allo Bernard*. Then there's the news that has sent shivers through the ranks of the French football hierarchy but has delighted a good many Marseille fans who still hold Bernard Tapie dear to their hearts. On 22 November 1999, the Council of State refused a request from the French Football Federation to indefinitely suspend Tapie's licence to run a football club. Despite the fact that he has stated that for the time being he has no desire to do so, and that from now on he'll concentrate on his acting career, he still maintains that his greatest memories date from his time with OM.

So will Tapie return to OM? Why not?

And what of the other players in the Valenciennes–OM affair?

Jean-Pierre Bernès is now a players' agent. Working alongside Alain Miglaccio, he is one of the major players in the field.

Boro Primorac can be found at Arsenal, where he is the highly respected assistant to Arsène Wenger.

Jean-Jacques Eydelie is still playing football. After a spell with Bastia in Corsica, the Champions Cup medal-winner is now playing for Servette of Geneva.

Jean-Louis Levreau is enjoying his retirement from the peace of his villa just outside Marseilles.

Jorge Burruchaga is in Argentina, where he is now a television pundit, and where, alongside his longstanding friend Diego Maradona, he acts as a scout for new talent to ship over to Europe.

Jacques Glassmann, dubbed by Bernès 'the Mr Clean of Football', endured a period of self-imposed exile on the island of Reunion, where he played for a nondescript team. He is now back at Valenciennes, where he is in charge of the youth team.

Jack Mellick stayed up north and dabbles in politics no more.

All that, and for what?

The circle is now closed. As the saying goes – and it applies to everybody in every circumstance – after the rain comes sunshine. And down here on the Canebière, we no longer dwell on this infamous affair. For the time being, everything in Marseilles is just fine, the sun is shining, and so are OM.

25

Nearly the Best Player in France – Ever: The Sad Story of José Touré

JOSÉ TOURÉ WITH PATRICK AMORY

I'm not normal, but you always knew that.

What is it that makes me say that? My life, and the virulent and long-lasting fever that took hold of me the very first time a football landed at my feet. My life's golden age was the age of football: of success, of recognition. But before all that, before the dream goals and the media attention, before the praise and the money, there was the passion. It was infectious, like one of those tropical diseases that periodically abate, only to rise again with greater vigour; it was the centre of my life. Reason is blind in the face of passion. Passion is absolute. I owe everything to passion. The irony is that all that my passion gave to me, it was to take back again.

My passion for the round ball gave me the strength to exceed my limits. It anaesthetised me to the gnawing pain in my muscles. It made me feel chosen – feel that maybe God was rewarding me for walking up the aisle of the tiny church in Cuges-les-Pins with my beloved Carméle. It wasn't hard for me, I became an irresistible showman. When they dubbed me 'Le Brésilien', a homage to Pelé the king and his footballing princes, I took this honour in my stride. I was happy to be known as a virtuoso. I considered myself an 'artist' as opposed to the donkeys who slogged their way round the pitch.

My head was full of dreams and I was flying. I failed to realise when it was time to come back down to earth to listen, look and reflect on the reality of events, facts and people. I was caught up in the blindness of youth and folly, in my fervent love of my art. That's where I went wrong. I was one of the few to believe in the art. I was on another planet, mixing with men who played by different rules. They were playing for high stakes on the back of my sweat and my skill. They bet heavily on my flair and my speed; they bought my freedom and my inspiration. And I sold my soul, without understanding that I had forfeited the right to question what was going on.

The pleasure of caressing the football had wormed its way into my brain. It had made my head swell. It had invaded my heart. Naïvely, I thought that one consumed by the passion was blessed with immunity. I was wrong. I blurred the lines. The stadium is not reality, the referee is not a judge, offside is not outside the law. My passion misled me. I gave plenty and received too much.

My love of football is, was, immense. I was lucky enough to be able to express my talent and to be recognised for it. But in my madness I never stepped back from my passionate state of mind: like a typhoon it finally sucked me in, the better to crush me.

I've decided to set everything down on paper so that no more young footballers, no more young sportsmen and women, consume themselves in the fire of their passion. Because there is nothing sadder at the age of thirty than to feel yourself reduced to dust.

I was playing well. My club were playing well. Nantes were winning. I was riding high. My life had always followed the rhythms of the ball. I was faithful to my passion. I knew how to handle it. I expressed myself best on the pitch, with a tone and vocabulary that were always spot-on.

That season, FC Nantes returned to the big time: we were

second in the French Championship. In the autumn of 1985 we enjoyed a brilliant run in the European Cup. I'll skip the details, but our games against Partizan Belgrade and Dynamo Moscow were superb, watched by millions on television. Against Belgrade I was the artist; against Moscow, the realist. My realism crucified Dasseïev, the great Soviet goalkeeper. My headed goal snatched us a victory, which I hoped made club president Fonteneau and Robert Budzinsky happy to have increased the value of my contract two years previously. Our European campaign filled the club's coffers nicely and whipped up a storm at the Beaujoire ground. The people of Nantes knew how to respond to the big occasions.

I gave one of my greatest performances in the match against Dynamo Moscow, along with the historic, hard-fought victory against a transcendent Uruguayan side which I helped to achieve as part of the national side. It was France's first-ever win in an intercontinental cup. That night we played for an unofficial world title, the champions of Europe taking on the champions of South America. Right from the off, the Uruguayan defence were out to get me. Only my sharpness kept me out of harm's way. I escaped their clutches, the better to play my own artistic game in the face of their cheating tactics and butchering tackles. Sadly, that night one of them managed to get at my left knee – the same knee that a few months later was to shatter my dreams and prevent me from travelling with my team-mates from the national side to Mexico for the World Cup.

But that match! What joy! I took a few knocks but came away with a goal as well as bruises. Success erases suffering. Henri Michel had put his faith in the new-look attacking duo: I played up front with Rocheteau. We both scored, set up by a tightly knit team with two maestros at its heart: 'Platoche' and 'Gigi' – Platini and Giresse.

The heavens were bluer than blue. The public exulted. The headlines in *L'Equipe* showered us with praise: 'Giresse and Touré, what class!' and 'Olé! Touré'. Their report on our exploits took on an epic flavour: '55th minute, on the half-

way line, Touré-la-classe beats three opponents, passes the
ball to Platini, who finds Giresse. He in turn plays a long
ball forward, over the heads of the Uruguayan defence. Touré
takes the ball with his chest and before it has a chance to hit
the ground, slams it into the opposition's net.' They dubbed
me the Brazilian, which was fine by me. I felt so full of football and happiness, my life was so dazzling.

This French side was marching towards Mexico, and we
qualified for the final phase of the World Cup. It was a team
that offered me some memorable encounters, both sporting
and human.

It was Jean Tigana who welcomed me aboard and took me
under his wing when I first joined the national squad. We
roomed together at the training camp at Jouy-en-Josas. He
was very solicitous of me. He was a real star, with a strong
and generous personality, but he was thin-skinned and
unyielding. People didn't argue with him, because he was an
awkward customer: small but formidable. At times our room
became an office where he consulted, advised, led. Jeannot,
too, had come up from the streets, but not the scrubbed pavements of the Blois estates. He hailed from the broken and
mean streets of north Marseilles. He retained the sing-song
accent, the piercing gaze and the scarcely concealed aggression.
He was crafty, with a good eye for business and for people.
The younger squad members were quick to seek out this most
accessible of mentors. He was very free with his advice, though
he could be a right pain on his off days, or when he was talking to pricks. But he gave his time generously to newcomers.

In 1986, when I arrived at Bordeaux, he welcomed me with
open arms. He had quite a clan down there and he lorded
it over the people of the Gironde. In a totally different way
Dominique Rocheteau was a partner whose company I enjoyed
both on and off the field. Without me ever having to open up to
him, we shared a great understanding that made our partnership
work beautifully deep inside tough opposition defences. But the
real trump cards lay elsewhere, playing behind Dominique and
me. Beginning with Platini, whom I didn't know and never really

got to know. He always turned up at the last moment from Juventus. He was the boss, but he let his feet do the talking. A player such as Platini has a status that sets him apart, even within the national side. At twenty-four years old I was becoming an adult, but with my handful of caps – eight – I was a mere kid compared to his thirty years and sixty caps. He was enormously experienced and projected a tremendous aura. Maybe this made him seem to me a bit unapproachable. But there's no doubting how much I respected him.

Gigi was another class act. I loved him. Alain Giresse was accessible, humble, a great character and I loved sharing victories with him. The Platini–Giresse duo plus Tigana the Star and Fernandez the Bold became a magic quartet. Back then the four of them were the unchallenged champions of our noble cause.

The 1985–6 season continued along the same lines as the previous year. I was still dancing around the pitch, scoring goals and savouring victories and qualifications all over the place, with the French team as well as with Nantes. And then, on 19 March 1986, Touré-la-chance had a date with destiny – a destiny that was about to change course. I'd been suffering from pains in my left knee ever since the game against the hard men of Uruguay. I'd kept quiet about it as knocks are all part of the game – you just have to grit your teeth and get on with it. Nantes' European campaign was physically hard. We Brazilians can come to grief because we fly too high.

I used to jump to avoid the knocks and at times I dished some out as well, to make opponents respect me. However, I preferred to counter the hard men of the defence by taunting them with my virtuosity rather than resorting to primal retaliation.

That March, during the first half of a difficult European Cup quarter-final against Inter Milan, the brother of the great Baresi, let's call him the not-so-great-Baresi, hit me from behind on my left knee. This time the pain was greater, different. By half-time the knee was swollen. But it was a vital match that was going to be tough to win, and I wanted to carry on. Everybody wanted me to carry on. I started the second half after being treated with a large dose of cold spray and some heavy-duty strapping. But fifteen minutes later, after I leaped up to take a header, my knee gave out. I collapsed to the ground. For me, the match was over. Nantes, too, would lose that night.

The usual stuff followed: back to the changing room, a session with the physio. The next day our doctor called Professor Leteneur at the teaching hospital in Nantes, the man who a few months previously had operated on Baronchelli.

I wasn't worried at the end of the match. I gave a few interviews after our defeat and left nobody with the impression that I was at all anxious about my chances of recovering in time for the World Cup. I found it unthinkable that our great team, under Platini and Giresse, would play without me. The pleasure I derived from it was too great. And it was in the land of the Aztecs that, as a child, I had first seen a player by the name of Pelé. The forthcoming World Cup was my destiny.

Next day, I went to the hospital. Professor Leteneur examined me. He was calm and professional. I stared at him as he manipulated my horribly swollen knee. My temples were pounding, the blood felt thick and hot in my head. Leteneur finished and thought for a moment, looking me square in the face. This look alone was enough for me to understand the truth.

'So, Doctor, what's wrong?'

'Well, there's a chance that you've twisted your ligaments, maybe more than that. You'll need an androscopy before we can be sure.'

'Any hope for the World Cup?' I asked him. There were only two months to go before it kicked off.

'Yes, if you do a lot of weight training to compensate, but I can't guarantee anything. And all it would achieve would be to push back the date for an operation that you are going to have to have.'

'OK, Ettore, I'll try some.' We'd left the restaurant and were now sitting in his powerful Mercedes coupé. Ettore removed a small mirror from the glove box. He very gently tapped his sachet to make a little pile of powder on the mirror. Using his gold AmEx card he chopped out four even lines, each a few centimetres long. He peeled a crisp note off the wad of 500-franc bills he always carried in his inside pocket and rolled it up like a straw. I signalled that he should go first. It felt like I was in a movie. He sniffed a line up each nostril then offered me the mirror, and I took my turn. It was as if my sinuses were instantly unblocked. There was a bitter taste at the back of my throat and I felt a tingling in my cheekbones. I was simultaneously excited and relaxed. Back then, taking coke was just another game.

The first time I had made a conscious decision to take cocaine was in Monaco. I'd already tried it in Paris a few months earlier with my friend Thierry, a denizen of the night and former big-time sportsman, now a pseudo-sophisticate who buried his disappointments in powder. We were in some trendy club in the Halles area of Paris. He offered, I accepted. It was before I left for Mauritius. But that time . . . well, I was on holiday. The season was over. Now, for me, in my head, football itself was over once and for all. I didn't want to hear about it any more. I especially didn't want to hear anything about what had been my life until then.

I often went out to eat in Ventimiglia with an Italian mate of mine, the one I am calling Ettore. Ettore cut a fine figure, always well turned out, around forty, a class act. I never knew exactly what he did for a living. I didn't care. He was good company, even-tempered, well-mannered and very discreet. I liked him very much. I never realised what his friendship would cost me.

I'd come across coke plenty of times before during my trips up to Paris. I'd noticed that in showbiz circles you could have a good night even if you didn't get a girl, but not without a snort of the white stuff. I saw that my night-time comrades in the trendy venues and clubs, the most famous and the most respected, always knew where to score. Often they didn't even need to ask, as a discreet delivery was made at the same moment as an offer. Dealers are like bankers who keep their tills open all night. Just like pizza deliveries, they'll come to you if you're a big customer.

When I went to people's houses I realised that there was a whole ritual that went with snorting coke. In the trendy and moneyed set, everywhere you looked – in the kitchen, bedroom, sitting room or on the terrace – the lines were racked out. Coke is a status symbol for these people. You know the sort of thing: 'Come round to my place, I've got top models and charlie.' In these circles you don't snort in the toilets like you do in restaurants and clubs; no, you organise a less sordid little ceremonial, a little secret to share. Sniffing together is like belonging to the same masonic lodge or having slept with the same girl: it creates a bond. I used to watch without, up till then, wanting to get involved. Before Berquez let me go I had too much respect for my body, which was the instrument I used for both work and pleasure at the time when playing was still a pleasure.

But now I was free. I'd nothing left to respect or to fear, not even mistakes. I finally had to take responsibility for my own life, for better or for worse. I wanted to decide.

The effect was immediate. I thought I was a superman. I felt invincible. The feeling lasted for some of the evening, then, having had another toot with Ettore, I went back to my place. I played the bass into the small hours, then went to lie down. But I couldn't sleep. Around 6 am, as the daylight began to filter in through the shutters, I came down with a crash. I felt so bad I started to cry, and I swore that I'd never touch that shit again for the rest of my life.

Fine words, fine words indeed. I hadn't yet understood that a loser thrives on illusions and flounders in lies. The same evening I went for a boozy dinner with Ettore. Euphoric, I told him I wanted to buy. 'Oh yeah? How much d'you want?' he inquired in his Italian accent. I knew nothing about cocaine, apart from that it came in grams. I said:

'Me, I've got no idea. Fifty grams?'

'You want fifty grams! You got the cash?'

'Not on me.' I had no idea how much what I'd asked for would cost.

'Stay here. I'll be back.' I spent nearly two hours waiting, chatting to the owner of the restaurant. When he returned, the ever-calm and straight Ettore announced, 'Come on, we're going to your place.' I became excited when we were in his car. 'You got the gear?' I thought I was some kind of Pablo Escobar, but I hadn't considered what I was getting into, hadn't thought about the dangers lying in wait for me.

When we got to my place Ettore went straight to the kitchen where, from his trousers, under his belt, he produced a plastic bag. Inside were five smaller bags of rock cocaine, ten grams in each. It was an enormous amount.

'Hey, Ettore, that's loads.'

'José, you ask me for fifty grams, I bring you fifty grams.' I was in much too deep to reproach him. The only thing I was interested in was getting some of that bloody gear up my nose. Ettore took one of the bags and I immediately hid the others in the cellar, at the bottom of a boxful of books. All that gear made me nervous.

'Pass me a sieve and a plate.' Using the round end of a mortar from the kitchen, Ettore ground up the rocks and the powder fell on to the plate. We piled into it. It was madness. I opened a bottle of Cristal Roderer, my favourite champagne, and drank and snorted. We talked, we ranted, we set the world to rights, slouching on the terrace with the lights of Monaco shimmering in the distance. 'Ettore, it's great here, isn't it? Together, far from the cares of the world. It's magic gear. You're a great guy. Tell me what I owe you. You know me, I want to sort you out, I never cause any problems.' Ettore looked straight at me, 'José, I'm going to give you a great price. I got the gear from a friend and I told him it was for you – he loves football. So you get a real bargain, 25,000 francs for fifty grams.' I had my snout in the stars and I didn't give a shit about what it might cost me.

Ettore returned to my house the next day, in the afternoon. I'd been to the bank to withdraw the 25,000 francs, plus a further 10,000 that Ettore had asked to borrow.

I didn't see my Italian friend again over the following two weeks, but I did begin to realise that I was poisoning myself.

I was freaking out with worry, as much about my state of health as about having all that charlie stashed at my place. On the spur of the moment I flushed the remainder of the first bag down the toilet. I told myself I'd give the other bags back to Ettore at the first possible opportunity. I was scared keeping it so close to me. I became totally paranoid.

Once again the night became my friend. My loser's itinerary had transformed my Parisian peregrinations into a permanent trip into the catacombs, peopled by all those Parisians of the night, screwed-up or famous, unknown or well known, all united by the nihilism which, at night-time, cloaks them in delusion. I don't know who, from David Lynch through to Pier Paolo Pasolini, could best have depicted the sordid scenes through which I lived for months at a stretch. In Fellini's *Roma* there is suffering and humour, the common and the grotesque. My film had only masks and the heads of the living dead. The coke connection was lying in wait for me at every turn, whatever the place, whatever the time. I lived in a city, Paris, where every night it snowed on the disenchanted in-crowd. It's the common currency, and you talk to people about it because you're all addicted to those same endless lines. It's the currency of relationships, because you're friends for the time it takes to open the tiny bag together, to keep warm, during that little period of illusion, the shroud that covers your dead-end lives. You stop flirting, you are no longer charming, you screw whores and fuck-ups who sell their bodies for a sprinkling of snow. You have many friends – as long as the dealers keep dealing. Feeblemindedness and hypocrisy are the guiding values in this world where everybody is somebody's whore.

Watch out! Too many of our role models and heroes by day are nose-powderers by night. Watch out! They're sold to us as heroes, but they are nothing but zeroes, and they know it so well that the only person they believe in any more is their dealer. Who are they? It doesn't matter. Everybody, singers and sportspeople, TV journos and trendy producers,

rebellious nymphets and champagne intellectuals, all career-
ing ahead into the vacuity of the age of nothingness. All
hooked on the same night-times filled with empty talk and no
action.

Mike Tyson, Diego Maradona, Ben Johnson, and how many
more have been hung out to dry in the name of sport as
business? I'm no judge, and have no desire to act as one. I
don't know exactly what Mike, Diego and Ben did to see their
lives shattered. Me, I never cheated, never committed a crime,
I was merely a football player, then a victim of the *commedia
dello sport*. Sport, that wonderful word, corrupted by
avarice. If today's top sports stars are too often competing on
a money-go-round in a farcical moral-free zone, they are
no more than accessories, and most often victims. Those we
brand as guilty carry the can for faults which our entire
society tolerates, and with which sport on the whole
co-operates. I'm against doping, against violence, against
cheating, but I can't stand idly by and watch people martyred
without a sense of revulsion. Because Tyson, Maradona and
Johnson, whatever their faults, are no more than the products
of the perverted culture of modern sport – the frenetic chase
for the big-business bucks which makes promoters and agents
more important than any judge or referee. Nobody will make
me believe that Johnson or Maradona set out to ruin their
own lives. Some people say they're guilty; I'd tend to the view
that they are accessories, and what I'm sure of is that they are
victims.

   My story is different. I at least had courage and respect
for myself and for the sport which had given me so much
pleasure. I retired, I gave up, I ran away rather than destroy
myself on the pitch. I'm like one of those elephants who
leaves the herd to go and die somewhere far away. I went off
to lose myself in my very own labyrinths, far from the light of
my passion.

26

Les Verts' Slush Fund: A Rock Built on Sand

JEAN-PHILIPPE LECLAIRE

He could have gone down in history as our very own Sir Matt Busby. A pioneer, a visionary, an originator, the man who built up the club most dear to French hearts: l'Association Sportive de St Etienne (ASSE), winners of the French Championship ten times (a record which stands to this day), nine of them while he was club president.

'*Allez Les Verts!*' went up the cry from 50 million supporters when Roger Rocher's players reached the final of the 1976 Champions Cup. Beaten 1–0 in Glasgow by Germany's Bayern Munich, despite twice hitting the woodwork, the Stéphanois carried on the typically French tradition of the *perdant magnifique*, or beautiful loser, previously exemplified by the cyclist Raymond Poulidor and Marcel Cerdan the boxer.

All this was twenty-two years before the France of Zidane won the World Cup. English clubs had by then already captured thirteen European Cups; the French were crowing about making their first final since 1959. But trophies aren't everything, so long as you've got your myths. You had your Reds; we had our Les Verts, with winger Dominique Rocheteau, a pirouetting romanticist nicknamed the Ange Vert (Green Angel), and the enigmatic coach Robert Herbin, alias the Sphinx Roux (Ginger Sphinx). And then there was the man himself, the club president with a pipe for ever stuck in the corner of his thin, pinched mouth: Roger Romulus Rocher. He was born in 1920, with his strange, Roman middle name and a surname carved in stone (*rocher* means 'rock'). It was the heritage of a firmly secular, Republican father, who was also to bequeath his eldest son a small construction firm.

In 1957, as boss of the Société Forézienne de Travaux Publics (SFTP), Roger Rocher built the north and south stands of the Geoffroy-Guichard Stadium, before going on to preside over the greatest moments of glory of the Stéphanois 'cauldron'. During the period he was club president, Bayern Munich (3–0 in 1969), Dynamo Kiev (3–0 in 1976), PSV Eindhoven (6–0 in 1979), and even the great Liverpool of the Keegan era (1–0 in 1977) all bit the coal dust that still blackened areas of the bumpy pitch at the *enfer vert*, or green hell.

Honoured by four French presidents (De Gaulle, Pompidou, Giscard, Mitterrand), received by the Pope, paraded at the head of his team down the Champs Elysées, Roger Rocher entered the annals of French sport as a living legend. The manner of his leaving would be a lot less exalted: head bowed and wrists handcuffed. Having been found guilty of embezzlement, the president of St Etienne was sentenced to four years' imprisonment, with thirty months suspended, as well as being fined 200,000 francs. Roger the Rock had built his career and his club in the image of Sir Matt: he finished it in prison like any common or garden Bernard Tapie. Even today, over on our side of the Channel, the affair of Les Verts' so-called slush fund continues to intrigue and fascinate, even though we've seen a lot worse since then. Claude Bez, president of the Girondins of Bordeaux, Champions Cup semi-finalists in 1989, and Bernard Tapie, boss of Olympique Marseille, winners of the Champions Cup in 1993, were both given ample time to ruminate on their falls from grace from behind the peephole of a dark prison cell. Nevertheless, ten years after its dénouement, the scandal that entangled St Etienne from April 1982 (when the police investigation began) until June 1990 (when legal proceedings ended) retains a symbolic notoriety that outstrips the others. 'The slush fund scandal was the first big scandal to hit French football, and the first money-laundering trial in France, predating even the inquiries into the corrupt financing of political parties,' explains Maître André Soulier, who at the time was a lawyer representing a certain Michel Platini. For the greatest player in the history of French football (at least while we wait to see whether Zidane can build on his exploits during the 1998 World Cup) also figured in this shady tale. Accused of having pocketed 880,000 francs in under-the-table payments, the man who wore the green shirt for three years, from 1980 to 1982, was found guilty, but has since received an amnesty.

Les Verts, Platini and Rocher: the idea for this *ménage à trois* was born on 12 May 1976, the evening at Glasgow's Hampden Park when St Etienne went down 1–0 to Bayern Munich in the final of the Champions Cup. Of the eleven players in the St Etienne team selected by coach Robert Herbin, nine had come up through the club. In the grandstand at Hampden Park, and subsequently on the Champs Elysées, where Les Verts were welcomed home as if they'd won, club president Rocher was scheming: put his 'Rocher babes' together with one or two top-notch players bought from other clubs and Les Verts would have what it took to become the first French club in history to win the Champions Cup.

Michel Platini was out of contract at AS Nancy-Lorraine, the club where he had started his career, and on 29 April 1979 he signed with St Etienne. The fee was derisory: a mere 1.4 million francs to cover 'training costs'. However, the ambitious 'Platoche' demanded a net annual salary of 1 million francs. That's the same amount as Nicolas Anelka currently earns in two weeks at Real Madrid, but at the time it was a fortune: Platini would be earning twenty-five times his previous wages. At St Etienne, the captain of the French national team would receive 83,300 francs each month, and as Les Verts' new number 10 was obliged to return around 50 per cent of his income in taxes, every month the club handed him a large envelope containing his monthly tax liabilities in cash.

So where did these huge wads of 500-franc notes come from? The answer is from the St Etienne slush fund, although it wasn't called that at the time. Roger Rocher was more delicate, referring instead to his precious 'nest egg'. 'Papy Rocher' must have had some serious holes in his nest egg: at least 17.3 million francs were diverted between June 1976 and June 1982, thanks to a complex web of 'levies' and 'tax exemptions'. Rocher and his accomplices skimmed off around 20 per cent of receipts from memberships of the honorary committee, gate money from friendly fixtures and the sale of souvenirs at the highly profitable club shop. The under-the-counter cash was spread around. It went to Michel Platini and his team-mates, but also, naturally, to club president Rocher, who used the slush fund to keep his business, which had been hit hard by the recession, afloat. After coming to light in the aftermath of the 1982 World Cup, where Platini and Les Bleus valiantly made it through to the semi-finals, the biggest scandal in the history of modern French football would drag on for eight interminable years. It is a fact that at the highest levels of state everything possible was done to bury the affair. Neither the Gaullists nor the Socialists wanted to be seen to be the ones tarnishing the dream. Despite the refusal of the Finance Ministry to take action, the requests for further details from the public prosecutor's office and the quashing of other findings by the Court of Appeal, one 'minor judge' continued to pursue the case. His name is Patrick Desmures.

Totally unknown at the time, he has since achieved great notoriety, for he is the magistrate, methodical and courteous, who is currently engaged in examining corrupt sources of financing of the RPR, the political party of President Jacques Chirac.

Twenty years before he began rummaging through the

head of state's dirty laundry, Patrick Desmures managed to drag the *crème de la crème* of French football before the courts: ten players, including eight French internationals – Platini, Larios, Battiston, Janvion, Lopez, Lacombe, Farison and Zimako – plus St Etienne coach Robert Herbin and president Roger Rocher. On the evening the verdict was handed down, 29 June 1990, they were all found guilty. The great St Etienne plunged into the depths of the Second Division, to finally resurface only in 1999. Having served his time, sold his business and even auctioned off his famous pipe collection, Roger Rocher died on 29 March 1997.

Michel Platini didn't go to his funeral. When challenged by a journalist friend over his absence, the man who was by then president of the 1998 World Cup organising committee, replied: 'I had a committee meeting that day, and anyway, I don't like funerals.'

VI

Les Supporters

27

Blood and Gold: The Best Public in France

CHRISTOV RÜHN

Go, Lensois, go! Go, club, go!
Hoist on high the flag!
We stand together under our colours.
Home stands, sing your passion!

Chant of the Lensois fans

While the current tendency in the international press is to conjure up concern about money, drug-taking and racism in sport, it is important to emphasise that in football there are still blessed places where fair play linked to a genuine passion for a local club still reigns.

Loyal followers of football are fairly regularly singled out by journalists, even though the press would be hard pushed to deny that the public remains the principal driving force behind the football business, from which the media reap great profits. The tension between fans and the press is due to an amalgam of football and violence, a mindset which dates back to the seventies when numerous incidents that took place in the English Championship signalled the birth of the first hooligan gangs. These should have remained no more than sad memories in the minds of the older generation, had the gruesome Heysel tragedy not occurred during the final of

the European Clubs Cup, which pitted Juventus of Turin against
Liverpool. It was a disaster that sullied for always the most
universal of team sports.

On that fateful day in May 1984, clashes between supporters from both camps led to a terrible outcome. Just minutes
before the confrontation, British hooligans – unwisely placed
high up in the stands of the Belgian stadium by unsuspecting
authorities – began, with mind-blowing rage, to bombard
their Italian counterparts with projectiles: seats, metal bolts,
bottles, whatever they could get their hands on. General panic
spread among the Juve supporters, who retreated down to
the lower levels of the grandstand to escape this frenzied
aggression to join their comrades standing below. A great
many of them got stuck between barriers in their attempt to
escape the British fans' attack and as a result an entire section
of the stand collapsed. Most of the victims were suffocated or
imprisoned in the trap which closed around them.

The whole of Europe witnessed this tragedy live on TV and
could only watch with horror as the full extent of the nightmare unfolded. The final count was high – nearly fifty dead
and many injured, some very seriously. Men, women and
children, all were affected. In the wake of this bloody day
a war on hooligans was openly declared. Fathers, the core
supporters, could no longer countenance taking their kids to
matches because it was so dangerous and such hatred presided
over the debates. But for a delirious press it became difficult
to separate truth from hysteria. Supporters equal violence has
since become the leitmotiv of scandal-ridden tabloids.

Events took a new turn when the football authorities made
a decision to ban British clubs from the European Cup for
five years. On a sporting level, this created a void for the
duration which the British clubs struggled to fill and which
nobody could forget. The governments of the European Union
elected to provide major support to UEFA to help control violence in stadiums, a determining factor being the resolute
influence of the British prime minister, the appropriately
named 'Iron Lady', who was keen that her country's image

should regain positivity. More police were drafted in to enforce law and order at football grounds, backed by Interpol, which kept a vigilant eye on the comings and goings of hooligans and filed their reports in dossiers across Europe. The wave of terror was cut short and football evolved in a more humane way. There was less violence in the stands and the excessive cheating and rude gestures of players on the pitch during the 1990 World Cup in Italy was its last manifestation. It was high time for change, because football could have been destroyed.

Hooliganism virtually went out of fashion as the nineties dawned. Calm was restored to a great majority of stadiums and the emergence of a new breed of fan was noticeable. They were far more peaceful and went to matches not to make trouble, but out of genuine support for their favourite team. This did not prevent further tragedies: at the FA Cup semi-final at Hillsborough in England, where ninety-six people died, and at Furiani in Corsica, where eighteen people died and around fifty were handicapped for life. But these disasters were largely due to the irresponsible conduct of the police and the authorities rather than to the behaviour of the hooligans. 'You'll never walk alone.'

In marked contrast, it is in a joyful spirit and family atmosphere that the stands of Stade Félix-Bollaert are regularly adorned with flags hoisted by the fans of Lens bearing the trademark 'blood and gold' colours of the club. They float in the icy wind of the Nord-Pas de Calais like banners from a distant age when the spirit of chivalry was still considered de rigueur. The people from the north, 'les Ch'tis', always show great respect for both teams on the pitch, which does not stop them from fervently supporting their own. Thanks to this, the supporters of RC Lens are regularly cited as great exemplars of French football. They can be proud of their reputation as 'the best public in France'.

Tales from the coal mines

The football section of the Racing Club de Lens was born

in 1906, in response to the demands of kids playing this new sport from across the Channel on public squares and wastelands during school holidays. Nearly thirty years later, in 1932, thanks to an alliance of managers and the mining brotherhood, the club turned professional. The local community, from which Les Houillères, the coal board, employed a majority of workers, endured a bleak spell when Europe was hit by the most serious economic crisis to date, the notorious stockmarket crash of 1929. The bosses had no choice but to make redundant a great many workers. Fortunately, 200 unemployed coal miners were needed to build a large stadium for RC Lens. The players of the 'blood and gold' club thus became the symbolic standard-bearers of the *gueules noires* (black faces).

The architectural design of the stadium was largely modelled on that of a neighbouring coal-mining town, Béthune, where colliery bosses had built 'the most beautiful stadium in France'. Stade Félix-Bollaert was constructed between seam 1 and seam 9 along the Paris–Dunkirk railway line. Félix Bollaert, an important local figure and president of the coal-mining administrative council, bequeathed his name on dying suddenly shortly after the stadium's construction.

Entire families worked underground in difficult conditions, and for these firedamp-fighters the hard fact that life expectancy was short was the likely source of local pride and humility. Ultimately, with faces blackened by coal, everyone looked the same: a mine is infertile ground for the cultivation of racism or intolerance. The warmth within this community of workers conferred on the club a stability that is apparent to this day in the Lensois grandstand. One for all and all for Lens. . .

Across the generations, many players wearing the blood and gold colours came from Poland. The Polish community arrived en masse in this mining region at the turn of the century, leaving an indelible stamp on the club. Thus the distinguished qualities of RC Lens and the style of football played are a blend of courage, abnegation and celebration.

Throughout its history the club has seesawed between the top of the First Division league table and long spells in the purgatory of the lesser divisions. For many years RC Lens has lived under the shadow of its northern big brother, Lille OSC, frequently national champions. For the blood and gold club rewards have been rare, though they have twice won the League Cup, in 1994 and 1999, and were finalists in the French Cup in 1948, 1975 and 1998. And the coal-mining community became French Champions for the first time in 1998, the year of the club's ninety-first birthday. The title was a welcome addition to its Second Division Champions honour of 1937, 1948 and 1973. Club president Gervais Martel's squad was in top form, outstripping other great sides. This was also one of the years in which Lens reached the final of the French Cup, in which this time it lost narrowly to Paris St Germain.

Of this mythical 1998 team only a few players remain at the Stade Félix-Bollaert stadium today. Their highly respected manager, Daniel Leclercq, formerly a player with Marseille and Lens, resigned in 1999 after a catastrophic start to the season. The fans miss him so much that every week a banner bearing his name is unfurled in the stands. Loyalty may be paramount at Lens, but it is important to appreciate one thing: that for the supporters here the loss of Leclerq is as great a trauma as the sudden loss of Wenger would be to Arsenal or that of Sir Alex to Manchester United. A huge void has been left by the man who empowered Lens to win the ultimate title for the first time ever. But most of all, the fans from Lens mourn the stars of that blessed era: Tony Vairelles, the brilliant international centre forward who crucified Arsenal at Wembley during the Champions League in 1998 and who is now playing for FC Lyon, one of the big names of the French Championship; Titi Camara, the fabulous striker from Guinea who ended up at Gérard Houllier's Liverpool (Houllier was himself a coach at Lens in the 1980s, before he became national technical director), along with another former Lens player, the Czech international winger Vladimir Smicer.

Former skipper Frédéric Dehu now plays for one of the largest clubs in the world, Barça; the talented under-Twenty-One international Stéphane Dalmat is basking in glory at OM and Stéphane Ziani is playmaker for Bordeaux, the 1999 French champions, having spent a year at the Spanish club Déportivo la Coruña. But it isn't the first time Lens has experienced a period of upheaval and its spirit of optimism is alive and well. In the grandstand over 35,000 Ch'tis regularly chant for their team.

The official RC Lens supporters' club, les Supp'r Lens, the most representative of its public, has numerous subscribers scattered through regional branches in the north and east of France: Aisne, Drôme, Bouches du Rhône, Pas-de-Calais, Oise, Somme, Seine et Marne, Puy de Dome . . . Les Supp'r Lens are usually based in bars and cafés in small villages. The existence of other supporters' clubs, such as Bollaert Boys, Génération Sang et Or, Les Ch'tis Gavroches, Kop Sang et Or and Red Tigers, may call into question the hegemony of the official organisation, and indeed are just as active.

Of the fans of First Division clubs, those of RC Lens are probably the most modern. They have created clever and regularly visited websites which provide a forum for debate for discussion groups and interesting information about the club and its history. For example, on the Red Tigers' site (www.tigers.citeweb.net), the fanzine *Rugir* calls on its members to get to their team's regional away derbies – by bike or moped, to assert their difference. This passion for the net also provides a major marketing tool for RC Lens itself. France Telecom are Lens' shirt sponsors through Ola, the mobile phone line targeted at the young, which enables club president Gervais Martel to communicate with its subscribers at RC Lens and to boost merchandising. Bubbling under those big guns of the French Championship, OM and PSG, the club ranks third nationally in sales of derivative merchandise – shirts, scarves, gadgets, etc. – with profits of around 25 million francs. On the home page of the site 'Allez les Sang et Or', President Martel addresses the fans: 'Since its birth in

1906, le Racing Club de Lens has always been supported by the best public in France ... within the framework of our development of the club, the internet is undoubtedly a crucial tool of progress which couldn't be passed by.'

Unquestionably, the fans experienced their greatest moment of glory away from their magnificent stadium, modernised for the 1998 World Cup, one evening in November of that year when they set off to 'conquer *perfide Albion* and avenge Joan of Arc' by taking on Arsenal at Wembley in the qualifying stages of the Champions League. For the first time RC Lens came out on top against a major British team in an official top-level competition. The amusing thing about their rallying cry is that the Blood and Gold supporters are the most 'British' of all French fans. This northern fan base is very similar to those of the Geordie clubs Newcastle and Sunderland, whose authenticity and seamless infatuation are rooted in a fusion of working-class traditions and foul weather. Lens is a town of middling importance where often there are almost more people in the football grandstand than in the town itself. The club's operating budget is infinitely less than that of the Magpies or Sunderland, but the passion that drives its supporters is the same and goes way beyond mere results on the pitch. They are all 'proud to be Lensois'.

Today, on the eve of centenary celebrations at RC Lens, the spirit of the *gueules noires* is truly alive. The Blood and Golds are not afraid to take on any other European football side, thanks to the ever-present support of its fans, who truly are 'the best public in France'.

> *In misfortune or glory,*
> *Defeat or victory,*
> *To our team we remain loyal,*
> *Our faith is eternal.*

28

Hooligans Made in France

PHILIPPE BROUSSARD

The day we beat the English

It was a Wednesday in February, back in 1984. The 29th to be exact – which just goes to show that you should always watch out for leap years. Because they don't come round very often, leap years somehow manage to make things stick in the mind, and they cause more mental mayhem than any full moon. That night, French football was to cross an historic threshold, though we didn't really appreciate that at the time. At the Parc des Princes, south-west Paris's very own Wembley, French hooliganism came kicking and screaming into life. The French crews took on the English 'masters' and helped to prepare the ground for the Stadium Wars which, one and a half years later, would reach their nadir with the tragedy at Heysel.

I'm sure that lovers of the game will have long forgotten the ironic fact that this was a 'friendly' fixture, and only the statisticians will recall that Peter Shilton's England team, unbeaten away from home since 1982, went down to two goals from Michel Platini. But this is mere detail: the relevance of the game lies elsewhere, in the memories of those dozens of young Frenchmen, by now fathers with families, who were part of the savagery that unfurled on the game's periphery. These were the lads who made 29 February 1984 a sort of punch-up D-Day, one of those memories that is handed down through the generations, with added satisfaction if you are able to say, 'I was there.' They certainly were, and I saw them.

At the time our stadiums had been pretty much spared the violence seen elsewhere. From time to time, a hundred or so Paris St Germain (PSG) fans would attack visiting supporters, but their assaults – ambushing coaches and throwing stones – were relatively innocuous. France considered hooliganism to be an English disease affecting England alone. France was wrong. In fact an entire section of its youth had been raised on the 'hooligan culture' born in England fifteen years before. The Chelsea, Millwall, and especially the West Ham 'crews' were heroes to the proto-hoolies from Paris, Lyons and Lille. Every Paris skinhead, dedicated lover of football and skinhead music, knew Oi bands like the Cockney Rejects ('War on the Terraces') and the Business. Home-grown hooliganism was waiting in the wings. It just needed kick-starting, and this was the game that did it.

The last time the French capital had played host to English fans had been in May 1975, when we had the chance to watch Leeds United fans in riotous action against Bayern Munich. Nine whole years: an eternity! The Paris 'skins', already dreaming of the battles to come, were anxious to gain recognition as fully fledged mashers of the international scene. Despite an allocation of only 600 tickets for English fans, several thousand ticketless visitors were planning to make the journey and regroup in Paris. They didn't turn up like the Italians, in tight and disciplined formation, but in English style, spread out in small groups, and they were therefore harder to keep tabs on.

This was in the days before the Channel Tunnel. It was such a long and tedious trek from England to Paris that 550 fans started as they meant to go on, trashing the ferry *Saint-Eloi*. Glass doors were smashed, lifebuoys thrown overboard and the duty-free shops pillaged. Lacking a French adversary, Chelsea and West Ham fans fought each other instead. Once they had disembarked at Dunkirk, they turned their attention

to a load of new British Leyland cars, pressing them into service for a spontaneous stock-car racing session. The horde
then descended on the train that was to take them to Paris,
causing £1,500 worth of damage and forcing the police to
board at Lens.

However, that night on the métro the first Englishmen I
saw didn't appear intent on causing trouble. They were blind
drunk, of course, but they seemed like OK guys. If I remember
rightly, they were from York or Preston, somewhere up north,
at any rate. To them, the Parc des Princes must have seemed
like the other end of the world, the apotheosis of an alcohol-
fuelled epic journey. As I talked to them, I realised that, the
match aside, there was only one thing on their minds: 'Are
the Paris skins waiting for us?' Rumours had already spread
through the cafés where they'd been drinking. When I reached
the Parc, I discovered that the rumours were well founded:
the French, armed with CS gas, had just attacked a métro
carriage.

As it turned out, all the extreme right-wing skins had come
out that night. They'd come from the suburbs to the west,
from Tolbiac in the east and from the Halles in the centre of
town. They were all seasoned fighters from the nationalist
band Tolbiac Toads' gigs. Numerically they weren't very strong
– around a hundred, including reinforcements down from
Normandy – but they'd worked hard on their battle plan,
making clever use of strategies that made the most of their
lack of numbers. Hooliganism, to these boneheaded thugs,
was nothing less than a tribal war, bound up with supremacy
and honour: 'us' against 'them', France against the rest of the
world. The eternal fascist mantra.

The area round the ground was under siege. The English
were everywhere: around the fountains, on the grass, in front
of the shops, lying on the pavements, sprawling on the benches.
They pissed on parked cars, threw up in doorways, belched in
the faces of old ladies. They even took over bistros usually
occupied by their rivals from PSG. They drank, drank and
drank some more. Beer from cans, wine from bottles. The

French stayed more sober; I guess they wanted to keep their heads clear for the rumble that would follow.

The 600-strong riot police, CRS, on duty didn't know where to turn. A brasserie window right outside the métro station was smashed in. In the next street a dozen thugs were laying into a youth in a white polo-neck. French? English? Nobody really knew. It was dark. Slightly further away, two policemen were beaten to the ground by a screaming mob. A sixty-something man was led away to a first-aid point, blood streaming from his cheek. Gangs chased each other down the ill-lit streets, screaming 'Fuck off!', and you couldn't tell which were French and which were English. Ambulances tried to thread their way through the frightened crowds. Parents who'd come with their kids turned and made their way back home; so what if TV wasn't covering the game.

The ground wasn't quite full. There were 4,000 or 5,000 spare places, enough room to leave gaps between rival gangs and to make retreat easier if fighting broke out. The English fans didn't have their own separate section. They were spread out across the different stands in larger or smaller groups, depending on which club they supported. By buying their tickets in Paris at the last minute, fans avoided having to travel with the official FA supporters, which would be far too restricting for their tastes. In these circumstances, they behaved just as uninhibitedly inside the ground as they had outside. Some groups scaled the fences to move from one section to another, causing panicked spectators to flee.

As far as the public, the players and the press were concerned, the trouble was all down to the Brits. However, there was one stand that they didn't manage to invade: the Boulogne corner, heartland of the PSG support. They were up above, on the balcony, like besieged warriors behind their ramparts. Below, on the pitch-side seating, they'd spotted several dozen English invaders. Easy prey, choice targets, they thought. The French started spitting; the English shouted insults, arms outstretched, giving them the finger.

There's a limited vocabulary in the international language of naked hatred.

They had only to go down one flight of steps to come face to face with the enemy. A challenge not to be ignored when recognition on the hooligan scene is what you crave. The upper tier, the Parisians, swept down as one on to the lower tier, the English, and the Battle of Paris was joined in furious close-quarter combat. It was no-holds-barred stuff featuring knuckle-dusters and steel-capped DMs. Pieces of seating ripped from the concrete terracing served as missiles. It was a funny old game, with the CRS, helmet visors down, acting as referees. They, too, had their clubs, but theirs were used to beat the two sides apart. One bent down and retrieved a bloody hatchet. My first impression was that it was English, and had recently been used to cut a French ear down to size.

Everybody in the ground, including the players, was riveted to the action in the corner. The atmosphere was such that the stewards decided to evacuate a party of schoolchildren from the Oise, north of Paris, who'd come with their teacher to watch their first football match. The kids were led back on to their coach during half-time. Other spectators followed their lead and left the ground well before the final whistle. They were the wise ones. In the crush to leave after the game, dozens of cars, windows and telephone booths were damaged, the first-aid service dealt with several dozen injuries, including two stabbings (knife and hatchet) and the police arrested twenty-five people.

The next morning, the same fire and fury could be heard emanating from both sides of the Channel. British prime minister Margaret Thatcher fumed: 'The name of Great Britain has been besmirched.' Future French president Jacques Chirac, mayor of Paris at the time, was quick to point the finger. 'I've had enough of English supporters.' Only a couple of newspapers – *The Times* in Britain and *L'Equipe* in France – blamed the trouble on the French supporters in the Boulogne stand. The Paris skinheads savoured what was to them a triumph. By taking on the acknowledged masters, they'd come of age.

In France, the Stadium Wars took off as a result of this game, but without ever becoming as widespread as in other countries. Although other clubs would have to face up to the phenomenon (St Etienne, Lyon and especially Marseille, with their 'Ultras'), Paris was always the heartland of hooliganism. In 1993, the PSG hardcore numbered up to 500, devotees of both extremist right-wing politics and the Boulogne corner. Since then, several dozen of these young men have ended up in prison, or banned from grounds, but fascination with the English (Casuals) and German (Hools) models remains intact. They still consider European Cup games against British teams to be something a bit special (Arsenal in 1994, Liverpool in 1997). It's one way of keeping alive that tradition born on 29 February 1984, the day the old-timers told themselves, probably somewhat prematurely, 'We've beaten the English.'

29

Marcel Desailly and the Second Liberation of Paris, July 1998

ONYEKACHI WAMBU

> *On the pitch, I concentrate – sometimes I don't even hear the crowd ... I'm just on the pitch: sweating, tackling, listening to the coach, keeping an eye on which corner I have to cover, which number I have to mark ... There are times when I would like to be like a supporter, and so enjoy the game more than the guy on the pitch.*
>
> Marcel Desailly

Pre-history

As the first hunting bands of men and women walked across the East African plains, they would often stop at a safe clearing. The hungry women and children would wait, while the courageous and able-bodied among the men would go off in search of game to feed everyone. A few men, resentful at not being allowed to accompany the hunters, would be left behind with the women, idly awaiting the first tales of the hunt. Later these dreamers would sit round the crackling fire, taking in the aromatic smells from the fat dripping off the roasting meat as the hunters gathered and the darkness crept in. They would listen with envy, like the first fans they were, as the hunters exaggerated and embellished their exploits.

These fire stories provided the basis of future mythologies

and would be the dreamer's only compensation for not being there, sharing the excitement and rewards of the hunt. Although it would remain a rather frustratingly visceral way of participating, during these stories an umbilical relationship developed between actor and listener, performer and fan, both of whom needed each other for the hunt-event to have meaning. These fire stories of the drama of the hunt would, in time, become even more important than the hunt itself. They would become ritualised – initially through formalised ceremonies and other rites of passage to decide which warriors were eligible for the hunt.

Such organised ceremonial games were symbolic recreations of the tests, dramas and skills involved in the hunt itself. They became the first controlled spectacles. But embellishment by the hunters was no longer possible. With the ritual being played out in front of the whole community, lies were no longer possible. The hero was to be tested in a very public way. It was now possible to see which warrior buckled under pressure; which one in his generation would carry the 'torch of ideals' for the tribe. In fact, the actual hunt would retain its significance as a symbolic group spectacle, played out in public, only where the fan could directly participate by teasing the hero mercilessly, and watching his shortcomings being openly exposed. It could be called the revenge of the fan.

But occasionally in the process of the public symbolic ritual, the hero hunters still manage to silence and then astonish the mocking fans by incredible moments of illuminating courage or skill – a human flash of magic. During such a moment, a hush, pregnant with wonder, descends on the crowd. Time seems for ever frozen, and when the excited fans eventually engage once more with reality, a tingling sensation remains, an indication that the body has, momentarily, undergone a process of genuine time travel to a magical place of distant dreams and transcendent ecstasy where they are reconciled with their fears; where they grasp the infinity of possibilities available to them. The hunters, through their flash of magic, become the 'Stargate' portals to a world of renewal. And having been to the world of renewal, when the fans return to the real world, they are slightly dizzy, but know that it is impossible to return to their old state. That it is possible to give birth to a new way of seeing, of feeling, of behaving, of being human.

The Greeks and Romans developed theories about this moment of magic, and the principle of genius that produced it. In the Greek concept of the daemon, the genius, though regarded as a personification of the individual's nature, tastes and talents, was also viewed as being divine, separate from him. So it was perfectly possible for a genius to be worshipped by its own charge or, more commonly, by others.

As a fan I wait for those instances of genius or transcendence, when the moment is transformed and in that transition a new way of being is given a possibility. I love the game: the beautiful game. To watch eleven warriors at the height of their powers playing as a team in a highly organised formation is like listening to jazz. Like jazz they can work together in skilful combinations to produce a sequence of movements, each flick adding to the impression of a highly choreographed display, leading ultimately to a dazzling moment of sublime magic. And as in jazz, an individual can be allowed a moment of solo enchantment, whereby through his own understanding of the flow and drift of the game he disrupts the melodic and harmonic structure being played out to impose his own vision on the game. As we recognise those great charismatic individuals with unique voices in jazz such as Miles Davis and John Coltrane, so we recognise their footballing peers – players like Pele, Maradona and Cruyff who can conjure the impossible out of thin air and turn a game.

American jazz trumpeter Wynton Marsalis has called jazz the most democratic of music forms, likening it to a conversation between equals with the ability to do a lot of on-the-feet thinking because they are responding to each other's thoughts, although in the end they must go in the direction the majority of the players want to go. 'The principle of American democracy is that you have freedom: the question is, how will you use it? Which is the central question in jazz. And in democracy and jazz, you have freedom with restraint. It's not absolute freedom, it's freedom within a structure.'

Football is singularly democratic in this way, which is why it is now the most popular spectacle on the planet. The World Cup final in Paris in 1998 was watched by over 2 billion of the earth's population. The single largest audience for an event, ever. Football has responded best to the developing democratic civilisation that is beginning to take shape around the world. And it offers a theatre for the resolution of all sorts of personal, national and international dramas, with the trials and accomplishments of the players providing the catalytic focus.

As a devotee I go for the magic moment of genius and transformation these players sometimes offer. When this jazz is missing and the game is humdrum, the mind drifts to other possible narratives that these eleven players we worship project into the world through the ritual of the spectacle of the games. Just as I imagine that, if the athletes at the ancient classical games could not breach the 'Stargate' to the magical world of renewal through their exploits in the arena, then the thoughts of those bards of the Greek and Roman *demos*, Homer and Virgil, would drift off towards myth. For them art would offer another way of escaping through the portal, by embedding the struggles of athletic genius in long, vivid narratives, such as the *Iliad* and the *Aeneid*, which spoke to their time, stirring the imagination and forming the con- sciousness of subsequent generations. In these accounts, both poets mentioned another Paris, and another great drama.

Paris: 70BC–AD1997

In our time, the name Paris is evocative of a beautiful city, as much a symbol of romance as of culture. Originally called Lutetia Parisiorum (the Mud Town of the Parisii) by Caesar, romantic and tragic echoes already haunted its name. Paris first appears in Greek legend. The son of Priam, King of Troy, and Hecuba, at his birth soothsayers prophesied that he would destroy Troy so his mother abandoned him. As an adult he reclaimed his royal inheritance through his athletic prowess at the games. Priam the spectator was so seduced by Paris's genius in the arena that he ignored repeated warnings about his destiny and brought him back into the royal household. Later, in his legendary judgement to decide who was the most beautiful between three quarrelling goddesses, Paris chose Aphrodite, goddess of love, over power and eternal beauty. Aphrodite had bribed him with the promise of Helen, and was to help in his most famous exploit – the abduction of Helen, which triggered the Siege of Troy, leading, as the prophecy had predicted, to its destruction.

Paris was the nemesis of Troy, and like Troy, Paris the city has been a contested site at the heart of an evolving nation and civilisation that would radically change the world. But the people of France have been experiencing much self-doubt over the last century, largely as a result of devastating defeats at the hands of their more powerful German neighbour. During the last Liberation of Paris at the end of the Second World War, its citizens overran the city, filling the boulevards around the Champs Elysées in a massive, emotional out-pouring, marking the recovery of freedom and independence. This celebration of the possibilities of the future was mixed with nostalgia for the past. The war dealt a severe blow to French illusions of power. World superpower status abruptly shifted to the US and Russia. And the French colonies began to slip away. First there was the humiliating retreat in Vietnam, then the debacle of Algeria. To losses on the battle-field were added losses on the culture field. French ceased to be the international language of diplomacy. Ironically, the destiny of French as a language of world importance is increasingly intimately bound up with its speakers in the former colonies in Africa; they outnumber all other French speakers, including those in France. Despite the large numbers of these Africans who reside in the main French cities and in Paris, the French have been ambivalent towards them. As France attempted to redefine itself within the European

Community, its internal racial tensions gave rise to the Front National, the largest mainstream anti-foreigner and racist political party in the whole of Europe. As an African visitor to Paris, I had always found it more uncomfortable and tense than London. For these reasons I had not visited the city for at least ten years. The 1998 World Cup, and the fate of one particular genius, Marcel Desailly, would change some of my perceptions.

Paris: June AD1998

During the closing stages of the 1998 World Cup, Marcel Desailly, the elegant, rock-solid, French central defender, came to my notice. It was he who was to bring together the confluence of global spectacle and personal drama that pro-vided, for me, the major symbolic narrative in an otherwise ordinary World Cup. I watched him closely through matches with Italy and Croatia and then in the final against Brazil. Before the final he seemed unable to do any wrong; then suddenly, in the final, already on a yellow card, he committed another foul. The referee lifted his hand for a second yellow card, then immediately produced the red. As Desailly walked off, I felt for him, becoming intimately bound up in his per-sonal drama. It was too big a stage for such a momentary loss of self-control. I felt for him because I knew that if the French were to lose their two-goal lead and succumb to the Brazilians, as a black footballer, his sending-off might assume other dimensions. It could seep into the realm of racialised politics; raise issues of loyalty and identity. Then I realised that my mind had begun to drift away from the game itself to another narrative, to do with race and the New Europe.

Usually, at World Cup level, the Brazilians, as purveyors of the beautiful game, were guaranteed my automatic support. But this time something was different. Uncharacteristically, in the semi-finals, I wanted the Dutch team to beat what was in any case a lacklustre Brazilian side lacking the genius of a Zico or Rivelino. The Dutch, on the other hand, were posi-tively daring; occasionally the genie even magically popped out of the lamp. Under enormous pressure, Dennis Bergkamp's deftly taken last-minute goal which destroyed the Argentinian resistance left me dizzy. I wanted this Dutch team to beat the Brazilians and meet the French in the final, largely to provide a broader racial drama. Both the Dutch team and the French team were so racially mixed that a final between these two sides, irrespective of the quality of the football, would have become a wider commentary about the state of the New Europe.

As it was, the Dutch didn't make it through, unlucky to lose to Brazil on penalties. Within France, the national side's success triggered an amazing celebration of the 'New France', and was a catalyst for a national debate about identity and the nation, which might have continued on a pan-European level had Holland been in the final. Before the massive celebrations on the Champs Elysées, the moment of Marcel Desailly's sending-off had already crystallised for me the moment of change. In victory, France would never be the same again. In defeat, it would not really be able to discover the new possibilities waiting on the horizon. Had his sending-off turned the final in Brazil's favour, something magical would have been lost. This was the closest I would ever get, in my life, to going to the biggest hunt in the world. I wanted to hear his story, for him to be my guide. This urge was enhanced when I found out that a great hero of his was Aeneas, the creator of a new city and a new people.

Aeneas, whose story is told in Virgil's *Aeneid*, was the son of Anchises, a Trojan prince, and Venus, goddess of love. After the capture of Troy by the Greeks, with the help of his mother he escaped from the burning city, with his father strapped to his back. But his wife was left behind in the confusion.

During a perilous, adventure-filled voyage which took Aeneas around the Mediterranean, the goddess Juno, who had always hated him, tried to drown him in a violent storm. He survived, finding refuge at Carthage on the African coast. Dido, the beautiful Queen of that city, immediately fell in love with Aeneas and begged him to stay with her. When he refused and set sail from Africa, she killed herself.

After several more years of wandering, Aeneas reached Italy and the mouth of the Tiber, where he was welcomed by Latinus, whose daughter, Lavinia, he would later marry and, through the intermingling of their blood, fulfil his destiny. His offspring founded Alba Longa, the mother city of the Romans and the Roman race.

Marcel Desailly's journey has not been quite as dramatic as that of his hero. He was born in Ghana and adopted by a French couple who took him to France. He began playing football from a young age, and was a gifted sportsman who could also have competed at a high level as a swimmer or a tennis player. He chose football because he valued the teamwork and camaraderie of the game, and disliked the intensely focused solitary repetition of tennis and the watery isolation of swimming. Hours and hours of practice in private resulted in what looked in public like an effortless rise through the ranks. Nantes, Marseille, the national squad, then Milan. In June 1998 he was on the precipice of great things. He relived the epic moment for me; the sending-off; how the relationship with his fellow players has changed him; the impact on his life of winning the World Cup. I lit the fire and listened.

The morning of the final

This is the greatest moment for a champion to live through. You begin by thinking that your career has been dedicated to such a day, in preparation for this one day. So you have to think about every movement you make. Some are super-stitious, so they go through their superstitious routine, wearing special things, taking off their clothes in a particular order: unbelievable. That morning . . . you wake up and think: 'Here we are.' You eat, go to the coach, have lunch and then you try to sleep. At that moment you make many resolutions – 'I'm going to do this, and that, and . . .' You're not sure if you will sleep. You're on the bed, tossing and turning, trying to calm yourself, relax. No, I did not talk to my family. I have two mobile phones; my friends have the number of one and the other is switched off. People want to greet you, help you, encourage you. If they are not close to you, it is not good to hear from them. You're in a bubble.

For me . . . I don't know whether it is a dream state, but it is the best moment when you are preparing yourself for the game. You have a small training session in the morning before the match and everything is positive – you try to be positive. Of all my life, on that one day I had to be positive: 'Everything is fine, nothing can hurt me. No problems, nothing can bring me trouble – not to my house, my children, nothing.' You dedicate your life only to one thing – I have worked hard for years and years. When I watched my first World Cup in 1978, and Argentina won, it was really something, truly unbelievable, a dream that you know you can never make real. And then Maradona in Mexico in 1986 held up the World Cup in the middle of the pitch, everybody was carrying him, he was kissing the World Cup, and he was crying. Even at that moment, it was such a strong dream, because just then I was only starting professionally.

The morning of the final: at this point, forget the coach, there are no more real words, only tactical words. He talked tactically, and at such a moment you have to listen because he is the coach, he has to have a tactical position for everybody or some technical instruction, because you will mark on the corner or some midfield position. Afterwards all other discussions are useless. You're in the final of the World Cup. How can he release the pressure, or motivate you? Everybody is looking out for himself. The coach is also talking for himself, to reassure himself that he has done a good job. He talks to be strong. But he doesn't need to talk to us: we will be strong. We were trying to find harmony. There was pressure in the country. All the newspapers, including Le Monde, one of the serious papers which normally only focuses on finance and politics, talked now about soccer and France. We tried to ignore it. If my picture was in the newspaper, I looked to see

*if I was looking good, but didn't read too much of all that
was written.*

I remember when France was eliminated in the semi-finals
of Euro '96, I went to Africa: Ghana. I was at the airport,
watching television. I had never experienced this before. I'm
usually playing on such occasions, or I am at home, alone,
watching. At the airport in Accra I saw so many people all
watching the smallest television I had ever seen, with a very
weak signal. It was the final, between the Czech Republic
and Germany. I don't ever get to see outside: how the people
enjoy football. And I thought, 'Oh, it means when I play,
people are like this: they are watching.' Later, in a small bar
in town which was packed, I saw everyone jumping up and
down shouting: 'Germany, Germany!' To think that such
a small television could even exist! The fans were dancing,
laughing, shouting. During the 1998 World Cup this remem-
brance put me under a bit of pressure, because I said to
myself, 'Look, do you realise? Remember Ghana, remember
the airport.' And this time it was all over the world, in many
countries, many towns, many houses. And most of all in France.

On one level, we were not really thinking about winning,
because we were so happy to be there. Because it was in
France. It was already magnificent. After the game against
Italy, for us the World Cup was wondrous because we'd
reached the minimum we had to reach. You understand? And
then, we just thought: we have arrived and we have to win,
because we are strong.

The semi-final, Holland against Brazil – I remember it was
penalties. We were all in front of the television, which might
surprise you! We all jumped when Brazil won. Because for us,
at that moment, the Netherlands was stronger than Brazil.
Football-lovers might not quite understand this, but those
who closely followed all the teams in this competition will
know what we meant, because then the Netherlands were
really strong. Brazil had had problems facing Denmark, and
nearly lost. They were surprised that France beat them 3–0 in
the final, but Brazil were not that good. Even in their first

game, they only just beat Scotland. It was not what we were expecting. When you say 'Brazil', in everyone's mind the word conjures the beautiful game – Pelé, Ronaldo, prestige. But we knew that on this occasion, the quality and prestige were not at that legendary level. So we jumped and were happy when Brazil beat the Netherlands. 'Brazil, yes!'

In the final it might have been special if we'd played Holland, given the make-up of both teams. We had a problem in 1996 during the European Cup in England, because there were a lot of players of foreign origin in the squad. Le Pen from the Front National began to say in the press that he couldn't understand, questioning why the players didn't sing the national anthem, and saying there was too much colour in the team, too many Arabs, too many Africans.

When you arrive at the game it is already a fait accompli, or rather, the pleasure is finished. The game is not magnificent. Of course there is pleasure, but it is your talent working. You don't really realise when you're inside the bubble. Football is my passion. Whether the stadium is full or empty, I enjoy playing. On the pitch, I concentrate – sometimes I don't even hear the crowd; the beauty of the moment. I'm just on the pitch: sweating, tackling, listening to the coach, keeping an eye on which corner I have to cover, which number I have to mark. As a fan watching on television, you have time to take in everything – the splendour of the stadium and the crowd. As a fan you're under pressure – when somebody scores, you roar, you hang on in there, and . . . he missed! But when you're on the pitch, if he misses, you say to yourself, sure, he missed, and you shout, but you have no time, every second counts: you must concentrate. There are times when I think that perhaps in football it is better to be like a supporter. There are times when I would like to be like a supporter, and so might enjoy the game more than the guy on the pitch. When I'm inside the game, it is done. I see nothing.

The game and finding new friends . . .

Revolution? There were no major technical innovations. I

don't think we learned anything special with this World Cup, about new things, tactics. I don't think there was a special player. Suker may have been the best striker of that tournament, but nothing really special, beyond being a good player, not oh so, so, special. Ronaldo's World Cup? Medium. I suppose it is because in all the teams, even if you play against Paraguay or Germany, the coaches don't always leave the possibility for the players to express themselves. You have to be in the tactical side: disciplined by the tactic; always study closely the power of the other team.

So when we were in the final, we said, there are three players to mark. We have to block Roberto Carlos, so we play with three midfields and put Karembeu on the side and he has to deal with Carlos. Karembeu was good; Carlos did not express himself. Then we said we have to put somebody on Rivaldo, because he is the guy who feeds Ronaldo. Ronaldo will not be at his best if Rivaldo is off. So we put one on Rivaldo, and any time he gets the ball, somebody has got to be there. Afterwards we say we have to put somebody on Dunga. You say go, go Dunga and they will be troubled, because he has no time to think and he is central to their thinking. They will not find the right position. For me the big surprise was Cafu. He had such a good match. He gave us some trouble, because we did not do anything to mark him, nothing special, so he expressed himself. But you see, Rivaldo: out; Roberto Carlos: out. Nowadays, for individuals, it's difficult at such a level. Now it is the collective which creates the possibility for the individual to express himself.

When I was sent off, I was not anxious. I thought, 'Even if we play with ten players, it will not be so big a problem; with our accumulated experience we are so, so, so strong.' How could they manage to score three goals and win the World Cup? They were at their level, but not enough to provoke trouble. That's why I was not worried by the red card. I knew I'd made a mistake, so I knew, 'Get out fast, now, and your team-mates will take positions.' No worries. No worries that we might lose it. No worries that if we lost, it could be my fault. It didn't even cross my mind. But it was difficult watching the rest of the match, not because I was afraid that my team-mates might blame me, but because I wanted to be on the pitch. Because if we won, it was different for me to be outside and to have to run on to see the guys. I was on the bench. To be on the pitch and appreciate the last minute with the guys, it's a big difference.

At the end, when I lifted the cup, it was for myself, for all the images I had of all the things I've experienced. When I was young, I remember looking at France when they won against Brazil in the quarter-final in Mexico. That quarter-final remains such a vivid memory. I remember I was in some square where there was a fountain in the middle and I jumped about in the water. So happy. I remember dreaming about it, really dreaming. And then I got it, I got the cup! Everything can happen. Now I have it! This was my first emotion. I had many things on my mind – my brother, my family, but these were my second emotions. The third wave of emotions which came were my thoughts about the long month and a half we had all spent together as players, the entire group. It was a magnificent moment, a real story in my life, apart from the game – the game is a game, but then a whole lifestyle followed. Twenty-two guys came together.

1996 was when we started together, then many players went off and new players joined. We began to be a bit worried about the relationship between the players. We needed to share all the moments and the same objectives. Everybody had to be positive in the build-up to the World Cup. Everybody was open, because you don't want trouble. There is competition on the pitch but afterwards you want to relax and feel free.

Thuram is really funny, he looks like a guy who is serious, but in fact he is very funny. Djorkaeff looks a bit serious, too. In the group there is no leader. A leader has to be the strongest. It would also have to be in my interests to follow him, and not because I'm afraid of him. But we were all big guys in our job, and it is difficult to defer to anybody; to give one guy, at this level, in the national team, that sort of authority and power without exceptional justification. No way can this happen. No way.

Old leaders . . . of course Platini was there at the stadium when the cup was lifted high. He was happy that the organisation of it all had been so magnificent and to see this generation get it, but it was a mixture of happiness and suffering, because he has been the best player, of Europe maybe, but certainly of France, and he never reached it. So there was joy because of the ramifications of his organisation, and suffering because of the player in him that didn't reach it.

Illuminating a new country in the aftermath

The Champs Elysées: there are many roads off it. Our coach started off miles away. Even so all the side streets were packed. People were jumping for joy, laughing. 'Look at how happy we are! We weren't expecting it.' By the time we got there we were already tired. Continuously showing the World Cup, your hands begin to droop. We were already happy about the people in the small streets, but when we arrived in the Champs Elysées, us players, we all looked at each other. We were surrounded by a sea of faces, all the way to the Arc de Triomphe. Impossible. Incredible.

The last time there were celebrations like this was after the Second World War, when Paris was liberated. It looked as though we had liberated Paris again, but this time it was the liberation of the frustration of France. This was a country that was used to coming second, and accepted this. France always came second. Now that some people in a team could win, suddenly everybody could win. Think positive. It is possible.

As we went through the crowd, I remembered the match against Italy. For me that victory was the best moment because I had just left that country, and many of the French players were playing there. When you live in Italy – it's a great country, magnificent style, women, everything – the Italians hit you with all these things and talk about themselves the whole time, to show you that after Italy, there is nothing else. They have great championships, but if you have a great championship in Italy it is also because of the foreign players. So now we had the chance to show them that France was strong, that we can play at the same level, and that we can bring so many things – experience, attitude, the practicals. There was pressure on that game, real pressure. A double pressure. Because it was like we were living in Italy and we were feeling a piece of the pressure of Italy, and all of the pressure of France.

In France, interest in the game has grown. It will never have the football culture of Italy or Spain or Portugal because it is not really in our culture. But I think because of the World Cup and the happiness that football brought at this time, people began to look at it in a different way. Before, they were not really convinced about soccer, just a game. But even those who were not interested in sport started to say, 'Oh this is interesting, France has arrived,' so it provided a fashionable thrill for the game and for the country. Before, people who did not give it much thought, like the wife at home – 'Ah, football!' – began to take notice. She and the others said, 'It's France playing, it's France, where I live, in the French society, so I have to be behind France. I have to put some emotion into it. I cannot stay cold.' Then they began to be positive because of sport; because of what the French national side represented. That is why they started to say that at that moment there was no trouble any more, no black people, no Algerians, just French people. Differences were momentarily set aside. Even the Algerians flew the French flag in the inner cities. These are people who normally live in Algeria in their minds, all their lives they have lived in France, but they live like they are in Algeria, with its religion, but that day in July they were hanging out of windows, waving the French flag. Unbelievable. Perhaps football gave them a chance to see their own country and let out emotions that were buried. Even if it was only for two hours, it's enough.

I don't know about long-term change. Perhaps 90 per cent

of the people may not change their ideas. But maybe the other 10 per cent of the people might have started to think differently. Let me put it another way: maybe people who had been negative started to think positively for a three-month period because France won the World Cup. They forgot some of their problems. They had a bit of time to think about positive things, about what they could achieve, about the happiness of the world. Afterwards . . . I don't know the end result. Maybe only one person has used the victory in the World Cup to do something really great, patriotic. But even if only one person has, it is something.

For me, the great thing is the friendships I have made with other players, especially in the three months after the tournament, when we went around the country together celebrating victory with the nation. We were like kids. I like my friend Deschamps, but there are other players I didn't initially appreciate – I didn't hate them, but I didn't appreciate them that much before the World Cup, even though we were working together – but today I can see they are really good guys and I can joke with them and talk seriously. They are real friends. You can see that now when I am with the national team. I am happy, smiling, because I'm going to see friends. Our destinies in the future will be linked for ever through that moment.

The new Europe

Yes, I have played in France, Italy and now Britain. Are we the heroes carving out a new European identity? I don't know. When I had the opportunity to come to England, I could think only about Ghana, and how it could represent trouble for me. Most people in Anglophone countries have a team in England that they follow. I said to myself, 'Oh, you will be known by the English people and the Italians. Is it something that is really good?' Now, it has become a problem for me because in Ghana I'm not free any more – even when I go there I cannot go into the village and relax and play soccer with the kids on the pitch with rough grass without people shouting 'Desailly!' Now I'm just 'Marcel Desailly' all the time, even in Ghana. Before the World Cup and coming to London, it was easy for me to appreciate the real life, the real smile, the real genuine behaviour of the people in Ghana. Now. . .

I suppose the positive thing is my experience. I didn't really think about being a European in that sense. It was more about, 'Is it easy for me to use that experience in England; for me, for my children?' That's all. I believe that when I stop football, I will be an ex-player who won the World Cup. The best moment of my life remains the time when I cut my daughter's umbilical cord. Sport is sport.

Afterword

The New Ambassadors, or the Reincarnation of the Temple Moneychangers?

DANIEL BERNARD, HIS EXCELLENCY THE FRENCH AMBASSADOR

Who hasn't – go on, admit it – when driving down a country lane, stopped the car at the sight of twenty-two red-faced lads playing football, if only for a few minutes, to watch them battling it out with a round ball that never seems to bounce the way it should, which is hardly surprising, given the state of the pitch. It doesn't matter who the teams are, what the score is, or what they're playing for, the sheer sight of teenagers desperately trying to win the ball and attack the opponents' goal is irresistible.

Today, tens of thousands of fans fill the stands, fanatical supporters of the blues or the reds, no matter, but always hoping to witness the most brilliant move ever, the bicycle kick, the 'nutmeg', that back-flick which completely outsmarts the opponent. Football has become universal precisely because it is a basic sport which kids pick up from their dads and from their friends. You don't have to be an athlete, sprinter or strong man to play it. Everyone can.

Invented by the British, like most sports, football has conquered the planet, developing and adapting to the morphology and talent of players all around the world. Today football has become a global phenomenon. However, if we're not careful, it could bring out not just the best, but the worst in us, too.

The beautiful game reflects society, societies. France swelled with national pride when her team won the 1998 World Cup, just as England did when she triumphed in 1966. The make-up of France's world champion team, a mosaic of players of different races and religions hailing from a huge variety of back - grounds, some far from metropolitan France, but all wearing the same blue, white and red strip of their country, is more than just a symbol: it is a source of hope, of promise for the future. Les Tricolores – second-generation North Africans, Basques, Arabs, Kanaks, Africans, West Indians and natives of Normandy – perfectly illustrate the multifaceted unity of the France of today and tomorrow.

Now many of these players are winning acclaim on British pitches, demonstrating why their team won the World Championship. Most are well aware that their role goes beyond that of professional players of a popular sport, and one awash with money. They are the new ambassadors, ambassadors who aren't confined to making suave diplomatic speeches. Like Cantona who, in his time, brought the Old Trafford crowd to its feet, inspiring thousands of British voices to strike up 'La Marseillaise'. No aggression, no chauvinistic fervour, just a love of the brilliant move, the display of pure skill sometimes bordering on art.

But danger threatens. To take an image from Roman times: the Capitol of the beautiful game is never far away from the Tarpeian Rock of marketing and merchandising, or worse. It would be criminal if football were to die suffocated by the excesses of money and profit, thereby losing its very essence – that heady mix of pure sporting skill and excitement – metamorphosing into a fixed-price business regulated by the global Internet network.

The people, it used to be said in Rome, need bread and games. Hence the celebrated Roman sports arenas, like the Circus Maximus, with its famous and extremely popular chariot races. If football should die through the fault of the temple money-changers, then I shall go back to my country lane and watch the kids finish their match.

Contributors

Patrick Amory is a freelance journalist who contributes frequently to the French national and sports press. He has had various book published.

Avi Assouly is reporter-in-chief for Radio France Provence. He has followed the fortunes of Olympique Marseille for over fifteen years and holds a special position as a leading authority on the club's remarkable history. He covered the sensational Valenciennes–OM court case for the French media in 1993 and was present at the Furiani disaster in Corsica. According to a local saying, 'Avi is to l'OM what pastis is to Marseilles.' His published works include *Mon OM à tout coeur . . . et ma Coupe du Monde 1998*.

David Baddiel is a writer and comedian. He is co-creator of three hugely successful BBC comedy series – *The Mary Whitehouse Experience*, *Newman and Baddiel in Pieces* – and *Fantasy Football*. He is also the author of two bestselling and critically acclaimed novels, *Time for Bed* – 'With his first novel David Baddiel goes straight into the first eleven of young contemporary British novelists' (Nick Hornby) – and *Whatever Love Means*. A sitcom, *Baddiel Syndrome*, is due to be broadcast on television in 2000.

Daniel Bernard, His Excellency the French ambassador, is married and has three children. His career has included the following posts: Seuxième Secrétaire à Dublin (1967–71), Direction des Nations Unies au Ministère des Affaires Etrangères (1975–7), Premier Secrétaire à la Représentation Permanente de la France auprès des Communautés Européenes (1977–81), Conseiller technique au Cabinet du Ministre des Relations

Extérieures (1981–83), Délégué aux Affaires Interationales au Ministère de l'Industrie et de la Recherche (1984), Conseiller diplomatique du Premier Ministre (1984–6), Inspecteur à l'Inspection Générale des Affaires Etrangères (1986), Détaché auprès de la Commission des Communautés Européennes (1987–88), Chargé de Mission auprès du Président de l'Assemblée Nationale (1988–90), Directeur de Presse, de l'Information et de la Communication au Ministère des Affaires Etrangères (1990–92), Directeur du Cabinet du Ministre d'Etat, Ministère des Affaires Etrangères (1992–3), Ambassadeur de France aux Pays-Bas (1993–5) and Ambassadeur, Rèpresentant Permanent de la France auprès de l'Office des Nations Unies à Genève (1995–8). He was nominated Ambassadeur Extraordinaire et Plénipotentiaire auprès du Royaume Uni de Grande Bretagne et d'Irlande du Nord in August 1998.

His decorations include the Chevalier de la Légion d'Honneur, the Companion of the Order of St Michael and St George (CMG), Commander of the Order of the British Empire and Chevalier de l'Ordre National de Mérite.

Patrick Barclay grew up in Dundee and supports Dundee FC. He has written for the *Guardian* (for which he covered the 1984 European Championship in France), the *Independent*, the *Observer* and, since 1996, the *Sunday Telegraph*. He was voted Sports Journalist of the Year in 1994 and has covered five World Cups for different newspapers. He lives in Barnes, south-west London.

Olivia Blair is a freelance football writer who cut her teeth on the ground-breaking football magazine *Four-Four-Two*, interviewing personalities as diverse as Terry Venables, Michel Platini and David Ginola, before moving on to the *Independent*, where she wrote an eclectic weekly column. Having edited Sir Alex Ferguson's highly successful diary of the 1995–6 season, *A Year in the Life*, and its follow-up, *A Will to Win*, she then co-wrote Glen Hoddle's controversial *World Cup Story*. She is now sticking to 'safer' projects by writing her own book about Arsenal and Spurs, to be published in summer 2000.

Philippe Broussard has been writing for *Le Monde* since 1989. One of its leading sports reporters, he received the Prix Albert Londres in 1993. He is the author of *Génération Supporter: enquête sur les ultras du football* and *Les rebelles de l'Himalaya.*

Will Buckley, sports feature writer for the *Observer*, is renowned for his incisive observations and humour. In the past he has pursued various careers, from barrister to game-show host. He is co-author of *Who Cares Who Wins: The SAS, the Final Cash-In.*

José Carlin is twenty-nine. His passion for the game dates back to when his Spanish grandfather told him bedtime stories about football before the Civil War. Several years later, José went on to write for *L'Equipe*. He was press officer for the World Cup '98 Organisation Committee and is the representative of the Union of French Sports Journalists. José now works for Paris St German, where is is responsible for the club's development of new Internet and audiovisual media.

Tam Dean Burn is an actor, most recently on film in Michel Blanc's *The Escort* and Mike Figgis's *Miss Julie* and onstage in a one-man adaptation of Irvine Welsh's book *Filth*. Live artist-in-residence at the New Foundry in London, he is also a writer. He is one of 'The Assassins'.

Charlie Hall is hitting forty and running. Behind him lie ten years of spinning vinyl as an acid house DJ and as part of the infamous worldwide spiral tribe techno traveller terrorist troublemakers: trance in Goa; techno in St Petersburg; house in Sydney; breaks in Belfast; ambient in Amsterdam. He has released three albums as part of Drum Club's techno combo and toured Japan, Europe and Iceland. A contributor to the 'chemical generation' bestsellers *Disco Biscuits* and *Disco 2000*, he now runs the Victoria Music record company, releasing electronic underground music to the world.

At six years old, **Amy Lawrence**'s life was changed for ever when a Liam Brady goal distracted her from the toy Wombles brought along to keep her entertained at Highbury. Later she began writing for *The Gooner* fanzine, graduating to *Four-Four-Two*, before moving on to the *Observer*, for whom she covered Euro '96 and France '98. Amy has written *Proud To Say That Name*, which chronicles thirty years of Arsenal, ghosted David Ginola's autobiography and made a documentary on Dennis Bergkamp for Sky. She has also contributed to *France-Football* and presents a world soccer feature for OnDigital's coverage of the Champions League.

Jean-Philippe Leclaire was born in Paris and grew up in St Etienne, behind the famous stadium. After acquiring degrees from l'Institut d'Études Politiques in Lyons and the Centre de Formation des Journalistes in Paris, he went on to become feature writer for *L'Equipe* magazine and, since 1992, for the daily sports paper *L'Equipe*. He covered the 1994 and 1998 World Cups and the 1996 Olympics. His first book, *Platini: le roman d'un joueur*, received Le Prix 'Post-Scriptum' du meilleur livre Français de sport in 1998.

Singer and novelist **Mounsi** was born in Kabylie, Algeria, and moved to the industrial Parisian suburb of Nanterre as a child. A 'wonderful writer' (Helen Stevenson, the *Independent*), his published works include *La cendre des villes*, *Territoire d'outre-ville*, *Ballade éléctrique*, *Le Voyage des Ames* and *La Noce des fous*. A short story, *Into the Void*, was published in *XCiTés: The Flamingo Book of New French Writing*.

Queen of the night for five years, **Paquita Paquin**'s favourite haunts were Club 7, La Main Bleue and Bains Douches. She ran Le Privilege for Fabrice Emaer, the legendary owner of Le Palace. In 1983 she turned to journalism. An uncompromising and accurate reporter for *Le Matin* and then *Vogue*, for which she wrote about Parisian life and fashion, she is currently one of *Libération*'s leading columnists. She is also a football commentator for various French national radio stations.

Alain Pecheral's career kicked off with his writing for the newspaper *Le Provençal* (1970–97). Chief reporter and feature writer for *L'Equipe* since 1997, Pecheral has also written authoritative books about Olympique Marseille, notably *La Grande Histoire de l'OM, Le Provençal raconte l'OM* and *Cent ans d'OM*.

Q is a Londoner. Clubland maverick and cult author, he has had stories published in *The Fred* and *Disco Biscuits*. He is the author of *Deadmeat*, which he self-published and sold in instalments in markets and clubs, and which was subsequently released by a mainstream publisher in a 'remixed' version. He turned *Deadmeat* into a multimedia stage show for West Yorkshire Playhouse, featuring live, filmed and 'virtual' characters. 'Websites, rap, DJs and audience participation: Q can see the future, which is a neat trick from behind his trademark glasses.' (Daniel Rosenthal, *The Times*.) Q has his own band, live show and website, www.deadmeat.com He is at present writing interactive films and games.

Arnaud Ramsay is twenty-eight. Precociously talented, he founded and edited his own magazine at the age of thirteen. In his early twenties he contributed to *L'Equipe*, *Le Nouvel Observateur*, *L'Optimum* and *La Cinquième Chaîne*, his particular focus being sport and its social and cultural context. Currently he is a writer-reporter for *France Football*.

Jean-Philippe Rethacker was editor-in-chief of *L'Equipe* and *France-Football* for forty-three years, during which time he covered twelve World Cups. He attended the 1998 World Cup as a passionate spectator. The author of numerous books about football, Rethacker is France's most revered football writer, 'a legend in his own lifetime'.

Ben Richards is the author of *Throwing the House Out of the Window*, *Don't Step on the Lines* and *The Silver River* and a fourth novel, published in 2000, *A Sweetheart Deal*. He has written a number of short stores for various publications and anthologies. He lives in London but spends a lot of time in Chile, where he supports Universidad de Chile, the current League champions.

Ian Ridley is a highly respected football columnist with the *Observer* and the author of five books, including *Cantona: The Red and The Black* and *Addicted*, the autobiography of the Arsenal and England player Tony Adams.

Salman Rushdie is the author of seven novels – *Grimus*, *Midnight's Children*, *Shame*, *The Satanic Verses*, *Haroun and the Sea of Stories*, *The Moor's Last Sigh* and *The Ground Beneath Her Feet* – and one collection of short stories, *East, West*. His non-fiction includes *The Jaguar Smile*, *Imaginary Homelands*, *The Wizard of Oz* and, as co-editor, *The Vintage Book of Indian Writing*. He has received numerous awards for his writing, including the European Union's Aristeion Prize for Literature. He is fellow of the Royal Society of Literature and Commandeur des Arts et des Lettres. In 1993, *Midnight's Children* was adjudged the 'Booker of Bookers', the best novel to have won the Booker Prize in its first twenty-five years.

Andy Thompson who was taken to Anfield while still in the womb, never had a choice in who to support, but never wanted one. A Kop season ticket-holder since the eighties, he has emerged as one of the greatest left-handed spellers in the modern game. One-time sports editor of *Time Out Amsterdam*, young Andy (who, at twenty-eight, still has a bright future) is currently knocking together a magazine for QPR-mad record label 'Wall of Sound'. He has also recently completed *This is Anfield*, a limited-edition history of some club or other to be published by Genesis in 2000.

Philippe Tournon grew up in the Tarn-et-Garonne. He has devoted his entire career to football. From 1966 to 1982 he was deputy editor-in-chief of the national sports newspaper *L'Equipe*. In 1983 he joined the Fédération Française de Football as chief press officer and masterminded media relations for the French national team during the period 1994–8, closely collaborating with Aimé Jacquet, trainer of the 1998 World Cup-winning team. Tournon co-authored Jacquet's autobiography *Ma vie pour une étoile* (1999), which has become a bestseller in France with sales of over 300,000 copies.

Onyekachi Wambu was born in Nigeria and arrived in Britain in 1970 following the Biafran Civil War. Columnist for the *Voice* and the *New Nation* and editor of the *Voice* from 1986 to 1988, Wambu has also directed and produced documentaries for the BBC and Channel 4, including the 'Beginner's Guides' series featured on *The A Force* on BBC2. Wambu left the UK in 1999 to work with Blackside Inc., the leading African–American production company whose credits include *Eyes on the Prize*. He is masterminding the production of a TV documentary, *Hopes on the Horizon*. Wambu edited the anthology *Empire Windrush: Fifty Years of Writing about Black Britain*.

Irvine Welsh was born in Leith. His first book, *Trainspotting*, has sold over 1 million copies in paperback. The film of the book was released in 1996 to huge acclaim and popularity.

This was followed by a collection of short stories, *The Acid House* (1994), which became a cult movie. Then came a second novel, *Marabou Stork Nightmares* (1995), followed by *Ecstasy – Three Chemical Romances* (1996), the first paperback original to become a number one bestseller. His most recent novel, *Filth* (1998), became an instant number one bestseller. In 1998 he produced his first play, *You'll Have Had Your Hole*. Welsh's talent does not lie in writing alone: his band, Hibee Nation, have released two singles. He is a keen DJ and has performed in some of Ibiza's top clubs.

Translators

After working in London and Paris in public relations and television production, **Philippa Bowe** and **Giles Smith** decided to move higher up the food chain. They now live in splendid rural isolation and work as writers and translators. They have a beautiful son, Raphaël.

Georgia de Chamberet was born in Paris to an artistic mother and an eccentric father. She spent a nomadic childhood travelling between England and France. Managing editor at Quartet Books in the 1980s, she left the company in the 1990s and founded the literary agency BookBlast Ltd (www.bookblast.com). In 1999, she edited the anthology *XCiTés: The Flamingo Book of New French Writing*.

Copyright Details